CREATING
A SUSTAINABLE AND
DESIRABLE FUTURE

Insights from 45 global thought leaders

CREATING
A SUSTAINABLE AND
DESIRABLE FUTURE

Insights from 45 global thought leaders

Editors

Robert Costanza
Ida Kubiszewski

Crawford School of Public Policy
The Australian National University

NEW JERSEY · LONDON · SINGAPORE · BEIJING · SHANGHAI · HONG KONG · TAIPEI · CHENNAI

Published by

World Scientific Publishing Co. Pte. Ltd.

5 Toh Tuck Link, Singapore 596224

USA office: 27 Warren Street, Suite 401-402, Hackensack, NJ 07601

UK office: 57 Shelton Street, Covent Garden, London WC2H 9HE

Library of Congress Cataloging-in-Publication Data
Creating a sustainable and desirable future : insights from 45 global thought leaders / [edited] by
Robert Costanza & Ida Kubiszewski (Australian National University, Australia).
   pages cm
  Includes bibliographical references and index.
  ISBN 978-9814546881
  1. Sustainable development. 2. Sustainability. 3. Environmentalism. 4. Environmental policy.
I. Costanza, Robert. II. Kubiszewski, Ida.
  HC79.E5C725 2014
  338.9'27--dc23

                          2013035772

British Library Cataloguing-in-Publication Data
A catalogue record for this book is available from the British Library.

In-house Editors: Lum Pui Yee/Chitralekha Elumalai

Typeset by Stallion Press
Email: enquiries@stallionpress.com

Printed in Singapore by World Scientific Printers.

Contents

Preface

As a society, we need to think more deeply and discuss more broadly the kind of world we really want. This book is an attempt to deepen and broaden that discussion. It is a collection of positive ideas about what a sustainable and desirable future might look like from a broad range of perspectives.

In the environmental community, there is a growing pessimism about the future. Climate disruption, biodiversity loss, overpopulation, and a host of other problems seem to be getting far worse with no sign of our ability to solve them. The majority of the business and political communities are still in denial about the severity of the problems. They are counting on the ability of "business-as-usual" (with perhaps some tweaking) to solve them. But, as Paul Raskin has said: "It is business-as-usual that is the utopian fantasy."

This book is **not** about business-as-usual. It is not about projections of future technologies or extrapolations of past trends. It is a collection of multifaceted descriptions of better worlds that are both plausible and possible. These are not predictions of what *will* happen, but visions of what *could* happen if we, as a society, put our minds to it.

Most of the chapters are versions of articles that have been published in *Solutions* (www.thesolutionsjournal.com), which has a regular section that challenges authors to envision a future society in which all the correct changes have been made. Think of it as a "best of" collection of *Solutions'* visions plus a few additional chapters from other sources. The chapters are written in a broad range of styles. We see that as an advantage. Describing the future we want must take many forms. We hope the reader will find in these chapters inspiration, hope, and motivation to help envision and then create a better world.

Acknowledgments

We thank, first and foremost, all the contributing authors for their visions, for sharing those visions with the world, and for supporting *Solutions*. We also thank Sung Lee and the Crawford School of Public Policy at Australian National University for their encouragement and support in putting this collection together, and Ms Chitralekha Elumalai and Ms Lum Pui Yee, editors at World Scientific for their advice and help throughout the process. Finally, we thank the late Dana Meadows and dedicate this collection to her, for her inspiration, strength, and personal vision of a better world.

Robert Costanza
Ida Kubiszewski
Canberra, Australia, 2013

About the Editors

Dr Robert Costanza is a Professor and Chair in Public Policy at the Crawford School of Public Policy, Australian National University. Prior to this, he was Distinguished University Professor of Sustainability, in the Institute for Sustainable Solutions at Portland State University (2010–2012), Gund Professor of Ecological Economics and Founding Director of the Gund Institute for Ecological Economics at the University of Vermont (2002–2010), Professor at the University of Maryland (1988–2002) and at Louisiana State University (1980–1988). His transdisciplinary research integrates the study of humans and the rest of nature to address research, policy, and management issues at multiple time and space scales, from small watersheds to the global system. He is cofounder of the International Society for Ecological Economics and founding editor-in-chief of *Solutions* (www.thesolutionsjournal.org). He is author or coauthor of over 500 articles and 24 books and has been named one of ISI's Highly Cited Researchers since 2004. More than 200 interviews and reports on his work have appeared in various popular media.

 **Dr Ida Kubiszewski** is a Senior Lecturer at the Crawford School of Public Policy at Australian National University. Prior to this, she was an Assistant Research Professor and Fellow at the Institute for Sustainable Solutions, at Portland State University. She is the Managing Editor of a magazine/journal hybrid called *Solutions* (www.thesolutionsjournal.org). She is also a cofounder and former Managing Editor the *Encyclopedia of Earth* (www.eoearth.org). Dr Kubiszewski is the author or coauthor of over a dozen scientific papers. She is a Fellow at the National Council for Science and the Environment and an Associate Research Fellow at the Institut Veblen pour les réformeséconomiques (Veblen Institute for Economic Reforms). She sits on the steering committees or advisory boards of various organizations including the Ecosystem Service Partnership and the Environmental Information Coalition.

About the Contributors

Gar Alperovitz Lionel R. Bauman Professor of Political Economy at the University of Maryland, is the cofounder of the Democracy Collaborative. He is the author of numerous books, including most recently *What Then Must We Do? Straight Talk About the Next Revolution; America Beyond Capitalism*; and, with Lew Daly, *Unjust Deserts*. He is a founding board member of the New Economics Institute and of the Committee for the Political Economy of the Good Society (PEGS). Alperovitz previously served as a legislative director in the US House of Representatives and the US Senate, and as a special assistant in the Department of State.

Peter Bartelmus is an honorary professor of the Bergische Universität Wuppertal, Germany. At the UN Environment Programme in Nairobi and the UN headquarters in New York, he developed international systems of environmental statistics and accounting. His latest book is the forthcoming *Sustainability Economics: An Introduction*.

William S. Becker is an executive director of the Presidential Climate Action Project (PCAP). PCAP has created a comprehensive plan for the Obama administration to shape US energy and climate policy. Becker also directs the Future We Want, which uses cuttingedge communication technologies to help the American people envision life in a sustainable, low-carbon society. He is the former central regional director for the US Department of Energy.

Wendell Berry is the author of more than 40 works of fiction, nonfiction, and poetry and has been the recipient of numerous awards and honors. His books include *Hannah Coulter* (2004), *Citizenship Papers* (2005), *The Way of Ignorance* (2006), and *Given: Poems* (2005). Berry's latest works include *The Mad Farmer Poems* (2008) and *Whitefoot* (2009). He lives and works with his wife, Tanya Berry, on their farm in Port Royal, Kentucky.

Ajay Bhave did his Bachelors and Masters in Environmental Sciences in India. He was a research associate at the Department of Environmental Sciences, University of Pune for a year, wherein he worked on solute transport in coastal aquifers and in river processes. His interest in policy making led him to join the Masters program in Environmental Science, Policy and Management. He is currently at the International Institute for Industrial Environmental Economics, in Lund University. His research interests include implementation and consequent effects of biofuel program, corporate social responsibility, and sustainability. His interests also involve social *entrepreneurship* and its importance in community development.

George W. Burns is adjunct professor of psychology at Cairnmillar Institute, Melbourne; adjunct senior lecturer at Edith Cowan University, Perth; and director of the Milton H. Erickson Institute of Western Australia. He is a clinical psychologist and therapist trainer who teaches internationally, and his numerous publications include his recent book, *Happiness, Healing, Enhancement*.

Ernest Callenbach's novel *Ecotopia*, a portrait of an ecologically sustainable future society, has sold almost a million copies and was translated into nine languages. His most recent book is *Ecology: A Pocket Guide*, a nontechnical guide to 65 fundamental ecological terms. Callenbach passed away in 2012.

Silvia Ceausu holds a bachelor degree in ecology and a master degree in systems ecology and sustainable development. Currently, she is studying at IIIEE in Lund as part of the MESPOM program. Her interests include environmental politics and policies, and the influence of mass-media in shaping environmental concepts.

Ronald Colman is founder and executive director of GPI Atlantic, a nonprofit research group dedicated to developing comprehensive accounts and measures of well-being and sustainable development. Since 2003 Colman has worked closely with the Royal Government of Bhutan to develop a national survey and measures of progress in line with that country's policy of integrating social, economic, ecological, and governance objectives.

Robert Costanza is a Chair of Public Policy at the Crawford School of Public Policy at Australian National University. He has authored or coauthored over 350 scientific papers, and reports on his work have appeared in *Newsweek*, *U.S. News and World Report*, *The Economist*, *The New York Times*, *Science*, *Nature*, *National Geographic*, and *National Public Radio*.

Tess Croner is pursuing a master's degree at the Yale School of Forestry and Environmental Studies. She graduated in 2009 with honors from Washington University in St Louis, where she earned a BA in environmental studies with a minor in anthropology.

Herman E. Daly is currently Professor at the University of Maryland. From 1988 to 1994, he was Senior Economist in the Environment Department of the World Bank. His interest in economic development, population, resources, and environment has resulted in over a hundred articles in professional journals and anthologies, as well as numerous books. In 1996, he received Sweden's Honorary Right Livelihood Award and the Heineken Prize for Environmental Science awarded by the Royal Netherlands Academy of Arts and Sciences. In 2002, he was awarded the Medal of the Presidency of the Italian Republic.

Anand Deshmukh obtained his Masters in Environmental Management from Shivaji University Kolhapur, India. His area of interests are Environmental impact assessment, corporate social responsibility, technology transfer and its role in climate change adaptation, industrial ecology for sustainable industry network, energy efficiency, and security. Currently, he is a student at the International Institute for Industrial Environmental Economic on the Erasmus Mundus Masters in Environmental Sciences Policy and Management program.

Joshua Farley is an ecological economist, associate professor in Community Development & Applied Economics, and fellow at the Gund Institute for Ecological Economics at the University of Vermont. His broad research interests focus on the design of economic institutions capable of balancing what is biophysically possible with what is socially, psychologically, and ethically desirable.

Richard T.T. Forman is the PAES Professor of Landscape Ecology at Harvard University, and teaches ecological courses in the Graduate School of Design and Harvard College. As a leader in landscape ecology, road ecology, and urban ecology, he links science with spatial patterns to interweave nature and people on the land. His books include *Land Mosaics* (1995), *Road Ecology* (2003), and *Urban Regions* (2008).

Carol Franco Dr Franco supports projects on forest mapping and monitoring and fosters climate change policies in Latin America. Her research has focused on environmental and socioeconomic policies, food security, and climate change policies. She has worked as the Carbon Finance Officer of the United Nations Development Program in the Dominican Republic, and prior to joining the Center, she was a Research Assistant Professor at the Institute for Sustainable Solutions at Portland (OR) State University. Dr Franco received her Ph.D. from the State University of New York (SUNY) College of Environmental Science and Forestry.

Gary Hart Former US senator Gary Hart served on the Armed Services committee, was a founder of the Congressional Military Reform caucus, and is currently chair of the American Security Project. He is chair of the Threat Reduction Advisory Council at the Department of Defense. Hart was cochair of the US Commission on National Security for the Twenty-first Century. The commission performed the most comprehensive review of national security since 1947, predicted the terrorist attacks on America, and proposed a sweeping overhaul of US national security structures and policies. Gary Hart represented the state of Colorado in the United States Senate from 1975 to 1987. In 1984 and 1988, he was a candidate for his party's nomination for president.

Anders Hayden is an assistant professor of political science at Dalhousie University, Nova Scotia. His primary research interest is the social and political responses to climate change, particularly the evolving balance between efforts to promote green growth and sufficiency-based challenges to the endless growth of production and consumption. He is the author of *Sharing the Work, Sparing the Planet: Work Time, Consumption and Ecology.*

Tim Jackson is a leading international expert on sustainability. Since 2000, he has been professor of sustainable development at the University of Surrey — the first such chair to be created in the UK. In 2004, he was appointed as economics commissioner on the UK Sustainable Development Commission, where he led a five-year project called Redefining Prosperity. This groundbreaking work culminated in the publication of his controversial book *Prosperity without Growth—Economics for a Finite Planet.*

Jessica Jewell's research focuses on energy security under long-term energy scenarios and as a driver for policy change. More broadly, she is interested in the interaction between national energy priorities and global energy objectives. She works in the Energy Program at the International Institute for Applied Systems Analysis.

Van Jones is president and cofounder of Rebuild the Dream, a platform for bottom–up, people-powered innovations to help fix the US economy. In 2008, *Fast Company* magazine said he had one of the 12 most creative minds on earth, and in 2009 *Time* magazine named him one of the 100 most influential people in the world. That same year he worked as the green jobs advisor to the Obama White House, where he helped run the interagency process that oversaw US$80 billion in green energy recovery spending.

Tim Kasser is professor of psychology at Knox College in Illinois. He has published numerous articles, chapters, and books on values, goals, quality of life, and environmental sustainability. Kasser also frequently consults with activist and civil society organizations in the United States and United Kingdom.

Ida Kubiszewski is a senior lecturer at the Crawford School of Public Policy at Australian National University. She is the managing editor of *Solutions* and a cofounder and former managing editor of the *Encyclopedia of Earth*. Kubiszewski is the author or coauthor of dozens of scientific papers and a fellow at the National Council for Science and the Environment.

Les W. Kuzyk is currently employed in urban planning in Western Canada, with a recent focus on sustainability research. He has authored several articles including two academic papers promoting the use of the ecological footprint. He is seeking to further a parallel freelance writing career through the composition, now in progress, of a novel.

Frances Moore Lappé is author of 18 books, including the three-million-copy *Diet for a Small Planet*. She is cofounder of Food First: The Institute for Food and Development Policy; and, more recently, with Anna Lappé, of the Small Planet Institute and the Small Planet Fund. In 2007, *Gourmet* magazine named her one of 25 people, including Thomas Jefferson and Julia Child, whose work has changed the way America eats.

Peggy Liu is chairperson of the Joint US–China Collaboration on Clean Energy (JUCCCE), a nonprofit with the goal of greening China for a healthier world. She was named a TIME Hero of the Environment and is an executive advisor to the Marks & Spencer department store on issues of sustainability. She has also been dubbed China's "green goddess" and in March 2012 was named by China Business News as one of the 50 Most Innovative Business Leaders.

Christine Loh is founder and CEO of the nonprofit think tank Civic Exchange, based in Hong Kong. A lawyer by training and a commodities trader by profession, she was previously a highly successful litigator in Hong Kong for nearly 10 years.

L. Hunter Lovins is president of Natural Capitalism Solutions, which helps companies, communities, and countries implement more sustainable business practices profitably. Over her 30 years as a sustainability thought leader, Lovins has written hundreds of articles and 13 books. A founder of the field of sustainable management, she has helped create several MBA programs and currently teaches sustainable business at the Bainbridge Graduate Institute, the University of Denver, and Bard College.

Bill McKibben is author of a dozen books about the environment, beginning with *The End of Nature* (1989), regarded as the first book for a general audience on climate change. He is a founder of the grassroots climate campaign 350. org, which has coordinated 15,000 rallies in 189 countries since 2009. The Boston Globe said in 2010 that he was "probably the country's most important environmentalist."

Donella Meadows, founder of the Sustainability Institute, was a professor at Dartmouth College, a long-time organic farmer, a journalist, and a systems analyst. She was honored both as a Pew Scholar in Conservation and Environment and as a MacArthur Fellow. Her weekly column, "The Global Citizen," in which she commented on world events from a systems point of view, appeared in more than 20 newspapers and was nominated for a Pulitzer Prize in 1991. Meadows passed away in the spring of 2001.

Mohan Munasinghe is chairman of the Munasinghe Institute of Development and holds professorships at universities around the world. He shared the 2007 Nobel Peace Prize as vice chairman of the UN Intergovernmental Panel on Climate Change. Highlights from 40 years of distinguished public service include working as senior energy advisor to the president of Sri Lanka, advisor to the US Council on Environmental Quality, and senior advisor/manager at the World Bank.

Catherine O'Brien is associate professor in the Education Department of Cape Breton University, Nova Scotia. She coined the term "sustainable happiness" at the Second International Conference on Gross National Happiness in 2005. In addition to the university course that she developed for Cape Breton University, O'Brien cocreated an online course on sustainable happiness for the general public.

David W. Orr is the Paul Sears Distinguished Professor of Environmental Studies and Politics, Oberlin College, and executive director of the

Oberlin Project. He is the author of seven books, including *Down to the Wire: Confronting Climate Collapse* and *Hope is an Imperative.*

Wayne Pan is student in the Erasmus Mundus Master's of Environmental Sciences, Policy and Management programme and is currently studying at IIIEE in Lund University. He has worked as a strategic management consultant, a web and print designer, and as an editor in the UN system. He most recently spent time as a Communications and Advocacy Advisor at UNDP China. He has interests in issues surrounding consumption, sustainable cities, and public awareness/value changing. He has lived and worked in the US, Europe, and China. He holds a BA from UC Berkeley.

Daniel Pauly is a professor at the Fisheries Centre of the University of British Columbia. Since 1999, he has been principal investigator of the Sea Around Us Project, devoted to documenting and mitigating the impact of fisheries on the world's marine ecosystems.

John Peet is the author of *Energy and the Ecological Economics of Sustainability* as well as papers on systems, sustainability, and the ethical requirements of stakeholder involvement. Since retirement, he has worked with a number of local, national, and international nongovernment organizations.

Jamie Querubin A young civil servant who believes in the power of community engagement, civic participation, and a stronger, more effective government.

Kavita N. Ramdas served as president and CEO of the Global Fund for Women from 1996 to September 2010. This fall, she was appointed visiting scholar and fellow to Stanford University's Center for Democracy, Development, and the Rule of Law (CDDRL) and the Center for Philanthropy and Civil Society (PACS). She also chairs the Expert Working Group of the Global Leaders Council for Reproductive Health of the Aspen Institute.

Paul D. Raskin is president of the Tellus Institute. He founded Tellus in 1976, Stockholm Environment Institute — US in 1989, the Global

Scenario Group in 1995, and the Great Transition Initiative in 2003. The overarching theme of his work has been envisioning and analyzing alternative scenarios of development, and identifying the strategies, policies, and values for a transition toward a future of environmental sustainability and human justice.

William E. Rees is a human ecologist, ecological economist, and professor emeritus and former director of the University of British Columbia's School of Community and Regional Planning. Best known as the originator and codeveloper of ecological footprint analysis, Rees has lectured on EFA and related topics in 25 countries. He has been recognized as one of British Columbia's top public intellectuals.

Katherine Richardson is professor of biological oceanography at the University of Copenhagen and leader of the Sustainability Science Centre. She was chairman of the Danish Commission on Climate Change Policy, which presented a 2010 roadmap for how Denmark can become independent of fossil fuels by 2050. She is also lead author of the book *Climate Change: Global Risks, Challenges and Decisions*. She was vice president of the European Science Foundation from 2001 through 2008.

Jane Roberts cofounded 34 Million Friends of the United Nations Population Fund in 2002. For this work, she has been recognized by the American Public Health Association, by *MS* Magazine, and by the United Nations Association. In 2005, she was one of 1000 women nominated for the Nobel Peace Prize as part of the 1000 Peace Women Project by UNESCO in Bern, Switzerland.

Penny D. Sackett is a physicist, astronomer, and former chief scientist for Australia (2008–2011). Sackett has held a research fellowship at the Princeton Institute for Advanced Study and appointments at the Kapteyn Astronomical Institute in the Netherlands and at the Australian National University.

Juliet Schor is professor of sociology at Boston College. Before joining Boston College, she taught at Harvard University for 17 years, in the

Department of Economics and the Committee on Degrees in Women's Studies. Her research has focused on work, consumption, and sustainability. Her "work and spend" cycle is an integrated approach to production and consumption. Most recently, her research emphasizes political consumption, new patterns of time-use, and alternative economic structures. As a member of a MacArthur Research Network, she is studying the emergence of collaborative consumption.

Martin Seligman is the Zellerbach Family Professor of Psychology and director of the Positive Psychology Center at the University of Pennsylvania, where he focuses on positive psychology, learned helplessness, depression, ethnopolitical conflict, and optimism. He is a best-selling author of several books, including, most recently, *Flourish*. In 1996, Seligman was elected president of the American Psychological Association by the largest vote in modern history.

Peter M. Senge is a senior lecturer at the Massachusetts Institute of Technology and founding chair of the SoL (Society for Organizational Learning) Council. He is author of *The Fifth Discipline: The Art and Practice of the Learning Organization* and, most recently, *The Necessary Revolution: How Individuals and Organizations are Working Together to Create a Sustainable World.*

Pahuna Sharma-Laden works as the Asia regional manager for Trees for the Future. She worked previously as an environmental reporter and researched the impact of bamboo flowering in northeast India for the Center for Science and Environment, New Delhi.

Daniel Sperling is professor of civil engineering and environmental science and policy, and founding director of the Institute of Transportation Studies at the University of California, Davis, and holds the transportation seat on the California Air Resources Board. He is author or editor of over 200 papers and reports and 12 books, has served on 13 National Academies committees, recently chaired the Future of Mobility committee of the (Davos) World Economic Forum, and testified seven times to the US Congress on alternative fuels and advanced vehicle technology.

James Gustave Speth is professor of law at the Vermont Law School. He is author of the forthcoming book *America the Possible: Roadmap to a New Economy*. In 2009, he completed his decade-long tenure as dean at the Yale School of Forestry and Environmental Studies. From 1993 to 1999, Speth was administrator of the UN Development Programme. Prior to this, he was founder and president of the World Resources Institute and chairman of the US Council on Environmental Quality under the Carter administration.

Barbara Elizabeth Stewart is a journalist, editor, and college teacher of writing and media studies. She has worked as a reporter for newspapers in Florida and New York, has written articles for the *Guardian*, *The New York Times*, and the *Telegraph*. She has taught in the City University of New York system, at Steven Institute of Technology. She is currently teaching media studies at Sherubtse College in Trashigang, which is part of the Royal Institute of Bhutan.

Brian Thomas Swimme is a professor at the California Institute of Integral Studies in San Francisco. He is coauthor of *The Universe Story*, the result of a 10-year collaboration with the cultural historian Thomas Berry.

Jigmi Y. Thinley The Honorable Lyonchhen Jigmi Y. Thinley is the first democratically elected prime minister of Bhutan. Prior to his election in 2008, he served as minister for Foreign Affairs and minister for Home and Cultural Affairs. He also served as prime minister from 1998 through 1999 and again from 2003 through 2004. The Honorable Y. Thinley is presently chairman of the National Environment Commission and the Ugyen Wangchuck Institute of Conservation and Environment.

Croix Thompson works as the Caribbean and West Africa regional manager for Trees for the Future. He previously worked for a television news station in Kansas City, Missouri, and served in the US Peace Corps in Niger.

Jana Timm is at the International Institute for Industrial Environmental Economics (IIIEE) Lund University.

Mary Evelyn Tucker is a senior lecturer and research scholar at Yale University, where she has appointments in the School of Forestry and Environmental Studies, the Divinity School, the Department of Religious Studies, and the Center for Bioethics. She also directs the Forum on Religion and Ecology at Yale with her husband, John Grim.

Maria Páez Victor is a sociologist, born in Venezuela and educated in Caracas, New York, Mexico City, and Canada. For several years, she taught the sociology of health and medicine as well as health and environmental policies at the University of Toronto. Páez Victor has national and international experience in policy analysis and impact assessment, with expertise in the areas of health, environment, and energy.

Peter Victor is an economist who has worked on environmental issues for over 40 years as an academic, consultant, and public servant. Victor was one of the founders of the emerging discipline of ecological economics and was the first President of the Canadian Society for Ecological Economics. Peter Victor is a Professor in Environmental Studies at York University and from 1996 to 2001 was Dean of the Faculty of Environmental Studies. This followed several years as Assistant Deputy Minister of the Environmental Sciences and Standards Division in the Ontario Ministry of the Environment. Prior to that, Peter Victor was a principal of VHB Consulting and Victor and Burrell Research and Consulting where he undertook many influential policy-related economic studies in Canada and abroad. He has continued to provide technical advice in areas such as air pollution and health, emissions trading, emerging issues, and education for sustainable energy development.

Ole Wæver is professor of international relations at the University of Copenhagen and director of the Centre for Advanced Security Theory. He originated the concept of "securitization" and was a central figure in developing the Copenhagen School in security studies. Among his main books are *Security: A New Framework for Analysis* and *Regions and Powers: The Structure of International Security*.

Brian Walker lectured at the University of Zimbabwe for six years and was professor of ecology at the University of the Witwatersrand, Johannesburg, until 1985, when he moved to Australia as chief of the Division of Wildlife and Ecology at CSIRO. He currently is a research fellow in the CSIRO Division of Ecosystem Science, chairs the board of the Resilience Alliance, is a fellow in the Beijer Institute for Ecological Economics in Sweden, and has a part-time appointment in the Stockholm Resilience Centre.

Dylan Walsh has a master's degree from Yale School of Forestry and Environmental Studies. He is currently an editor at *Solutions*.

Eckart Wintzen (1939–2008) was an unconventional Dutch entrepreneur and a pioneer in the field of sustainability. He built BSO/Origin, an IT company of 6000 employees with offices in 21 countries, and was one of the first to publish an annual environmental report. After selling his software business in 1996, Wintzen initiated Ex'tent Green Venture Capital.

Part 1

Introduction

Why We Need Visions of a Sustainable and Desirable World

Robert Costanza and Ida Kubiszewski

Creating a shared vision of a sustainable and desirable future is the most critical task facing humanity today. This vision must be of a world that we all want, a world that provides permanent prosperity within the Earth's biophysical constraints in a fair and equitable way to all of humanity, to other species, and to future generations.

Society is currently at a critical turning point. There is significant uncertainty about how environmental, social, and economic problems can be solved. However, there is growing consensus that the decisions we make as a society at this critical point will determine the course of our future for quite some time to come.

There is a tendency in thinking about the future to simply extrapolate from past trends. For example, if we have been getting materially richer in the past, then the future would be more of the same; if the environment has been deteriorating, then it will continue to do so. But one of the lessons we can learn from history is that trends often do not continue smoothly. There are tipping points and discontinuities that are impossible to predict from past trends. Many past civilizations have collapsed. The dissolution of the Soviet Union, the Berlin Wall being knocked down, attitudes changing toward smoking, and landing a man on the moon are recent examples of changes that were difficult or impossible to foresee.

We are learning more about the "process of change." For example, a necessary ingredient to making changes in a positive and specific direction is having a clear vision of the desired goal that is shared by a large fraction of the members of the organization or community.[1,2] A shared vision can change the world. In fact, it is one of the few methods that really can.

The challenge for the current generation of humans is to develop a shared vision that is both desirable to the vast majority of humanity and ecologically sustainable. This book is an attempt to contribute to a broad discussion on what a positive vision of the future is, should be, or can be. As Yogi Berra once said, "If you do not know where you are going, you end up somewhere else." We have to decide where we want to go, and balance that with where it is possible to go. It is the only way to change the world.

Visionaries and theorists have often been characterized as mere impractical dreamers. People become impatient and desire action, movement, measurable change, and practical applications. Yet we must recognize that action and change without an appropriate vision of the goal, and analyses of the best methods to achieve it, can be worse than counterproductive. In this sense, a compelling and appropriate vision can be the most practical of all applications. To some extent, we can change the way the world *is* by modifying our vision of what we would *like it to be*.[3]

Envisioning can also be seen as a key, but often missing, element in a true democracy. Democracy is about much more than simply voting for representatives.[4] It is about building consensus around the kind of world we really want. The New England town meeting is a good example of real democracy. It is a gathering where an entire town sits down, once a year, to discuss where they are, where they want to go, and how to get there. Can we scale up this process? In order to do that, we need an ongoing discussion about how that world might look. That is one of the issues this book is intended to stimulate. The global communications made possible by the Internet might make sharing visions and scaling up real democracy possible.

As ecological, economic, and social crises deepen, we desperately need new visions of a sustainable and desirable world. Isolated initiatives will not form an adequate response to our interconnected plights. Envisioning must also be seen as an ongoing process in which community members collectively identify shared values, describe the future they seek, and develop a plan to achieve common goals (in Chapter 2). Envisioning complements more traditional forms of planning, serving as a tool for determining community desires and initiating the process of change. This needs to happen at multiple scales, from small groups and communities, to states, nations, and the entire planet.

Our civilization's challenge is thus to create positive and detailed visions of a sustainable and desirable future. This not only needs to be a future with sustainable quality of life as the overarching goal but also a future that captivates and motivates the public. In this future, living in harmony with nature is recognized as enhancing everyone's quality of life and can create a world that we are proud to bestow on our grandchildren. Until we create and widely share this vision, we have no hope of achieving it.

The 46 chapters in this collection all describe what a sustainable and desirable future might look like from a broad range of perspectives. They are written by some of the world's leading thinkers, representing all aspects of society.

The collection is divided into four parts covering: (i) the process of envisioning; (ii) "future histories," which describe the envisioned world from the future, looking back; (iii) detailed descriptions of certain elements of the vision; and (iv) ideas about how to get from here to there. The contributions cover a broad range of questions, including, What does a sustainable and desirable world look like? Which worldview, or shared belief system, should predominate? How should we design society's physical infrastructure (including our buildings, transportation systems, energy networks, and industries)? How should we manage natural capital (the goods and services provided by nature)? How should we educate ourselves? How should we govern and make decisions? What should the economy look like? What should characterize our social interactions?

The four parts of this book

Part 1 includes this introductory chapter and three others about the process of envisioning. The first of these, by the late Donella Meadows, describes the process of envisioning and how we can, and urgently need to, do it better. The following two chapters by William S. Becker and Frances Moore Lappé encourage us all to envision and think differently about the kind of future we really want.

Part 2 is devoted to future histories. All the chapters assume that we are in the future and have already created the world we want. They describe this future and, to different extents, explain how we reached it. The first chapter in this section, by Robert Costanza and colleagues, describes what the worldviews, built capital, human capital, social capital, and natural capital might be like in 2050. The next two chapters, by Ajay Bhave and colleagues and Paul Raskin, outline some of the guiding principles, values, and hopes that exist in 2050.

The next three chapters each take a unique perspective on presenting a futuristic vision. Les Kuzyk describes a student taking a history exam in 2052, explaining how the world has changed since the beginning of this millennium. In his chapter "A Virtual Visit to a Sustainable 2050," Robert Costanza uses a hypothetical virtual reality system to allow people today to envision a world in 2050, walk through it, and experience this new world. Joshua Farley takes a different approach in his chapter by describing the world from the point of view of a man on his deathbed, thinking about his family and the world they live in.

The chapter by Ron Colman, although providing a global vision, describes a path that the world took to reach it. It describes a turning point occurring during a meeting in Bhutan in 2013. The last two chapters in this part, by John Peet and Barbara Elizabeth Stewart, describe how a specific country (New Zealand) and a city (New York, USA) look in 2050.

Part 3 describes various elements that the world we want will need to incorporate. The first chapter, by the Prime Minister of Bhutan Jigmi Thinley, describes the development philosophy of Bhutan, based on well-being and happiness, as a model for the world we want. Martin Seligman describes "positive psychology" and how it captures the elements of human well-being that we want to enhance, both now and in the future. Wendell Berry describes his wish for the coal economy of eastern Kentucky to change to a sustainable local economy. Jane Roberts, Kavita Ramdas, and Jamie Querubin envision worlds with gender equality. The chapters by Bill

McKibben and by Dylan Walsh and Tess Croner form an interesting pair of quite different narratives told from the perspective of the year 2100. They explain two versions of what our path looked like to get back to 350 ppm CO_2 in the atmosphere. Daniel Pauly describes how changing our baseline in fisheries can help to get the bad old things to shift away and the good old things to shift back into focus. Richard Forman describes a future with roads that integrate with nature rather than dissecting it. Senator Gary Hart describes how the military will require resetting, rebuilding, and reform to address 21st century security issues. Peter Bartelmus discusses how green national accounting can help us achieve a sustainable future. And in the final chapter of this part, James Gustave Speth lays out a comprehensive vision for a new sustainable American economy — America the possible — that could again be a positive model for the world.

Part 4 is about getting from here to there. It includes 21 chapters covering a broad range of topics and issues. William Rees lays out how we can achieve the reductions in material throughput, energy use, and environmental degradation necessary to meet humanity's needs within planetary boundaries. Mary Evelyn Tucker and Brian Swimme provide an integrating story of our connection with the cosmos to guide the future. Bill McKibben encourages us to get angry about the current state of affairs to stimulate movement. David Orr describes how we can avoid the "perfect storm" threatening humanity. Ernest Callenbach shows how a smaller economy can be stronger, more sustainable, and provide a higher quality of life. Brian Walker shows how to apply resilience thinking to help us achieve our sustainability goals. Penny Sackett describes the need to conserve the chemical building blocks of all life and economic production. Anders Hayden shows how work time reduction can lead to a better and more sustainable work–life balance. Mohan Munasinghe lays out millennium consumption goals to compliment the millennium development goals for a sustainable future. George Burns shows how a focus on psychological well-being and happiness can help create the world we want. Van Jones describes the new green economy based on production, thrift, and ecological restoration while Hunter Lovins describes an economy based on sustainable happiness rather than gross domestic product (GDP) madness. Christine Loh shows how ecological restoration can be the basis for a sustainable future while Eckart Wintzen advocates ecological accounting and taxation to fund this restoration. Pahuna Sharma-Laden and Croix Thompson show how agroforestry can be a key component in this restoration. Katherine Richardson and Ole Wæver describe the new science–policy links needed to achieve the world we want. On a lighter note, Maria Páez Victor describes how bringing classical music to the underprivileged in Venezuela has transformed people's lives and can serve as a model for education. Peter Senge moves beyond industrial age education to a description of what education for a sustainable future would look like, based on systems thinking and learner-centered engagement. Tim Kasser shows how fundamental values can be changed to achieve the world we want, while Catherine O'Brien shows how we can do this with courses in sustainable happiness. Finally, Peggy Liu shows how changing values can lead to sustainable consumerism.

We hope that this collection paints a picture of the kind of world we want, one that is sustainable, fair, and prosperous. But it is certainly not the end of the story. It is only the beginning since, as Donella Meadows points out in her chapter, the process of envisioning is critically important and we need to develop innovative ways to broaden people's engagement in that process in order to build a shared vision that can motivate positive change. We hope that this book helps stimulate that process and that everyone will participate.

References

1. Senge, PM (1990). *The Fifth Discipline: The Art and Practice of the Learning Organization.* New York, USA: Currency-Doubleday.
2. Weisbord, M and S Janoff (2010). *Future Search: Getting the Whole System in the Room for Vision, Commitment, and Action.* San Francisco: Berrett-Koehler.
3. Jones, RA (1977). *Self-Fulfilling Prophecies: Social, Psychological, and Physiological Effects of Expectancies.* New York, USA: John Wiley and Sons.
4. Prugh, T, R Costanza and H Daly (2000). *The Local Politics of Global Sustainability.* Washington, DC: Island Press, 173 pp.

2

Envisioning a Sustainable World

Donella Meadows

This is an edited transcript of part of a talk given by Donella Meadows at the 1994 meeting of the International Society for Ecological Economics in San José, Costa Rica, and recorded by Peter Griesinger. Meadows, cofounder of the Balaton Group, passed away in 2001, but she has inspired a generation to hold onto, build, and share their visions of a sustainable world. A video of her full talk can be viewed at: http://www. youtube.com/watch?v=oiUJaliYw5c.

We need clarity about our goals. We need to know where we are going. We need to have vision. And that vision has to be articulated, it has to be socially shared, and discussed, and formulated.

There's a tendency when we get involved in the problems — as a result of the lack of implementation, of money, of resources, of models and information, and vision — to go immediately to implementation, and talk first and primarily in that arena. How do we get governments to work better together? How do we get the money raised? But before that we need to be sure that our models are clear, that our information is accurate, and above all we need to be sure that we know where we're going.

Bob Costanza reminded me that the title of this session was "Creating a Sustainable and Desirable Future." And I realized that I had fallen into the trap that we modelers, and the politicians, and almost everyone falls into, which is to take the last steps first. To talk about the implementation or the model, skipping over or taking for granted the vision and goal.

I want to talk about vision and encourage all of us to do that — a subject, by the way, which I could say I am completely unqualified to talk about, having had no training. In fact, I would say, in the scientific, northern training I have had, I've been systematically *untrained* to find and communicate vision. But, in another sense, I don't think any of us *need* training. I think what we need to do is to brush away some of our training and rediscover our ability to vision, to see goals, to make the idea of a sustainable world a living picture in our minds and other people's minds so that we know what we are talking about and know where we're going.

> *I think what we need to do is to brush away some of our training and rediscover our ability to vision, to see goals, to make the idea of a sustainable world a living picture in our minds and other people's minds so that we know what we are talking about and know where we're going.*

What I'm going to do is to try and share the little bit I have learned by playing with the idea of vision and incorporating it into my own life. I think I probably don't have to tell you that when we, particularly we on the environmental side of things, start talking about a sustainable world, we somehow engender a vision of sacrifice, a vision of having much less, a vision of tight central control, of deep regulations, a loss of freedom. Whether we communicate that because it's in our heads or because it's in the culture we're communicating to, I think you probably know that most environmentalists are not considered people that put forth exciting visions. They generally are assumed to be people who are calling for great sacrifice. And this must say something about the vision in our culture of what a sustainable world is like.

I think that we are all born with a sense of what the world should be like and what we deeply want the world to be like. You ask a child to make a vision of a sustainable world and it comes flowing forth and there's not a bit of resistance. So this is clearly something we have had engendered into us by two things. One is the general culture, particularly the scientific, objective culture. And second, by our disappointments: as we grow old, we've tried things, they haven't worked, and instead of using disappointments to learn lessons and become more effective in pushing toward our vision, we've let go of our vision.

Remember, when you envision, that you are trying to state, articulate, or see what you really want, not what you think you can get. It's very quick for most of us rationally trained people to go out to the farthest envelope of what we think is *possible*. We are putting all kinds of analysis and models in there of what is possible. I never would have said that it was possible for apartheid to end in South Africa, or for the whole of the Eastern world to come back towards democracy. And yet it happened. So that tells you something about our model of possibilities. You have to throw them away. You have to think about what you want. That's the essence of vision. What is a sustainable world that you would like to live in? That would satisfy your deepest dreams and longings?

Second, if you can get there, to that picture, you are under no obligation, whatsoever, to tell us how to get there from here. The easiest way to shoot down a visionary is to have someone express a vision, and you say, "Oh yeah, but how do we get there from here?" And if the visionary can't tell you, you sweep away the vision. This is our rational left-brain working again. My experience in having, now many times, created a vision and then actually brought it, in some form, into being, my experience is that I never know at the beginning how to get there but, as I articulate the vision, put it out, share it with people, it gets more polished, and the path reveals itself. And it would have never revealed itself if I were not putting out the vision of what I really wanted and finding that other people really want it, too. Holding on to the vision reveals the path and there's no need to judge the vision by whether the path is apparent.

As I said already, the visioning, wherever it comes from, I don't understand this at all, it isn't a rational place, and it doesn't come from figuring out. But visions do have to be honed by rationality. There does need to be a responsibility in vision. I can envision climbing to the top of a tree and flying off. I may really want to do that but my rationality and my knowledge of how the world works tells me that's not a responsible vision.

Visions become responsible through all sort of processes, the best one I know is sharing it with other people who bring in their knowledge, their points of view, and their visions. The more a vision is shared, the more responsible it gets, and also the more ethical.

Another thing I've discovered is that once I'm clear and have worked on a vision, it becomes more and more real to me. I can literally see it. I've been working on this vision of a sustainable world for a long time. I can literally see it in Technicolor, in some detail, and it gets better and better the more I learn, the more I ask other people. It lives in me, a sustainable world that isn't a sacrifice or a bunch of difficult regulations, a sustainable world that I would love to live in. And having such a vision

> *I've been working on this vision of a sustainable world for a long time. I can literally see it in Technicolor, in some detail, and it gets better and better the more I learn, the more I ask other people.*

alive in me prevents me from selling out to something less that someone may be offering me, such as a vision of perpetual economic growth, which is pretty much the vision that the entire field of economics gives us. Growth isn't what I want. Growth has nothing to do with what I want. And I think that the only reason growth — which is a terribly abstract and, when you think about it, stupid vision of the future — can be sold so easily in every policy arena is that there's no alternative vision.

An alternative, sustainable world is, of course, where resource regeneration is at least as great as resource depletion. It's a world where emissions are no greater than the ability of the planet to absorb and process those emissions. Of course it's a world where the population is stable or maybe even decreasing; where prices internalize all costs; a place where no one is hungry or desperately poor; a place where there is true enduring democracy. These are some of the things I have in my part of the vision. But most of those are physically necessary or socially necessary parts of the vision. They form the responsible structure that you know has got to be part of the vision. But, then, what else? What more? What would make this a world that would make you excited to get up in the morning and go to work in?

I'm going to ask you now to close your eyes, because that's the best place to find a vision: within yourself, without distractions. And I'm going to lead just a little, ask you to look at, literally with your mind's eye, a sustainable world. And what I caution you to do, since I've now done it many times, is don't push it, don't feel you're a failure if nothing comes, and don't grasp too hard to see something. Just notice what happens. That's all you have to do. This needs to be a very relaxing exercise.

Start near home, in your home, whatever your home looks like, a home you would love to live in. One that's comfortable and beautiful and sustainable. Look around. What does that home look like, inside and outside? Who's there? What does it feel like to live there, to work there, to eat there, to get up in the morning? What does it feel like to walk out the door into your community, your neighborhood? Rural or urban or in between? What's the neighborhood like — the one that you would love to live in, that is sustainable, and knows itself to be sustainable, a world that can be handed down, intact, to the children and the grandchildren of that neighborhood? Physically, what is the neighborhood like? What does the built environment look like? Where is nature, and what is it like? What kind of energy is powering this neighborhood? What types of materials? Where does the water come from, where does it go? Who's living there? How do they make their living? Where do they go to make their living? If out of the neighborhood, how do they get there? How do you communicate in the neighborhood and with other neighborhoods? How often? By what means? About what?

And now, if you can, move up a little bit, to a bigger view of several neighborhoods together, a whole city, or a whole rural area, a whole state or province where you live, working sustainably in a way you would love it to work. Look at your whole nation. What does it look like? What does it feel like? How are decisions made? How are conflicts resolved? What kinds of technologies are being used and being born?

Now go to the whole world, sustainable, full of nations and neighborhoods, cities, and rural areas where people love to live, where they know their children and their grandchildren will have an even more intact, more sustainable, more exciting world than the one they live in. What kind of world is that? How do people of different kinds, colors, and cultures communicate? How do they learn from each other? How do they get along with each other? How do they resolve conflicts?

Spend just another few seconds in your sustainable world, looking at anything you want to look at, envisioning anything you want to envision about this world in which you would love to live. And when you're ready, open your eyes and come back to the unsustainable real world.

Visioning is the first step, and a continuous step, because visions continue to get revised and shared and built and elaborated and made more rich and more true.

3

Why Everyone Should Be a Futurist?

William S. Becker

In hearing rooms, hallways, and conferences where the world's policy-makers are wrestling with the big issues of our day, something important is missing.

Vision

By vision, I do not mean those forward-looking policy papers that tell us how we might shape the future with a global Green New Deal, or the Millennium Development Goals, or a Copenhagen Accord. Those intellectual constructs are critical, but they are not enough.

We are missing visions of the right-brain variety — immersive, lifelike visual images of the future we want, conveyed with the same powerful technologies that moviemakers use to entertain us, and the advertising industry uses to sell us things. Think about it. Would not it be interesting if we mobilized our visual arts and tools to change sustainable development from an abstraction into something we all can see?

In the brutal battles over public policy these days, visions of the kind I am describing seem fluffy, as though we are entering the arena with swords made of cotton instead of steel. However, as the late Donella Meadows put it, "Vision is the most vital step in the policy process. If we don't know where we want to go, it makes little difference that we make great progress."[1]

This is not to say our communications industries do not show us anything about the future. But they focus on the future we must avoid rather than the future we must create. It is likely that the apocalypse is coming right now to a theater near you. Think of *The Day After Tomorrow*, *The Road*, *An Inconvenient Truth*, *The 11th Hour*, or *2012*, to name a few movies in recent years. We have seen endless television shows on the frightening prophecies of Nostradamus and the Mayan calendar. The Discovery Channel has shown us in nightmarish detail *Ten Ways the World Will End*. Apparently thinking it is a public service to help us prepare, the channel is airing a series called *Doomsday Shelters* in which families who call themselves "preppers" are building underground shelters stocked with food, weapons, and ammunition. News media are governed by the "if it bleeds, it leads" rule, showing us economic collapse, homelessness, war, terrorism, natural disasters, and other symptoms of social collapse every evening at dinnertime. We revel in our fears but do not reveal our dreams.

For what would seem to be sound tactical reasons, environmental advocates also focus on fear as a motivator. The "fight or flight" reaction seems to be a more powerful force for change than happy visions of security and abundance. The prominent British environmentalist Jonathon Porritt notes that there is a:

> continuing lack of any compelling narrative focusing on the *upside* of living within environmental limits rather than on the multiple *downsides* of exceeding those limits. Many more people count themselves as environmentalists out of a desire to avoid a potential ecological apocalypse rather than out of a belief in some "Promised Land" flowing with organic milk and rainforest honey.

He continues:

> This lack of a compelling upside narrative exposes environmentalists to the rabble-rousing charge of being anti-progress and anti-aspiration — a charge that sounds more and more convincing as more and more environmentalists let it be known that they believe it is either "already too late" to do anything about the gathering apocalypse, or, in order to avoid it being too late, that we need to go onto an instantaneous "war footing" to combat accelerating

climate change — whatever the consequences for democracy. For wholly understandable historical and intellectual reasons, today's environmental discourse is still shaped far more powerfully by the language of "scarcity" and "limits" than it is by any compelling upside narrative. But fear of the future does not empower people; it debilitates and disempowers.[2]

We can find a corollary in international negotiations, where the conversation is about which nations will sacrifice growth to cut carbon emissions, rather than who will be the first to seize the enormous opportunities in a global transition to sustainability.

The resulting stalemate makes us pessimistic that our international institutions can deal with this century's global problems. That pessimism can easily become a self-fulfilling prophecy. Paul Ray and Sherry Ruth Anderson, authors of *The Cultural Creatives: How 50 Million People Are Changing the World*, write, "Today as we are besieged by planetary problems, the risk is that we will deal with them in a pessimistic and unproductive style. Transfixed by an image of our own future decline, we could actually bring it about."[3]

In the best case, problems push us to action. But to find its sense of direction, the "push" needs help from the "pull" of positive vision. The Transition Town movement, a grassroots network that began in the United Kingdom, helps communities become more resilient against threats such as peak oil, climate change, and economic instability. That is a response to "push." But the movement's founder, permaculture expert Rob Hopkins, also understands the power of "pull":

> It is one thing to campaign against climate change and quite another to paint a compelling and engaging vision of a post-carbon world in such a way as to enthuse others to embark on a journey toward it. We are only just beginning to scratch the surface of the power of a positive vision of an abundant future.[4]

Business has long understood the power of vision in attracting customers. General Motors (GM) illustrated it more than 70 years ago at the New York World's Fair. In the hangover of the Great Depression, GM commissioned theatrical designer Norman Bel Geddes to create *Futurama*, a pavilion in which an estimated 20 million visitors were conveyed through models of life 20 years in the future. At its core, GM's vision was a dynamic, highly mobile, car-centered society — an appealing alternative to the life many of the visitors were experiencing. A case can be made that GM's vision built public support for the way we have designed cities and transportation systems ever since.

But the 1930s GM model does not work anymore. We need a new vision (Box 1).

Box 1. Today's Visionaries

Nongovernmental organizations

2020: Shaping the Future, a series of videos from Ericsson Worldwide with thought leaders offering their ideas for the future (www.ericsson.com/campaign/20about2020).

Adaptive Edge, specializing in futures thinking, strategy, and innovation. It describes itself as "pathfinders for leaders on the brink of change" (www.adaptive-edge.com).

America 2050: Journey to Detroit, a video visualization of transportation options of the future (www.america2050.org/2010/02/journey-to-detriot.html). Produced by the America 2050 program at the Regional Plan Association, New York.

Collective Invention, which develops experiential future scenarios to help leaders innovate for the common good (www.theworldcafecommunity.org).

Monday Morning, whose Project Green Light has published *The Guidebook to Sustainia*, the vision of a sustainable future (http://greengrowthleaders.org/project-green-light).

My Green Dream, a project of the UN Institute for Training and Research (UNITAR) and the CIFAL Network. It has deployed "dream catchers" to 15 countries (at last count), taping short video interviews in which people state their aspirations for the future (http://green-dream.co.uk/dreams).

One Earth Initiative, whose objective is to "rethink the Good Life" and to transform unsustainable consumption and production (http://oneearthweb.org).

(Continued)

Box 1. (*Continued*)

Our Cities/Our Selves: The Future of Transportation in Urban Life, a project of the Institute for Transportation and Policy Planning (www.ourcitie ourselves.org).

The World Café, a place where visitors gather to share experiences and explore collective action (www.theworldcafecommunity.org).

US PIRG: Transportation of the Future, a video produced by a nine-year-old, one of the entries in a US Public Interest Research Group's video contest. (www.youtube.com/watch?v=sbX38qeVCqo).

Corporate visualizations

Arnold Imaging, a Kansas City company that facilitates green development with videos and animations showing how sustainable design and technologies benefit the built environment and quality of life (www.arnoldimaging.com).

Corning's *A Day Made of Glass* (www.youtube.com/watch_popup?v= 6Cf7IL_eZ38&vq=medium).

Enel on imagining the smart grid (www.youtube.com/watch?v=sV6o3t_ bNN4&feature=related).

General Motors' *Dreams of Flight*, imagining the future of air transportation (www.ge.com/thegeshow/future-flight). Also, GM's electric networked vehicles (www.scientificamerican.com/article.cfm?id=electric-networked-vehicle-gm).

Kjellgren Kaminsky Architecture's video, *Super Sustainable City — Gothenburg* (www.youtube.com/watch?v=aMFnmpNsaqg&feature=related).

Microsoft's Vision of the Future videos (www.singularityweblog.com/ microsofts-vision-for-the-future-videos).

Siemens' Sustainable Cities Vision, including Changing Your City for the Better, a video competition to show how people are using technology to overcome humanity's challenges (http://zooppa.com/contests/changing-your-city-for-the-better). Also, the company's video on how to make sustainable cities (www.usa.siemens.com/sustainable-cities/?stc=usccc-025107).

(*Continued*)

Box 1. (*Continued*)

Solutions

Design with the Other 90%: Cities, the latest in a series of exhibits featuring design solutions that address the 90% of the world's population not traditionally served by professional designers (www.designother90.org/cities/home).

Young Voices for the Planet, a film series featuring young people working on reducing the carbon footprint of their schools, homes, and communities (http://youngvoicesonclimatechange.com/climate-change-videos.php).

Inspiration

Apple's *Here's to the Crazy Ones* (www.youtube.com/watch?v=4oAB83Z1y dE&feature=related).

Make your own visions

Make a Comic Strip about sustainability in your community (www.pixton. com/overview#video and www.pixton.com/ca).

The future we want

In 2009, Michael Northrop, the director of the Rockefeller Brothers Fund's sustainable development program, convened 30 sustainability and communications experts to explore why the public was not more engaged in fighting for a more sustainable world. We who participated talked about "apocalypse fatigue" — the tendency for people to withdraw from solving problems that seem overwhelming and unsolvable. We also observed that today's social media and

> *We decided that we need to help the broad and largely disengaged public understand the future we can build, based on visions that are realistic, achievable, and positive.*

the Internet make it possible to have a global conversation about "push" and "pull." We decided that we need to help the broad and largely disengaged public understand the future we can build, based on visions that are realistic, achievable, and positive.

That was the inception of a project now called "The Future We Want." We are inviting people around the world to share their ideas about what they want their communities and lives to be like 20 years from now. We are mobilizing world-class technologists, designers, planners, and artists to show us what life would be like if we confronted today's challenges head-on and built a world that reflected people's hopes.

In 2011, we took the project to the United Nations, which was planning Rio+20 — its Conference on Sustainable Development in June 2012 on the 20th anniversary of the first Earth Summit. With agility uncharacteristic for such a large institution, the United Nations' entire chain of command adopted "The Future We Want" as the official tagline for Rio+20. Secretary-General Ban Ki-moon announced it on 22 November 2011; a few months later, he embraced it as the theme for his next five-year agenda at the United Nations.

As the project progressed, we found we were not the only organization engaged in exploring vision. My Green Dream, led by May East from the Findhorn community in Scotland, has deployed "dream catchers" around the world to collect short videos of people describing their aspirations for the future. Sustainia, a project of the Danish think tank *Monday Morning*, has organized a competition to identify the 100 best ideas to achieve sustainable societies by 2020. Rather than awarding its annual cash prize to an individual in 2012, TED launched City 2.0, calling for concepts on the city of the future. The Institute for Transportation and Policy Development in New York commissioned architects in 10 cities around the world to draw what sustainable development would look like at specific blighted locations in each place.

Corporations, who see the future in terms of markets, are entering the dialogue too. Siemens has its own exhibit of the cities of tomorrow, as does its competitor, General Electric. Corning has produced a video on a futuristic "day made of glass."

Some of the leaders in the world's principal oil patch also are thinking about the future — in their case, the post-petroleum world. Years ago, a Saudi Arabian oil minister warned that oil reserves would not be depleted before renewable energy takes over the world's energy markets. (In a quote for the ages, the minister, Sheikh Zaki Yamani, observed that the Stone Age did not end because we ran out of stones.) Today, the royal family in Abu Dhabi is positioning the United Arab Emirates as a global thought leader on sustainable energy, sponsoring an annual World Energy Futures Conference and working on the world's first carbon-neutral city.

The contributions of these change agents and visionaries have not yet penetrated the world's policy circles. We remain in a rut of oil and coal, flirting with even worse forms of fossil energy and with technologies we do not know how to control, such as nuclear energy, geoengineering, and carbon sequestration. The entrenched and well-financed fossil energy industries are so far more interested in finding ways to extend the oil age than they are in helping us achieve a new energy economy — an economy that would sustain them, too, if they made the transition with the rest of us. Lacking a better vision, the developing world still considers the Western model of consumption and car-dependent cities the highest expressions of progress.

But in this time in which our old institutions and systems are failing us; in which powerful and entrenched vested interests are fighting to maintain a status quo that cannot be maintained; in which the impacts of climate change are becoming more frequent, severe, and undeniable; and in which our confidence in the old economic order has been shaken, we have reached a teachable moment not unlike the one that GM seized in 1939.

It is time to envision the future we want, to get the global community talking about it, and to insist on the public policies that will allow us to achieve it. Given the finality of problems such as species loss, peak oil, and climate change, every day we delay makes the "upside narrative" less credible. But if we decide to grasp it, a future we want is still within reach. Buckminster Fuller had it right: "We are called to be architects of the future, not its victims."

References

1. Meadows, D (1996). Envisioning a sustainable world. In *Getting Down to Earth, Practical Applications of Ecological*, R Costanza, O Segura and J Martinez-Alier (eds.), Washington, DC: Island Press.
2. Porritt, J. (2011). Scarcity and sustainability in Utopia. *Insights Paper*, 4(4), Durham University and the Institute of Advanced Study, 12 pp.
3. Ray, P and SR Anderson (2000). *The Cultural Creatives: How 50 Million People Are Changing the World*. New York: Three Rivers Press.
4. Hopkins, R. (2008). *The Transition Handbook: From Oil Dependency to Local Resilience*. Cambridge, UK: Green Books.

Think Like an Ecosystem, See Solutions

Frances Moore Lappé

For the coming generation, the critical challenge is an interior one — a shift inside us that could trigger a tectonic shift outside.

Feel-good hokum, you say? Let me attempt a logical case.

As we watch ice caps dissolve, forests burn, and species vanish forever, we have to ask: Is our species really so dense that we cannot see that we are destroying our own life-support systems? Or, are humans so evil — narrowly self-interested and grasping for immediate reward — that we care not about the suffering we are creating?

The next generation must have good answers to such questions — a good working theory about *why* we are in this mess — in order for Rio+40 to bring better outcomes than its predecessors. So here is what I propose. Let us stop merely fighting to save our ecological home. *Let us learn from it.* What if our real problem is that we have not yet begun to "think like an ecosystem"? And what if the real solution is to start doing so right now?

For me, thinking like an ecosystem means moving from a fixation on limiting or growing quantities of things — from greenhouse gas to food calories — to focus increasingly on the quality of relationships, that is, whether they further life.

Thinking like an ecosystem means appreciating that all organisms, all elements of a system, are shaped by all others in a relational world characterized by three qualities: (i) connectedness, (ii) continuous change, and (iii) cocreation.

In biological systems, "there are no privileged components telling the rest what to do," writes Oxford physiologist Denis Noble. "There is rather a form of democracy [involving] every element at all levels." The shape of life, Noble explains in *The Music of Life*, emerges through the interactions of all elements.[1] At its deepest, this insight lies at the heart of great wisdom traditions, and scientists now tell us that it is the nature of nature.

And we are beginning to get it in regard to the natural world. But what if, simultaneously, we applied the same insight to our *human* ecology?

For, clearly, it is this ecology — that of human organisms relating to one another — that is at the heart of the matter. Since few of us live pre-industrial lives directly interacting with plant and animal life on its own terms, how we impact the natural world is today almost entirely *mediated through social ecology* — through our political and economic rules and norms determining, or at least greatly shaping, our personal options and our impact.

To readers of *Solutions*, this is obvious: Even cultures with roughly comparable physical amenities and infrastructure differ markedly, for example, in CO_2 output per person. Even a supermotivated American environmental activist, who cut her emissions to almost half that of her neighbors', would still disrupt the climate as much as the statistically average German, who makes no special effort to reduce her environmental impact, does.[2]

And we know why. For one, public choices made Germany — cloudy Germany — the producer of almost half of the world's solar power in 2010, though the country ranks 63rd in land area worldwide.[3,4] Germany's Feed-in Tariff policies, which reward households with a good rate of return for the clean energy they produce, have made it relatively easy and economical to become a household energy producer.[5]

Or, consider that the average American recycles and composts about half that of the average German.[6,7] A key reason is not the German's greater personal virtue, but each society's public choices: Two decades ago, for example, Germany launched a Green Dot labeling system requiring companies either to take responsibility for recovering their own packaging (impractical for most) or to contribute to the cost of the government's recycling it. Now, in 23 European countries, the Green Dot fee structure rewards companies for minimizing their packaging.[8,9] Plus, Germany makes recycling especially convenient with at-home receptacles plus color-coded neighborhood bins, including one for household waste.

It is obvious that differences among our societies flow from public choices, which create the context in which the individual functions.

Thus it is the quality of the decisions we humans *make together* that determine the fate of our earth. And, I argue, the "quality" of these common decisions, their effectiveness, is largely determined by *how* they are generated:

- How inclusive are the voices participating in decision making?
- How complete is the relevant input considered?
- How transparent is the process?
- To whom are decision makers accountable?

Still, many of us environmentalists in and outside government devote scarce attention to this all-important *how* in the making of common decisions. More often, we focus intently on the design of, and choice among, policies. We berate, beg, and shame politicians to do the right thing, and outside the chambers, we regale and rally citizens to make better personal choices.

In choosing these foci, we are implicitly saying that the real challenge is *inside* people — can we get laggards to do the right thing? In so limiting ourselves, we can miss the key lessons of thinking like an ecosystem: What is happening on the *outside*? What is the influence of context? Our species is, after all, like any other in an ecosystem, where the traits that individuals express depend a lot on external stimuli, that is, on the conditions in which they operate.

Conditions that elicit our best

From there, we can ask, simply: What conditions bring out the best and the worst in our species? We know that human beings, having evolved in tribes, retain the social capacities for cooperation, empathy, and fairness that enabled our species to thrive over eons of time.[10,11] Yet history and laboratory experiments on us *also* confirm, just as certainly, that most of us — not just an evil few — can be callous, in fact, unspeakably cruel to one another.[12,13]

Over the grand — err, not so grand — sweep of human history, three conditions seem virtually certain to elicit the very worst in us: (i) the extreme concentration of power, (ii) secrecy, and (iii) a culture of blame.

But there is great news here as well. With an eco-mind focused on context and the quality of relationships within the system, what to do appears pretty straightforward: we strive to flip this proven-negative context.

In other words, we work for the ongoing dispersion of power through inclusive decision making, transparency in human relationships, and moving from the "blame game" to a culture of mutual accountability.

With an eco-mind we see that, since we are all connected, we are all implicated. So the blaming can stop and the problem solving can take off. Or, more accurately, the manifestation of solutions can take off, for right now solutions to each of our great crises are *already known* or well within reach, be it for mass poverty, an out-

> *With an eco-mind we see that, since we are all connected, we are all implicated.*

of-whack carbon cycle, or species destruction. Exemplary, effective approaches are here, ready to take to scale. Our task is to generate the specific conditions, such as the three I have suggested above, in our social ecology that have proven to be most likely to elicit our pro-social capacities.

But how?

Leverage points to change a system

We circle back to the rewards of thinking like an ecosystem.

Systems maven, the late Professor Donella Meadows, taught us to think in patterns of connection and therefore to focus on leverage points: those points of entry into a system at which a small change triggers big change. In her seminal 1999 article, "Leverage Points: Places to Intervene in a System" assessing the power of 12 such points of leverage, Meadows ranked those involving the paradigm — the set of assumptions from which the system emerges — as most powerful.[14]

Taking her advice to heart means challenging the mechanical paradigm out of which today's policy choices too often arise. We work, for example, to crack the mindset in which the environment is the "other" with which we have to negotiate our existence: as in bargaining for the best trade-off between environmental health and job creation, or between ecological thriving, on the one hand, and comfort and beauty, on the other. Through evidence, metaphor, and story, we expose such framing as baseless.

But right up there among leverage-point royalty, according to Meadows, is "the goal of the system." *Affect the goal, and you affect the whole*, is how I think of it. And how is a goal set?

Certainly, the four aspects comprising the "how" of common decision making — who is included, how transparent the process is, what input gets considered, and to whom do decision makers report — end up determining the quality of societies' goals.

Okay. Now we are getting somewhere. We can focus on the improving quality of our common decision-making process and be certain we have got real leverage in creating the world we want.

We can start by acknowledging that today, in most of the world's most powerful societies, the goal-setting process is grossly lacking. Typically, highly exclusive processes determine who can get to the table and, even in nominal democracies, those few at the table are typically more accountable to interests funding their candidacies than to the people who elect them. Plus, the range of input which decision makers are required to consider is often narrow.

It is not working. It cannot work, and now it is clear why. It ends up creating conditions perversely aligned with human nature, that is, bringing forth the worst and tamping down the best. With this clarity, we are energized to create the opposite, the dimensions of common decision making — such as those I offer above — that both embody and potentially create conditions positively aligned with our nature, that is, eliciting our pro-social qualities while keeping our capacity for brutality and callousness in check.

And there is a word for it: democracy! We cannot let that word be discredited because it is been a victim of abuse. With an eco-mind, however, we might add a modifier and call it *Living Democracy*, suggesting an ever-evolving culture of engagement and mutual accountability that, of course, includes formal political decision making but goes far beyond it, too.

As environmentalists, seeing through an eco-mind lens, our vision changes. We perceive the Arab Spring, not as a separate political development emerging "over there," but as tender green shoots essential to planetary environmental flowering. And we participate wholeheartedly in campaigns pursuing, for example, full disclosure of political contributions, and transparency in government more widely, as well as public funding of elections, as the very foundation of effective environmentalism. In the United States, for example, public passion for these issues is growing, and in the US Congress today, legislation is pending for "fair elections" via the funding of campaigns from public sources combined with small donations from citizens.[15]

And we celebrate and help to further the proliferating examples of less formal, small "d" democracy that are already manifesting environmental solutions.

One example is community forestry, in which central governments are effectively devolving authority for forest protection to local management by citizen groups. From Mexico to Rwanda to India and beyond, it is working. In India, 10 million households are involved in officially sanctioned Forest Management Groups.[16–18]

Small "d" democracy is also emerging in the large, southern India state of Andhra Pradesh, hard hit by farmer suicides and pesticide-related illness. Today, almost one million Self-help Groups led by women are taking the lead in village organizing to move toward sustainable farming practices, now supported by state agencies.[19,20]

Yet another sighting of Living Democracy at the community level is the citizen-jury process that brings diverse voices together to weigh critical issues, with opportunity to learn from experts from all sides. Here, the pioneering work of the International Institute for the Environment and Development is taking the tool global. In West Africa, since 2010, several citizen juries, after weighing agricultural development priorities, have come out strongly for the involvement of farmers in setting the direction of agricultural research and rejected a focus on hybrid and genetically modified seeds that make farmers dependent on corporate suppliers.[21]

From fair elections to citizen juries, all are examples of people standing up to protect and create forms of common decision making that embody precisely the qualities of inclusion and accountability necessary to create effective solutions. They are examples of thinking like an ecosystem in which we become as excited about generating effective, democratic decision making as we are about our distinct issue passions. Al Gore was right when he reminded us that, "in order to solve the environmental crisis, we have to solve the democracy crisis."[22]

References

1. Noble, D (2006). *The Music of Life*. Oxford: Oxford University Press, p. 53.
2. World Bank. World Development Indicators: CO_2 Emissions (Metric Tons per Capita) [online]. Available at data.worldbank.org/indicator/EN.ATM. CO2E.PC/countries [accessed on 8 August 2013].
3. Renewables 2011 Global Status Report [online] (2011). Paris: REN21, p. 23. Available at www.ren21.net/Portals/97/documents/GSR/REN21_GSR2011. pdf [accessed on 8 August 2013].
4. World Factbook [online] (2012). Washington, DC: Central Intelligence Agency. Available at www.cia.gov/library/publications/the-world-factbook/ rankorder/2147rank.html [accessed on 8 August 2013].
5. Mendonca, M, D Jacobs and B Sovacool (2010). *Powering the Green Economy: The Feed-In Tariff Handbook*. London: Earthscan [accessed on 8 August 2013].
6. Municipal Solid Waste in the United States: 2007 Facts and Figures [online]. Available at www.epa.gov/osw//nonhaz/municipal/pubs/msw07-rpt.pdf [accessed on 8 August 2013].
7. EU27: Half a ton of municipal waste generated per person in 2007 [online] (2009). Available at www.recyclingportal.eu/artikel/21517.shtml [accessed on 8 August 2013].
8. Emergo Europe. Frequently Asked Questions about the Green Dot System [online]. Available at www.greendotcompliance.eu/en/common-questions. php [accessed on 8 August 2013].
9. Earth911. Trash planet: Germany [online]. Available at earth911.com/news/ 2009/07/13/trash-planet-germany [accessed on 8 August 2013].
10. Blaffer Hrdy, S (2009). *Mothers and Others: The Evolutionary Origins of Mutual Understanding*. Cambridge, MA: Belknap Press.
11. Tomasello, M (2009). *Why We Cooperate*. Cambridge, MA: MIT Press.
12. Zimbardo, P (2007). *The Lucifer Effect: Understanding How Good People Turn Evil*. New York: Random House.

13. Browning, CR (1998). *Ordinary Men: Reserve Police Battalion 101 and the Final Solution in Poland.* New York: Harper Perennial.

14. Meadows, D (2010). Leverage points: Places to intervene in a system. *Solutions* 1(1), 41–49. Available at www.thesolutionsjournal.com/node/419 [accessed on 8 August 2013].

15. Fair Elections Now [online]. Available at www.fairelectionsnow.org [accessed on 8 August 2013].

16. World Future Council. Celebrating the World's Best Forestry Practices, Future Policy Award [online] (2011). Available at www.worldfuturecouncil.org/fileadmin/user_upload/PDF/2011_Future_Policy_Award_Brochure_En.pdf [accessed on 8 August 2013].

17. Agarwal, B (2010). *Gender and Green Governance: The Political Economy of Women's Presence Within and Beyond Community Forestry.* London: Oxford University Press, pp. 11, 369.

18. Agarwal, B (2011). Personal communication, 2011 [accessed on 8 August 2013].

19. Misra, SS (2011). Community managed sustainable agriculture: Interview with Raidu DV [online]. Available at agrariancrisis.in/2011/06/25/1442/ [accessed on 8 August 2013].

20. Misra, U (2010). Back to the roots for Andhra Pradesh farmers. *Forbes India* [online]. Available at forbesindia.com/article/on-assignment/back-to-the-roots-for-andra-pradesh-farmers/17822/1 [accessed on 8 August 2013].

21. Pimbert, M, B Barry, A Berson and K Tran-Thanh (2010). *Democratising Agricultural Research for Food Sovereignty in West Africa* [online]. London: International Institute for Environment and Development, pp. 4–5. Available at pubs.iied.org/pdfs/14603IIED.pdf [accessed on 8 August 2013].

22. Gore, A (2008). Closing session: Technology, Entertainment, and Design Conference, Monterey, California. Available at www.wired.com/epicenter/2008/03/al-gore-makes-i [accessed on 8 August 2013].

Part 2

Future Histories: Descriptions of a Sustainable and Desirable Future and How We Got There

5

What Would a Sustainable and Desirable Economy-in-Society-in-Nature Look Like?

Robert Costanza, Gar Alperovitz, Herman Daly, Joshua Farley, Carol Franco, Tim Jackson, Ida Kubiszewski, Juliet Schor, and Peter Victor

The most critical task facing humanity today is the creation of a shared vision of a sustainable and desirable society, one that can provide permanent prosperity within the biophysical constraints of the real world in a way that is fair and equitable to all of humanity, to other species, and to future generations.

We need to fill in the details in a coherent vision that is tangible enough to motivate all kinds of people to work toward achieving it. Without a coherent, relatively detailed, shared vision of what a sustainable society could look like, there will be no political will nor united effort to take us from here to there. The default vision of continued, unlimited increases in material consumption is inherently unsustainable and undesirable, but we cannot break away from this vision until a credible and widely shared alternative is created.

Below we sketch out one version of such a vision as a starting point.[a] There are several other visioning exercises that have created similar descriptions, including the Great Transition Initiative (www.gtinitiative. org) and the Future We Want (www.futurewewant.org). Ultimately, this vision must be shared and further developed through participatory democratic processes.

If humanity is to achieve a sustainable and desirable future, we must create a shared vision detailing what we as a society want to sustain and incorporating the central shared values that express our hopes for the future. This vision must incorporate a diversity of perspectives and be based on principles of fairness, respect, and sustainability.

This draft vision is divided into five parts: (i) worldviews, (ii) built capital, (iii) human capital, (iv) social capital, and (v) natural capital, encompassing the basic elements of the ecological economics framework. This vision is written from the perspective of the year 2050, describing the world we have achieved by implementing the policies outlined in previous sections.

Worldview

Our worldview no longer divides the planet into "humans vs. nature." People now recognize that humans are a part of nature, one species among many, and must obey the laws and constraints imposed on all of nature.

---

[a]This vision is adapted from one created at a workshop held at Oberlin College in January 2001, attended by the following: Audra Abt, Gar Alperovitz, Mary Barber, Seaton Baxter, Janine Benyus, Aiza Biby, Paul W. Bierman-Lytle, Grace Boggs, William Browning, Diana Bustamante, Warren W. Byrne, Mark Clevey, Jane Ellen Clougherty, Robert Costanza, Tanya Dawkins, James Embry, Jon Farley, Joshua Farley, Harold Glasser, Becky Grella, Elaine Gross, Gerald Hairston, Sarah Karpanty, Carol Kuhre, George McQuitty, Peter Montague, Dondohn Namesling, David Orr, John Petersen, William Prindle, Tom Prugh, Jack Santa-Barbara, Claudine Schneider, Ben Shepherd, Megan Snedden, Karl Steyaert, Theodore Steck, Harvey Stone, Paul Templet, Mary Evelyn Tucker, Sarah van Gelder, Rafael Vargas, and Verlene Wilder. A version was also included in: Costanza, R, G Alperovitz, H Daly, J Farley, C Franco, T Jackson, I Kubiszewski, J Schor and P Victor (2012). *Building a Sustainable and Desirable Economy-in-Society-in-Nature.* New York: United Nations Division for Sustainable Development. Available at http://sustainable-development.un.org/index.php?page=view&nr=627&type=400&menu=35.

Nevertheless, humans bear responsibility that other creatures do not — we do not blame deer for overgrazing — yet we expect humans to recognize their "overgrazing" and stop it. We recognize that nature is not something to be subjugated, but instead is something we depend upon absolutely to meet physical, psychological, cultural, and spiritual needs. We recognize that natural resources are scarce and must be invested in. Our goal is to create conditions conducive to life in the broadest sense.

For centuries, the worldview of mechanistic physics dominated Western society. Within this worldview, each action has an equal and opposite reaction, and only by studying systems at smaller and smaller scales can we come to fully understand these reactions. As more and more people have come to understand the inherent complexity of ecosystems and human systems, we have come to realize that results cannot always be predicted and that irreducible uncertainty dominates the provision of life-support services by healthy ecosystems.

An ecological worldview of complexity and indeterminacy, inspired by nature as mentor — holistic, integrated, and flexible — has replaced the worldview of mechanistic physics. Unfettered individualism is appropriate and even necessary in a world of vast frontiers and unlimited elbow room. Individualism is still extremely important in 2050, but is far more tempered by a concern for the common good. This has led to a system where communities promote individual liberty as long as individual actions do not have a negative impact on the community. Individuals in return accept that they are a part of society, and it is unfair and illegal (even uneconomic) to impose costs on society for private gain. This attitude was necessary to wean ourselves of our dependence on heavily polluting single-occupancy vehicles, for example.

Further, ever-increasing consumption is no longer considered an integral component of human needs as it was in the early part of the century. People pay attention to their other needs and desires, such as joy, beauty, affection, participation, creativity, freedom, and understanding. Building strong community helps us meet these needs, while working ever harder to pay for more consumption deprives us of the time and energy required to fulfill them. Thus, status is not conferred by high incomes and high consumption (individual ends), but rather by contribution to civil society and community ends. With the recognition that consumption beyond limit is not only physically unsustainable but also does little to improve our quality of life, we now understand that a "steady-state" economy — prosperous but within planetary boundaries — is our goal. A steady-state economy does not mean an end to development; it simply means that we limit the input of raw materials into our economic system and their inevitable return to the ecosystem as waste to a level compatible with the ecological constraints imposed by a finite planet with finite resources. We now live happily and well within the safe operating space of our planet. We do not know the precise location of these planetary boundaries, and they are subject to change. Therefore, "adaptive management" has become the guiding principle.

The economy is now powered by our incoming solar energy — direct sunlight captured by solar panels — as well as wind, hydro, and the traditional forms of solar energy capture (agriculture, forestry, and fisheries). Economic production now focuses on quality, not quantity, on everyone having enough, and on fulfilling employment. Rather than the earlier focus on the production of goods, we now focus on the production of the services provided by goods and how those services are distributed. We do not need cars, we need transportation. We do not need televisions, we need entertainment and information. Goods are only a means to an end — the larger end of sustainable human well-being — and by recognizing this, our economy has developed as never before without growing in physical terms.

Built capital

Built capital is the human-made infrastructure used to meet human needs. Technological advance over the last century has had a large impact on the type of built capital we find in 2050. Different priorities have had as much or even greater impact.

Housing

Communities have been dramatically redesigned to integrate living space, community space, and workspace with recreational needs and nature. Workspace includes the stores that supply our everyday needs as well as production facilities for most of the goods those stores supply. People now live very close to where they work, where they shop, and where they play. The huge cities of the early 21st century did not disappear, but they have been dramatically reorganized. Cities are now aggregations of smaller communities in close physical proximity but where each community meets the housing, employment, social, recreation, and shopping needs of those who live there. The "20-minute neighborhood" idea — that all basic services should be no more than a 20-min walk away — has taken hold as an urban design principle. Natural areas have also made a big comeback in cities. The specifics of community size and design are, of course, determined by local physical and cultural conditions, and there is enormous diversity.

In addition to these very practical aspects, communities have been designed as soul-satisfying spaces that resonate with our evolutionary history. Most communities include natural areas and incorporate parks and other green spaces (though "green" is a misnomer in drier parts of the world, where xeriscaping is the norm), and such spaces also serve as common space for community members. They also foster social interaction and community. Rather than something new, this is simply a resurgence of a millennial tradition of settlement patterns.

Because community space is abundant and well designed, private homes are generally smaller (hence cheaper and easier to care for) and are much more energy efficient. Private lawns have virtually disappeared, though lawn-like community green spaces still exist, and private gardens abound. Private gardens in fact meet a substantial portion of community food needs. Walking and bicycle riding have effectively become the dominant forms of transportation, except in the worst weather. Rapidly increasing energy costs provided the initial incentive, but people then discovered the enormous benefits of such pedestrian communities.

One of the biggest impacts was simply getting people out of their cars. Walking to work, to the store, to community meeting places, or to nature preserves brings people into direct contact with the other members of the community. People walking together in the same direction naturally converse, establishing friendships, informing each other of current events, and discussing issues of relevance to the community. In fact, developing community and social capital has become one of many explicit goals for designing built capital. Modern communities are very healthy places for humans and other species. Invigorating exercise and nurturing social interaction have replaced the stress of hour-long commutes, road rage, and the pollution of vehicle exhaust, improving both physical and mental health. Air quality is very high. Many roads and parking lots have become redundant, and in their spaces stand parks, streams, and greenways, providing clean air, clean water, and healthy recreation, among numerous other vital ecosystem services. The dramatic reduction in impervious areas has reduced flooding and allowed the land and the ecosystems it sustains to filter water, restoring waterways to health.

With scarcer resources, the practice of destroying still useful buildings to build others on the same site has diminished, and stable populations have further decreased the need for new construction. But from time to time new buildings are still required. Ecologically designed "living buildings" have become the norm for new construction.

Transportation

As already mentioned in the description of communities, single-occupancy vehicles are now rare. The dominant modes of transportation within communities are walking and bicycling; between communities people use high-speed rail. Public transportation is important within communities and is designed to transport goods as well as passengers, making it convenient for grocery shopping and the like. Because so many people use public transportation, it is abundant and extremely convenient. Rail is common, but so are electric buses and taxis. "Traffic" is a thing of the past, and public transportation gets people around much more quickly than private vehicles used to, at a fraction of the cost. Dramatically fewer vehicles on the roads have also cut maintenance costs to a fraction of what they were, and new roads are unnecessary. Some people still own private vehicles, but these vehicles are expensive and their owners pay a higher share of the costs of road maintenance. Most communities have shared electric cars, such as ZipCars, available for rent when private transportation is absolutely required. When not being driven, these cars provide electric energy storage.

Energy

Renewable resources now meet virtually all of the world's energy needs. The conversion from hydrocarbons was facilitated by continuous increases in efficiency of energy use, combined with appropriate full-cost pricing of all energy sources, including environmental and health costs and risks of the full fuel cycle. Photovoltaic tiles are ubiquitous roofing materials, and roofs alone meet over half the world's energy needs. Large-scale hydropower has decreased in importance as more and more rivers are restored to their natural states, but low-impact mini-turbines are increasingly common. In spite of the abundance of renewable, nonpolluting forms of energy, energy-efficiency research is still very important and advances are still being made in both renewable-energy supply and demand management. The "smart grid" has done much to help this transition. In many places, municipalities and/or cooperatives now locally manage the generation, supply, and distribution of renewable energy resources, keeping prices affordable and ownership democratically controlled.

Industry

Industry has changed dramatically. Industrial design is now based on closed-loop systems in imitation of nature, where the waste product from one industry becomes the feedstock of the next. Wasted heat from industrial processes is used to heat nearby homes and workspaces. When possible, industrial production uses local materials to meet local needs, and wastes (the few that are not put to use) are processed locally. Most smaller-scale industries consist of a mix of locally owned proprietary firms and smaller corporations on the one hand, and cooperatives and new community-based commons institutions on the other. While these characteristics do not always maximize productive efficiency, the benefits outweigh the costs.

First, local production dramatically reduces transportation costs, helping to compensate for sometimes-higher production costs. Second, it makes communities directly aware of the environmental impacts of production and consumption. Costs of waste disposal are not shifted elsewhere. Third, industries are more a part of their communities. Most of them are locally owned by the workers they employ, by new cooperative and municipal institutions, and by the people whose needs they meet. Rather than simply trying to maximize returns to shareholders, industries strive to provide healthy, safe, secure, and fulfilling working conditions for workers.

Those who produce goods and those who consume them know each other, so workers take particular pride in the quality of what they produce.

Fourth, the decentralization of the economy means that the economy as a whole is much less susceptible to business cycles, increasing job, and community stability — a central requirement of local sustainability planning in general. Fifth, an emphasis on local ownership and production for local markets has reduced the importance of trade secrets and patents; competition has been replaced to some extent by cooperation.

Sixth, a significant number of larger firms are structured as public and quasi-public enterprises jointly owned with the workers involved. They are designed, on the one hand, to help target and anchor jobs to help achieve local stability, thereby also supporting sustainability planning, and on the other, to be less dependent on very short-term profit considerations necessary to meet stock market expectations that foster excessive growth.

Finally, decreased competition has led to a dramatic decrease in the size of the advertising industry. This means that money once spent on convincing people to buy one brand over another is now spent on making those products better — or simply not spent, making those products more affordable.

Markets and competition, of course, still play an important role. Industries are free to sell to distant communities, though having to pay the full cost of transportation provides a natural barrier. Still, this threat of competition means that communities need not rely solely on the good will of local industries to keep prices low. Trade secrets play less of a role in competition than in the past due to the resurgence of sharing information. The development of open-source software shows that freely sharing knowledge can lead to more rapid technological innovation than the profit motive provided by privatizing knowledge through patents. The problems with patents have became more obvious with the tremendous growth in green technologies, which have proven themselves capable of slowing climate change, reducing pollution, and decreasing demands on scarce ecosystem resources, but only by being used on a large scale. Patents on these technologies (and the accompanying monopoly profits) would mean that much of the world would be unable to afford them. The global community has come to realize that it cannot afford the price of people not using these technologies.

Fortunately, the free flow of information has led to impressive new innovations, often making patents obsolete. Some industries retain substantial economies of scale, using fewer resources per unit when producing in enormous factories. This is still the case for solar cells, for example. Large corporations still exist to produce such goods, but many are structured in ways that broaden representation on boards and in certain cases entail public ownership or joint public/worker ownership. Corporate charters have largely changed to the "benefit corporation" model that explicitly acknowledges a firm's responsibility to produce a social benefit rather than merely a private profit.

Human capital

Human capital was defined in the early part of the century as the practical knowledge, acquired skills, and learned abilities of an individual that make him or her potentially productive and thus equip him or her to earn income in exchange for labor.

The definition of human capital itself has changed — no longer emphasizing solely productivity in terms of income exchanged for labor. The primary emphasis instead is now on knowledge, skills, and abilities that make people productive members of society. The goals of society are far more than simply earning income. Education is now integrated into everyday life, not simply something we do for a few hours a day before we grow up. And it is not always confined to classrooms — schools are an institution, not a physical place. Nature offers us an amazing laboratory every time we step outside, and is valued every bit as much in urban settings as in rural. This is even more true in 2050, when our communities are designed to maximize exposure to healthy ecosystems. Education about civic responsibilities and roles is heavily stressed, and such topics are taught by direct exposure to the decision-making process or hands-on participation in activities that benefit the community. Youth are schooled in civic responsibility by actively participating in the community. And what better place to learn skills required for economic production than at the workplace? Apprenticeships are now an integral part of the learning process. Technology also plays an important role in education. Online learning environments are used where appropriate but by no means replace direct interaction. Education is now an interactive balance between online tools and content acquisition, and on-the-ground problem solving in the community.

Education and science no longer focus solely on the reductionist approach, in which students are only taught to analyze problems by breaking them down into their component parts. While the reductionist approach and analysis still play an important role in education, the emphasis is now on synthesis — how to rebuild the analyzed components of a problem into a holistic picture to solve problems. Synthesis is critical for understanding system processes, and system processes dominate our lives.

Beyond analysis and synthesis, learning also now emphasizes communication. Researchers skilled at communication are able to more readily share ideas, and ideas grow through sharing. Workers skilled at communication are able to work together to solve production problems. Citizens skilled at communication are able to contribute to the ever-evolving vision of a sustainable and desirable future that is the motivating force behind policy and governance. Citizens are also able to communicate their knowledge with each other, so that education, livelihood, family, and community become a seamless whole of lifelong learning and teaching, everyone simultaneously a student and teacher.

Education also now emphasizes much more than just scientific understanding of the material world. Critical thinking and research are important, but so are creative expression and curiosity. Knowledge and science are not portrayed as value-neutral endeavors; students now learn that the very decision of what to study is a moral choice with broad implications for society. The goal of education is to cultivate wisdom and discernment, to cultivate the emotional maturity to allow responsible decision making in every type of human endeavor.

The whole notion of work has also changed, and the word itself has lost the connotation of an unpleasant chore. Work hours have been reduced through work sharing and more generous leave policies to allow for a more reasonable balance of family and work life. Moreover, people now recognize the absurdity of applying technology to the problem of producing more goods to be consumed during leisure time regardless of the drudgery involved in the production process itself. Instead, to recruit the needed workers, industry is now forced to redirect some of its technological prowess toward making work itself a pleasurable part of our days that engages both mental and physical skills. A typical job now involves far more variety, not only to make work more exciting and interesting, but also to take advantage of the full range of a person's skills. There is less distinction between what would have earlier been considered gainful employment and volunteer work.

Everyone participates in civil society, both in decision making and in maintaining the public space. This is not an onerous chore, but a pleasurable time for socializing with neighbors and community. Nor does it take time away from private lives, since the typical work week in traditional jobs now averages only 15 h. Education deemphasizes the old "more is better" mindset and promotes a greater understanding of the linkages between economic production, nature, human development, and society. This has made people more aware of the true costs of excessive consumption.

With years of technological advance and diminished "needs," society is now able to provide a satisfactory living wage to all who work and to meet the basic needs of those who do not. Participation in the various types of work is expected and supported, but not forced. Because work is now more a fulfilling experience than an onerous necessity, there is little resentment of those who do not work but rather a feeling of concern that these people are not developing their potential as humans. Living in more tightly knit communities where social goals are actively discussed, people now better understand the importance of their work and feel greater obligation to contribute to the common good. Remuneration for work has been restructured to provide the greatest awards to those who provide the greatest amount of service to the community, such as teachers, childcare providers, and so on.

Human capital is also directly related to human populations. The population has stabilized at a level compatible with the safe operating space of our planet.

Social capital

Social capital refers to the institutions, relationships, and norms that shape the quality and quantity of a society's social interactions. Social capital is not just the sum of a society's institutions, which underpin that society; it is the glue that holds them together.

The dominant form of social capital in the employment and economic sphere in the early part of the century was the market. The interaction between employer and employee was that of buying and selling labor. In this model, employer loyalty exists only as long as the continued employment of the employee increases profits. Employee loyalty exists only as long as no other job offers a greater salary or better fringe benefits (which may include location, working conditions, etc.). The interaction between producer and consumer is even more market based in this model. People buy a product only as long as it is perceived to provide the greatest value in monetary terms, though admittedly advertising may play as large a role in shaping perceptions as the actual price and quality of the product.

In 2050, worker and worker/community ownership of many industries and local production for local markets has changed these relationships. Such enterprises logically pay more attention to worker and community well-being than enterprises driven by the need to generate shareholder profit. Well-being, of course, includes profit-shares but is increased by working conditions that are healthy, that stimulate creativity, and that create feelings of participation, community, and identity. While not all enterprises are owned in these ways, when a significant percentage of enterprises began to offer these conditions, they put pressure on the others to do so as well. In the absence of strong social capital, local production for local markets can be a disaster. In many cases, it might be inefficient to have a number of firms providing similar products for a small community. This could lead to monopoly provision of certain goods. If the market had remained the dominant form of social capital driving interactions between producers and consumers, high profits and poor quality would have resulted. However, when worker-owners also live in the local community, they have to answer to their neighbors for both the price and quality of what they produce. High-quality production is a source of pride, while low quality and high prices are perceived as incompetence and laziness, decreasing the individual's social standing in the community.

Local currencies also now contribute significantly to locally based production and consumption. Such systems existed in many communities in the early part of the century, such as in Ithaca, New York (www.ithacahours. org), and the Berkshires in western Massachusetts (www.berkshares.org). These currencies are backed only by trust that other members of the community will accept them in exchange for goods and services, and therefore require strong social capital to function. They also build social capital every time a community member accepts the currency. They are virtually immune to national and global economic instability and provide communities with greater autonomy.

For local markets to work, social capital must be strong. As discussed in the section on built capital, the very physical structure of communities now works to create that social capital. Abundant community spaces, parks, and recreation areas stimulate social interaction, build friendships, and generate a sense of responsibility toward neighbors and community. With single-occupancy vehicles almost gone and people living in smaller communities, just getting from place to place brings people in close contact with their neighbors.

At the beginning of the century, public transportation was primarily found only in large cities, and fellow passengers were strangers, not neighbors. Under these circumstances, public transportation did little to build social capital. But this is no longer the case in 2050. Some neighborhoods coalesced around different ethnicities and cultures, and these too served as sources of social capital. However, the world has rid itself of the racism, sexism, regionalism, and other prejudices that were all too prevalent earlier. People have more time for family, and family life is characterized by more balanced gender roles.

The process of government itself now creates social capital. Many countries are no longer weak representative democracies, but strong participatory ones. In a participatory democracy, the people must discuss at length the issues that affect them to decide together how the issues should be resolved. In the old world — of high-pressure jobs, little free time, and large communities of anonymous strangers — this approach to government seemed impractical, unwieldy, and too demanding. Now, with smaller communities of neighbors, a far shorter work week, and engaged, active citizens, participatory democracy is a privilege of citizenship and not an onerous chore. Of course, this required that civic education form an essential part of education and development of human capital from childhood on. This approach to government is particularly effective at the local level. As citizens come together in regular meetings to discuss the issues and work together to resolve them (even when substantial conflict exists), it creates strong bonds of social capital and plays an essential role in forging a sense of community.

Government, of course, implies action, and action implies purpose. The purpose must be defined by the people, who in these civic meetings also forge a shared vision of the future to guide their actions. This vision is not static but must adapt to new information and new conditions as they emerge. Of course, not all issues can be decided on the local level. Institutions are required at the scale of the problems they address. It is at the local level where people will feel the consequences of ecosystem change, for example, but causes may be distant, perhaps in other countries. On the national level, it is not feasible to bring together millions of people to discuss the issues and decide on actions, so some form of representation is required. But representatives are now chosen through direct participation by people to whom they have strong social ties and obligations, so these representatives are far more likely to truly represent their communities and not some large corporation that funds their rise to power. Additionally, new intermediary representative institutions on the regional scale exist to bridge the gap between local and national governance.

Social capital, the glue that holds society together, also include basic moral values and ethics such as honesty, fair dealing, care for the disabled, and a common set of cultural practices and expectations that for the majority do not have to be enforced by law. Both markets and government bureaucracies fail without these common values. These values are rooted in community and nurtured by the religions of the world and other systems of thought and practice. Social capital has deep roots, and has been reestablished in many areas.

Natural capital

Natural capital consists of all the world's ecosystems — their structure and processes that contribute to the well-being of humans and every other species on the planet. This includes both mineral and biological raw materials, renewable (solar, wind, and tidal) energy and fossil fuels, waste-assimilation capacity, and vital life-support functions (such as global climate regulation) provided by well-functioning ecosystems.

The absolute essentiality of natural capital is now so completely accepted that it is taken for granted that we must protect it if we are to survive and thrive as a species. Any schoolchild is able to tell you that you cannot make something from nothing, so all economic production must ultimately depend on raw material inputs. Economic production is a process of transformation, and all transformation requires energy inputs. It is equally impossible to make nothing from something, so every time we use raw materials to make something, when that product eventually wears out, it returns to nature as waste. It is therefore incumbent upon us to make sure that those wastes can be processed by the planet's ecosystems. Waste-absorption capacity is only one of many critical but still scarcely understood services provided by intact ecosystems. These ecosystem services include regulation of atmospheric gases, regulation of water cycles and the provision of clean water, stabilization of the global climate, protection from ultraviolet radiation, and the sustenance of global biodiversity, among many others. Without these services, human life itself would be impossible.

While by 2050, we have made substantial efforts to protect ecosystem services, uncontrolled human economic activity still has the capacity to damage them sufficiently to threaten our civilization. Obviously, well-functioning ecosystems are composed of the same plants and animals that serve as raw material inputs to the economy; and, all else being equal, increasing raw material inputs means diminished ecosystem services. Extraction of renewable raw materials directly diminishes ecosystem services, while the extraction of mineral resources unavoidably causes collateral damage to ecosystems. Ecosystem services are also threatened by waste outputs. While waste outputs from renewable resources are, in general, fairly readily assimilated and broken down by healthy ecosystems, ecosystems have not evolved a similar capacity to break down waste products from mining and industry, concentrated heavy metals, fossil fuels, and synthesized chemicals. In 2050, we have dramatically decreased our reliance on these slow-to-assimilate materials.

Natural capital is also economically important because it provides so many insights into the production process. The more we have learned about how nature produces, the more we have realized the inefficiency, toxicity, and wastefulness of former production techniques. It has now become a standard approach when seeking to solve a production problem to examine healthy ecosystems and strive to understand how they "solve" similar problems.

A recognition and high level of awareness of the importance of natural capital have led to dramatic changes in the way it is treated. The negative environmental impacts of nonrenewable resource use, even more than such materials' growing scarcity, have forced us to substitute renewable resources for nonrenewables, reversing the trend that began with the Industrial Revolution and making renewables more valuable than ever. Passive investment in natural capital stocks — that is, simply letting systems grow through their own reproductive capacity — is insufficient to meet our needs. Active investment is required. We are actively engaged in restoring and rebuilding our natural capital stocks by planting forests, restoring wetlands, and increasing soil fertility. The former philosophy of natural capital as free goods provided by nature has disappeared. This change has required and inspired significant institutional changes. For example, notions of property rights to natural capital have changed. Most forms of natural capital are now recognized as intergenerational assets. For example, legislation in many countries now explicitly prohibits the extraction of renewable resources beyond the rate at which they can replenish themselves, which would leave future populations dependent for survival on nonrenewable resources in danger of exhaustion and for which no substitutes exist.

Property rights to land are explicitly extended to future generations, and there are steep fines or even criminal penalties for leaving land in worse condition than when it was purchased. While ecological factors determine the total amount of natural capital that we can safely deplete, market forces still determine how that natural capital should be allocated. In addition to these fixed limits on resource use, green taxes now force both consumers and producers to pay for the damage caused by resource depletion and waste emission. When these costs are unknown, those undertaking potentially harmful activities are forced to purchase bonds or insurance that guarantee reimbursement to society for whatever damages do occur. These policies have dramatically increased the costs of degrading natural capital. As a result, most countries are rapidly weaning themselves from dependence on nonrenewable resources, having developed renewable substitutes for most of them. Many countries are competing to become global leaders in green technology. While we once relied on hydrocarbons as a feedstock for many industrial processes, we now rely heavily on carbohydrates produced by plants. This allows us to build non-toxic, biodegradable carbon polymers from CO_2 extracted directly from the atmosphere. As this technology came into its own, it helped to stabilize and even reduce atmospheric CO_2. Whether we will be able to continue to reduce global warming is still an open question, but one with growing cause for optimism.

Our understanding of ecosystem function has progressed dramatically and we continue to discover new ecosystem services. Yet for every puzzle we solve, we uncover three others. And we remain unable to accurately predict impacts of human activities on specific ecosystems, in part because of ongoing changes induced by continued global change. While the rate of warming has slowed, ecosystems are still slowly adapting to the impacts of that warming. The precautionary principle therefore now plays a critical role in deciding how we treat the environment when there is doubt over the potential impact of resource extraction or waste emissions on ecosystem goods and services. We choose to err on the side of caution. Continuing ecological-restoration efforts have begun to reverse the massive degradation that took place from 1950 through 2020, but continued global warming still threatens dangerous disruptions in ecosystem services. In keeping with the precautionary principle, we now consider it an imperative to develop extensive ecological buffers and to take the idea of planetary boundaries seriously.

Acknowledgments

From: Costanza, R, G Alperovitz, H Daly, J Farley, C Franco, T Jackson, I Kubiszewski, J Schor and P Victor. (2012). *Building a Sustainable and Desirable Economy-in-Society-in-Nature*. New York: United Nations Division for Sustainable Development. Available at http://www.un.org/esa/dsd/dsd_sd21st/21_reports.shtml

6

Vision Statement for the Planet in 2050

Ajay Bhave, Silvia Ceausu, Anand Deshmukh,
Jessica Jewell, Wayne Pan, and Jana Timm

We are a diverse group and we envision a diverse world. Although we are outlining a vision for 2050, we are aware that places in the world will look very different based on history, culture, and perspectives. Our vision attempts to outline some guiding principles, values, hopes, and aspirations, but in no way do we envision a homogenous utopia. We believe, and we hope, that these principles will manifest themselves in diverse ways in different parts of the world.

In 2050, our societies will transcend the narrow focus on material goods and wealth generation that we see today. They will instead strive to meet the deeper needs of human beings, addressing happiness and spiritual and emotional fulfillment. Indicators of success, now often measured in purely financial terms, will instead encompass ideas of happiness and satisfaction. The world will reallocate its energy and resources away from merely pursuing economic growth to addressing issues of poverty, equity, gender equality, and access to health care and education. Political structures will no longer disenfranchise those with limited social and economic standing, instead empowering all who wish to participate in determining their future with the right to do so.

Resources that are unvalued, or undervalued, in many of our current systems — notably the environment, the family, the community, culture, and cultural heritage — will grow to be the centerpieces of our societies.

This will allow us to situate ourselves within a more holistic vision of the world, bringing understanding of our interconnectedness and relationships not just to each other but to the natural and historical world.

The city is, in many ways, a reflection of society. Cities are built with and evolve with societal structures in mind, in ways that best meet the demands of our societies. Yet in the course of this evolution, many cities have lost touch with the needs of their own inhabitants, instead filling only a role in the political or economic systems of their countries. Cities of 2050 will hold links to history, tangible pieces of the past, to remind us of our place within time and space and to confer a perspective of the future.

Today the world is focused on the individual. In 2050, communities, relationships between people, and personal responsibility toward society will be the key principles in the construction of our cities. The structure of the city will support stronger communities by bringing people together in more cohesive spaces, which are then tied together in larger and larger webs. This idea of a polycentric city and urban nodes renders the issue of mobility moot; people will have greater access to urban functions not only within their own nodes but through convenient mass transportation connections between cities. Denser urban nodes will also eliminate the need for cars within these communities and will provide more space for parks, urban agriculture, and places for social interaction.

Cities of all sizes will also be more self-sufficient. Provision of necessary city services such as food, water, waste handling, and energy will be more localized, integrating these services into the fabric of the city. Bringing these services closer will also reconnect people with the earth, giving people better insight into their resource use and impacts. On the other side, cities will require drastically fewer resources through the widescale implementation of bioclimatic building design. With solar power generation, wind power, super-insulating windows, natural ventilation systems, gray-water usage, and rain water collection, buildings will annul the need for the massive infrastructure that sustains cities today. Waste volumes will be further reduced through highly efficient waste sorting, recycling, and composting. Additionally, wastewater will be processed locally, using natural wetlands and treatment processes.

Food production is one of the greatest limiting factors for self-sufficiency in cities, big and small. However, cities of the future will be built to overcome as many of the challenges as possible. People will eat lower on the food chain, thus decreasing the energetic requirements for food production. Likewise, their diets will better reflect local growing conditions and seasonality. Additionally, small cities and rural areas will provide not only for themselves but will also form symbiotic relationships with larger, neighboring cities, augmenting the urban agriculture that will take place in most cities. These cities will form unofficial regional units that will allow residents to benefit from both urban and rural lifestyles.

Bringing service provisions back into the city will be just one component of a radically different economic structure. In 2050, the economy will be based on product services, not products. This economy will shift from selling goods (such as electronics or appliances in today's world) that are designed for disposal to selling the services that these goods provide. This will have the effect of not only reducing waste but also encouraging manufacturers to design for reuse. The economy will no longer focus on producing the most products with the fewest resources, valuing instead the contributions of people. This will help mitigate unemployment in parts of the world and will create stronger social and professional communities.

In these ways, cities will be more sustainable and more self-sufficient. Just as nodes in a city create a greater whole, so will the cities of the future play a role in a better, more equitable, more satisfying world.

7

Scenes from the Great Transition

Paul D. Raskin

I'll let you be in my dream if I can be in yours.

Bob Dylan

Mandela city, 2084

The world today, a century after George Orwell's nightmare year, stands as living refutation of the apocalyptic premonitions that once haunted dreams of the future. This dispatch from our awakened future surveys the contemporary moment, scenes in the unfolding drama we call the Great Transition.

What matters

The whole edifice of contemporary civilization rises on a foundation of compelling human values. The prevailing pretransition ethos — consumerism, individualism, and anthropocentrism — has given way to another triad: quality of life, human solidarity, and ecocentrism. These

> *The prevailing pretransition ethos — consumerism, individualism, and anthropocentrism — has given way to another triad: quality of life, human solidarity, and ecocentrism.*

values spring from a sense of, a yearning for, wholeness at all levels: self, species, and biosphere. They are manifestations in the human heart of the interdependence of the world, the defining feature of the present historical era, the Planetary Phase of Civilization.

It has become clear that enhancing the quality of people's lives, not expanding the quantity of their possessions, is the only valid goal of development. The principle of material sufficiency, now widely held, has roots in the early decades of the transition, a time of turbulence and conflict that spawned a search for more meaningful and satisfying ways of living than the work-and-buy treadmill offered. Today, people may be as ambitious as ever, but fulfillment has displaced wealth as the primary measure of success and source of well-being.

The second pillar of the contemporary Zeitgeist — human solidarity — affirms a strong connection felt for strangers in distant places and descendants in a distant future. This capacious camaraderie draws on wellsprings of empathy in the human psyche, the Golden Rule that threads through the great religious traditions. By mingling the destinies of all, the Planetary Phase has stretched *esprit de corps* across space and time to embrace the whole human family of today and tomorrow.

Perhaps most profoundly, affirming humanity's place in the web of life, this sense of connectedness extends beyond our own species to our fellow creatures who share our planet's fragile skin. The lesson was hard won, and much has been lost, but at last, our highly evolved ecological sensibility has consigned the predatory motive of the past — the domination of nature — to the dustbin of history. Indeed, people today, understanding any compromise to ecological integrity as both morally wrong and foolishly self-destructive, are mystified by past indifference to the natural world. Our relationship to Earth is guided by humility in the face of our dependence on her bounty and by reverence for the exhilarating wonder of existence.

One world, many places

Buoyed by this enlarged sense of place, globalism has become as deep-rooted as nationalism once was, perhaps more so. After all, gazing back from space, we behold an integral blue planet, not the imaginary boundaries of political states. Philosophers and prophets have long envisioned a ring of community encircling the entire human family. But the cosmopolitan dream of One World had to await an unsentimental partner: mutual self-interest. The emergence of an interdependent world confronting common risks aligned subjective aspirations and objective imperatives. Idealistic and pragmatic concerns — the "pull of hope" and the "push of fear" — combined to forge the global citizen.

Thus, it has become axiomatic, self-evident to the average global citizen today, that the globe is the natural political unit for managing our interdependent affairs — not only sustaining the biosphere and keeping the peace, but cultivating an organic planetary civilization. Our thriving world culture and demos, for all its tensions and disputes, is perhaps the highest achievement to date of the Great Transition. The old skeptics, who could not see beyond nationalism, were myopic; the visionaries and activists who felt the stirring of a new consciousness and polity had the perspicacity to see the potential latent in the Planetary Phase.

Still, our enthusiasm for One World has been balanced by an equal commitment to Many Places. A century ago, it was common to speak of a unitary project of "modernity," a process of convergent development that would replicate the institutions and norms of industrial societies everywhere. Instead, the transition has demonstrated in the crucible of history the counter proposition of many oppositional thinkers that plural paths to modernity were possible. Today, modern ideals — equality, tolerance, rule of law, and universal rights — find myriad expression across our landscape of distinct places.

Thus, the fabric of planetary society is woven with hundreds of regions of astonishing diversity of character and size. Some took shape around old national boundaries or metropolitan centers; some followed the perimeters of river basins and other bioregions. Some are small and rather homogenous, while the larger ones are complex structures with sundry internal areas. The formation of regions was not without conflict, and tensions remain. However, aided by our highly effective negotiations bodies and adjudications of the world court, our regional structure has largely stabilized.

The different regions can be clustered into three broad types, often referred to as Agoria, Ecodemia, and Arcadia. The whimsical names draw on Greek roots to evoke the classical ideal of a political community — active citizens, shared purpose, and just social relations. In Athens, the *agora* served as both marketplace and center of political life; the neologism *ecodemia* combines the word roots of economy and democracy; *arcadia* was the bucolic paradise of Greek myth. Thus, commerce figures prominently in Agoria; economic democracy is a priority in Ecodemia; and local community and simple lifestyles are particularly significant in Arcadia.

Agoria's more conventional lifestyle and institutions would make it most recognizable to a visitor from the past. Ecodemia's collectivist ethos and socialized political economy depart most from classical capitalism. Arcadia's self-reliant economies and face-to-face democracy (at least in cyberspace) have antecedents in small-is-beautiful localism, long a strong current in environmental subcultures.

Some argue that these regional forms are direct descendants of the three great "isms" of the past: capitalism, socialism, and anarchism. This claim does have a degree of validity: Agoria's free-market emphasis gives it a capitalist orientation ("Sweden Supreme" according to one recent critic); Ecodemia's insistence on the primacy of social ownership was the foundation of socialism; and Arcadia's stress on small-scale, local effort was the essence of the humanistic anarchist tradition.

However, such ideological labels mask as much as they reveal. Its social democratic structure notwithstanding, Agoria's dedication to sustainability and rights is of a different order than, say, the old Sweden (a paragon of its time). Ecodemia's commitment to democracy and environmentalism bears little resemblance to the autocratic socialist experiments of the 20th century. Arcadia's highly sophisticated societies are enthusiastic participants in world affairs, not the pastoral utopias of the old anarchist dreamers.

Governance

Planetary decision making flows through an intricate web of local, regional, and global nodes and connections. The prime challenge in building and maintaining the governance structure lies in finding a balance between the competing imperatives of global responsibility and regional autonomy. In the early decades of transition, stale ideological dualities polarized political discourse — cosmopolitanism versus communalism, statism versus anarchism, top–down versus bottom–up. The solution, remarkably simple, and germinating for decades, had been masked by the nationalist mystifications during the decades of the Cold War, the Era of the Hegemon, and the Time of Troubles.

Today, the *principle of constrained pluralism*, our guiding political philosophy, transcends the seemingly intractable dualities of the past. This principle contains three complementary subprinciples — *irreducibility*, *subsidiarity*, and *heterogeneity*. The *irreducibility principle* sets the scope for global decision making, affirming that the adjudication of certain transregional issues — universal rights, biosphere resilience, world peace, fair use of common resources, and shared cultural and economic endeavors — is necessarily and properly retained at the global level of governance. The *subsidiarity principle* sharply limits the scope of irreducible global authority, ceding decision-making authority to the most local level feasible. The *heterogeneity principle* validates the rights of regions to meet global responsibilities in diverse ways compatible with their forms of development.

Our world constitution has enshrined these principles, and few find them objectionable. To a considerable degree, the governance system achieves the three goals embodied in the slogan "As global as must be, as local as can be, as diverse as need be." Still, with the devil in the details, the framework is implemented through an animated process of popular political contestation (almost always peaceful). In particular, agreement on which decisions should be considered irreducibly global is a work in progress, an evolving tug-of-war between advocates for a more tight-knit world state and those for a more decentralized commonwealth.

The world assembly includes representatives of regions as well as at-large members selected by popular vote in worldwide elections. At-large representation gives voice to One World politics, stimulating vibrant world parties as a counterweight to regional parochialism. Strong regional representation ensures that the Many Places are not forgotten. This balance provides safeguards against tyranny from above or below.

Regional democracy takes many forms: the representational systems typical of Agoria, the vigorous workplace nodes of political activity in

Ecodemia, and the direct citizen engagement found in many Arcadian communities. People are highly engaged in the political process at all levels of the governance structure — such involvement is considered a right and duty of citizenship. The boundless bandwidth of modern cyberspace enables authentic mass participation throughout the multiscale governance structure: the quantum entanglement of our computational processes breeds popular entanglement in our political processes.

Economy

We view contemporary economies as means for attaining social and environmental ends, not ends in themselves. Thus, setting global and regional goals for people and planet that define the legitimate operating space for economies comes first. Then, governments at all levels from global to local, prodded by vigilant civil-society watchdogs, must ensure that the scale and patterns of production and consumption remain within these socioecological boundaries.

Even in Agoria, where competitive markets are given the freest reign, they are highly fettered. Comprehensive regulatory frameworks align business and consumer behavior with nonmarket goals. Notably, large privately held corporations were long ago rechartered to make social purpose, not just profit, a fundamental bottom-line aim. Broad stakeholder participation ensures that workers and relevant community members have real influence on decision making.

Ecodemia's systems of "economic democracy" have expelled the capitalist from two key arenas of economic life. First, the conventional firm, based on private owners and hired employees, has been replaced by worker-owned enterprises, complemented by nonprofits and highly regulated small businesses. Second, private capital markets have given way to socialized investment processes. Publicly controlled regional and community investment banks, supported by participatory regulatory processes, recycle social savings and tax-generated capital funds. To receive funds from these banks, capital-seeking entrepreneurs must demonstrate that their projects, in addition to financial viability, promote larger social and environmental goals.

Despite their localist Zeitgeist, Arcadians prize their connections with cosmopolitan culture and world affairs, facilitated by advanced communication technology and efficient transportation systems. Some regions have become centers of innovation in such technologies as ecological agriculture, modular solar devices, and human-scale transport devices. Abuzz with artistic ferment, Arcadia is the source of more than its share of contemporary music, modern forms of folk and craft traditions, and creative digital media. Export of these products and services, along with ecotourism, supports the modest trade requirements of these relatively time-rich and slow-moving societies.

Overall, the forms of economic enterprise are much more varied than when huge corporations dominated the economic landscape. One reason for this transformation is the surge in nonprofit entities nearly everywhere as people strive for purposive and ethical work. Another is the diverse forms of privately held businesses, such as the social corporations of Agoria, the worker-owned cooperatives of Ecodemia, and the small private operations of Arcadia. A third is the explosion of the labor-intensive secondary economy, offering a breathtaking array of aesthetic goods and skilled services as well as many an outlet for creative expression. Social policies that shorten work weeks in the formal economy encourage this "peoples' economy."

Of course, the world economy is far more than the sum of these many parts. Global institutions play an essential role in marshaling "solidarity funds" for needy areas, developing transregional infrastructure, conducting space exploration, and promoting education and research for the common good. Moreover, world trade, while controversial, plays an important role in our interdependent economy. Except for small parties advocating extreme autarky, consensus holds that rule-governed interregional trade is a legitimate and important feature of planetary society.

World trade policy aims to bind a global culture and counter anachronistic nationalisms — when goods stop crossing borders, it has been said, bullets start. Also, trade enriches lives by providing access to locally unavailable products, sometimes, as with food imports to water-parched areas, reducing environmental pressure. In short, contemporary trade advances the larger social goals of solidarity, sustainability, and fulfillment.

Still, the debate on how to create rules that do not subvert regional prerogatives can be fierce. The tilt today is toward a circumscribed trade regime, fostering a meaningful degree of economic interdependence in a framework of regional semiautonomy. Regions exhibit great variation in their participation in world trade, some embracing the economic vitality and product diversity it offers, others erecting high barriers to imports, and most falling somewhere between open and protectionist extremes.

The way we live

Fascinated with 20th century history, people are mindful of the dreadful worlds that might have been and appreciative of the opportunities they have been given. Committed to advancing the transition in their public lives, they prefer, in their personal lives, lifestyles that combine material sufficiency with qualitative fulfillment — "Rich lives, not lives of riches," in the motto of the old movements.

The pursuit of money is giving way to the cultivation of skills, relationships, communities, and the life of the mind and spirit. Indeed, those still enthralled by conspicuous consumption are considered aesthetically impoverished and spiritually backward.

Our maturing egalitarian ethos has fostered greater economic equality. Within regions, policies maintain income spreads within rather narrow bounds through fair remuneration policies supported by redistributive taxes and sharp limits on inherited wealth. In tandem, global policy has marshaled resources to close the grotesque pretransition gap between rich and poor regions. With tighter income distributions, the material wellbeing of the average world citizen is far higher than at the turn of the century. The right to a basic standard of living is a universal right of citizenship, provided through a guaranteed minimum income, a full-employment policy, or a more traditional welfare system, depending on the regional approach. Except for a few nagging pockets, absolute poverty has been eradicated.

> *The pursuit of money is giving way to the cultivation of skills, relationships, communities, and the life of the mind and spirit. Indeed, those still enthralled by conspicuous consumption are considered aesthetically impoverished and spiritually backward.*

These profound cultural changes have been made possible by the surfeit of a once-scarce commodity: discretionary time. Where higher labor productivity increased output in the past, now it shrinks work weeks. Equally important to "time affluence" has been squeezing out the vast waste from pretransition economies that increased the social labor budget with no tangible benefit. That means the end of long commutes, inefficient resource use, and product obsolescence, and shrinking such unproductive sectors as defense, finance, and litigation.

Demographers report that world population has peaked at about eight billion people. Although far lower than turn-of-the-century projections, many believe this figure remains too large for a small planet. Still, the moderation in human numbers is a remarkable achievement, especially considering how average life expectancy has increased to about 100 years. Several developments led to the decrease in fertility rates, chief among them the education of girls, the empowerment of women, and the near-universal access to birth control. All this was supported by the tenacious world program to reduce poverty, a *sine qua non* of the Great Transition development paradigm.

Longer lives and fewer children have led to adjustments in family structure. While transitional and nuclear families are still common in most regions, and prevalent in Agoria, alternative forms have proliferated. Collective living communities, often built around workplace collectives, are popular in Ecodemia, and communal experiments abound in Arcadia. Diversity in living choices is part and parcel of this time of tolerance and pluralism.

Settlement patterns remain in flux, whether in urbanized Agoria or the rural precincts of Arcadia. A "new metropolitan vision" guides the redesign of neighborhoods into integrated mixed-use neighborhoods that place home, work, commerce, and leisure in proximity. This nurtures a sense of community within cities and, with sophisticated public transportation networks, radically reduces automobile dependence. One can see the day when sustainable urban development forms will replace the dysfunctional conurbations we have inherited.

The transition has achieved momentous victories in the long struggle for social justice. The emergent solidarity culture of respect and care for every person steadily eroded atavistic prejudice. The extension of the rights of citizenship to include material security and access to knowledge was key. These guarantees, by diminishing fear and ignorance, diluted the twin ingredients that throughout history have fed xenophobia and bigotry. Of course, this shift would not have happened — and would remain vulnerable to stagnation or even reversal — without the persistence and vigilance of the movements for the rights of women, indigenous peoples, and minorities of all stripes.

The great turn toward environmental sustainability is a proud chapter of the transition. The battle has been waged on many fronts: the reduction of the material consumption in households; the adoption of closed-loop industrial ecologies; the development of technologies that radically improved energy efficiency; the renewable resource revolution that brought down the curtain on the fossil fuel age; the explosion of ecological agricultural systems; and the greening of transport systems. With far more work to do, the restoration of Earth's vitality remains a passionate enterprise of the citizens of this damaged planet.

Now, the unfinished journey of transition arcs toward a new century of challenge and opportunity. As we look ahead with hope, let us also look back with gratitude. Our lives confirm what the pivotal generations of the Great Transition could only imagine: another world was possible!

8

Environmental History Exam 2052: The Last Half-Century

Les W. Kuzyk

She double-checks the name of the essay final exam — Global Environmental History 302 — complete with her student ID number and the date, 23 May 2052. Deciding to use voice and gesture interface for input and edit, she is ready. She thinks *OK, Jiera, just keep it organized. You studied for hours and you need to keep up those honors grades. Think chronologically and prioritize events by importance. The last half-century involved a series of crises and sometimes chaotic attempts at resolution, accompanied now and then by the influence of previously initiated trends and general circumstance.* She watches the time on the screen switch to 11:00 hours and she takes a deep breath. The entry screen changes color and the exam voice invites her to begin.

> **She watches the time on the screen switch to 11:00 hours and she takes a deep breath. The entry screen changes color and the exam voice invites her to begin.**

The first decade

Before the economically pivotal year of 2008, global citizens had gradually become aware of sustainability, but they and their governments had taken very little significant action. The primary global environmental predicament was climate change, which overlapped population, biodiversity loss, the soil nitrogen cycle, and a host of other issues. Various measurements of sustainability had been developed in the late 20th century, including the ecological footprint (EF), published in 1996, with the carbon footprint as one subcomponent. EF data showed that, while only half a planet's worth of resources were used in 1960, the significant one-planet mark of resource use was crossed by the early 1980s, and resource use was up to a completely unsustainable 1.52 planets by 2012, according to a report by the World Wildlife Fund. That report showed an ongoing upward trend into the future highlighting and summarizing the global environmental crisis at that time. *With one student-interest theme in human geography, her favorite sustainability measure is the EF, as it can be measured in global hectares as well as planet earths. Hectares lend themselves well to display on a map, and both units are intuitively understood. She recalls the paper she wrote profiling the footprint, but she knows she needs to stick to the broader picture for this exam.* Primary contributors to the dilemma were cultural (belief in unending increases in material living standards on a finite planet and consumerism viewed as the basis of cultural status and success); economic (a traditional outlook supporting a growth economy with a finite resource base, a market-driven influence over the general populace based on advertising and controlled media, as well as support for corporations as the basis of employment creation); and political (traditional partisan political systems in democracies based on mutual criticism, faultfinding, and a strict focus on short-term goals).

The second decade

The downturn — to use a traditional economic term — of 2008 was only the beginning of what has historically come to be known as the social-economic rollercoaster of the next decade. Traditional players in the global economy made ongoing attempts to kick-start its growth. But peak oil, now known to have arrived in 2017, as well as the obvious situation of peak planet (*the EF measure is right there*) contributed to the ongoing economic crisis. Each time the economy was able to begin to "recover," speculative investment would begin, petroleum prices would leap again as they had in 2008, and the economy would "crash" again. In parallel with peak petroleum, the global economy was being affected more and more directly by climate change, specifically droughts, floods, wildfires, and major weather events. Drastic increases in food prices led to social unrest, including repeated food riots in developing countries, which ricocheted into the increasingly unstable global economy. One positive outcome of this circumstance in developed countries, fueled largely by the price at the pumps, was a strong movement toward finding energy sources cheaper than hydrocarbons. Beginning in Europe, there was a significant move toward the deserts, where the algae lipids grown in the sun of the Sahara and sourced for biofuel became an essential source of liquid energy. Extensive solar arrays in the African deserts were also connected to the European power grid. The same pattern developed later in the Southern deserts of North America, along with parallel development of geothermal heat-sourcing at an industrial level. The destruction of rainforest for oil palm plantations ended when European tax incentives were adjusted to reduce the use of any biofuel based on a forest or food crop source. This decade is referred to by many as the first transition, the social-economic transition.

The third decade

In the early fall of 2023, the North Pole became briefly, and for the first time, ice free. Environmental activist film stars traveled there for a swimming photo op: images of some in dry or wet suits, and some not, appeared across magazine covers and screens around the globe. This symbolism of this event triggered considerable popular dialogue that continued throughout the 2020s. In those same years, frustrated by the lack of action from countries most responsible for carbon pollution and the resulting climate change, a group of countries came together to form High Impact Climate Change Countries (HICCC). HICCC included those concerned and affected most by desertification, rising sea levels, and major weather events. Bangladesh was hit by storm surges from two cyclones in 2024 and the Maldives was forced to initiate moves to abandon several islands the next year. When, in 2027, HICCC disclosed its plan to carry out a geoengineering project that would reduce the global temperature by, according to their estimate, 2°C through a sulfur dioxide release in the stratosphere, the global reaction was calamitous. Though China was not officially an HICCC member nation, the looming national climate change threats were seen by some to motivate their silence. *Her mom sometimes talks not only about all the fear at the time, like the Cold War of the 20th century, but also about the global awareness it engendered.* The popular community was aware by then, through a very well-known set of drama movies, of the dangers of such a one-time attempt to adjust a system as complex as the earth's climate. This was referred to as the political crisis, and sometimes as the second transition.

Throughout the teens and 2020s, two trends had noteworthy impacts: (i) the inclination toward Green Party power in democracies (ii) and an increase in the sway of women in politics. As democratically elected governments grew in number worldwide, with increasing youth support, they one-by-one voted Green Parties in as majorities or as parts of coalitions. Some political leaders still came to power through coups, or were democratically elected based on radical right platforms, and several regional military conflicts broke out. In spite of this, many Green Party members were able to educate populations on the benefits of a reduced economy. By the late 2020s, *reduce* became the keystone word from the token expression of the four R's — reduce, reuse, recycle, and recover. After a grassroots campaign to randomly paste social shaming sticker labels, such as the popular GROW UP on any gas-guzzling vehicle in North America, bans were put in place on all recreational vehicles. Images of the Rambo-man in his bush-crashing truck and the high-profile, sport utility vehicle (SUV)-driving consumer became relics of the past. Instead, biodiversity was advanced and protected through advertising images of threatened species beside small, efficient personal transportation units, including those made available through vehicle sharing programs. Major efforts to sequester carbon in soils and forests, partially in response to the HICCC threat and partially due to popular demand, were financially supported by carbon taxes and cap-and-trade policies that were, by then, in global use. Another North American grassroots campaign began to encourage reduction in animal protein consumption, looking toward Asian traditions where meat is often consumed as a condiment. The EF, which clearly shows that personal reduction of animal protein consumption results in a significant footprint reduction, made the news at that time. *She laughs at one of the jokes that came out then about the dog tax, when the animal protein tax on pet food made it clear how much the have-a-large-pet life-style was contributing to the demise of the pet owner's family future.*

For almost two years, in 2027 and 2028, three countries out of the G8 had simultaneous women heads of state who came to be known as the W3, and were sometimes compared to Gandhi, Mandela, and Martin Luther King Jr. In 2029, the long-term growth of women's involvement in politics reached the 50% mark in spite of major regional variation. *Her mother had served three terms on their regional council and is now sitting on several committees.* This was seen to have an important influence on the positive negotiations between HICCC, the G8, and the Organisation for Economic Co-operation and Development. Furthermore, with this equal gender representation came educational campaigns speaking to the universal benefits of equity in education, income, health care, access to the common biosphere, and each child's future. *The ecological footprint had become a standard measure by then, known to each European and North American household through real estate transactions as well as property tax forms, and to each individual through income tax returns from national statistics departments.* There was also a major shift to redistribution of paid-work hours and a reduction in formally recognized weekly work hours. The human population was mined globally for human capital, a search for naturally occurring intelligence, leadership potential, traditional beliefs on sustainability, and traditional methods of conflict resolution. A drastic reduction in spending on the military was carried out, recognizing this huge resource waste and acknowledging that security comes from the ability to cooperate with and help neighbors. Many female political figures, and especially the W3, spoke out about and financed the global education of girls and Planned Parenthood. This was also the beginning of the G8 cultural exchange program, first voluntary but now mandatory, where the selection of places available for exchange included Kerala in India, Costa Rica, Bhutan, Tuvalu, the Maldives, Iceland, New Zealand, Norway, Samso Island in Denmark, and British Columbia in Canada.

The fourth decade

By the early 2030s, the class action lawsuits against the major oil companies for their record of advertising and contribution to the climate crisis were in full swing. Many precedents had been set in previous lawsuits, including those citing health-care costs against tobacco companies. In 2034, the case of five western American states versus Exxon Mobil established a classic precedent, bringing forward everything from crop losses and wildfire damage to rising sea levels, surge tide damages, and flash floods from heavy precipitation events. Mention was even made of Standard Oil's historic purchase of streetcar systems with the business objective of promoting travel by automobile. This was referred to as the third transition, the legal crisis. But this time period was also known as the decade of peaks. The EF was first to peak, having reached 1.84 planets by 2032. Then, in 2038, global population peaked at 8.73 billion, lower than projected and highly influenced by women in political positions. Finally, in 2039, greenhouse gases in the atmosphere peaked at 465 ppm of carbon dioxide equivalent. Global concern over potential climate change tipping points was still a serious item of discussion and debate. Global awareness came to be clearly focused on cleaning up the problems created in the past and maintaining a healthy biosphere.

The fifth decade

By the 2040s, post-partisan democracy was coming into play. Democratic governments were becoming much more local and the idea of council and consensus decision making was rapidly replacing that of a president or any one person making decisions for the community. This system was found to work naturally, especially for women council members. Over the late 2040s and the first year and a half of the 2050s, the use of executive decision making was decreasing, going the way of the monarchies and dictatorships of the distant past. Local governments made most community decisions while the far off federal body was responsible for global security cooperation, national services, and management of the currency. *The global EF is now almost down to the one planet mark again, but still with significant regional variation.*

She is reminded by voice that she has 5 min remaining. She reads the essay over quickly, correcting minor discrepancies. When the screen fades back to its original color, she acknowledges the submission request, sending her exam in for grading. She has a good feeling about this exam, quite confident it will, in fact, keep her with honors-level grades.

She relaxes and thinks about the afternoon, when she will schedule her six-month community engagement term, mandatory but flexible. Her choice is to directly experience, observe, and learn in an alternate cultural and sustainability outlook setting — everything from studying how their local council makes decisions, to cultural traditions that have been determined to be valuable, to their societal outlook on the earth's biosphere, and its value to current and future human generations. She really looks forward to attending regional council meetings to observe how they come to resolution. She has chosen Costa Rica for its advanced methods and progressive positive cultural model, which made it the first nation-state in the world to attain a carbon-neutral status. It has also been influential assisting neighboring Central American countries to achieve carbon neutrality. Twenty-six hours on the Pan-American bullet train will get her there. Her evaluation and written thesis on the benefits of the learned lifestyle and their application in her home country will be credited toward her education and will be seen on her curriculum vitae as highly beneficial toward her future career.

> *She has chosen Costa Rica for its advanced methods and progressive positive cultural model, which made it the first nation-state in the world to attain a carbon-neutral status. Twenty-six hours on the Pan-American bullet train will get her there.*

9

A Virtual Visit to a Sustainable 2050

Robert Costanza

There is a new very advanced virtual reality system that just came out (almost like the holodeck on *Star Trek*). The "reality" it simulates is generated by a cross between a real-time systems simulation model of the biophysical environment, an agent-based personality simulator (a super-Sims), and an advanced "future search" consensus building system. It basically allows participants to create a future world that represents their overlapping hopes and dreams, tempered by the constraints of human nature and biophysical reality. Assumptions about these constraints are programmed in (by mutual agreement of the participants) at the start of the session. For our session, we agreed on a set of what we considered to be realistic assumptions, both about people and the rest of the world, that embodied the latest scientific research findings. We did not assume any major technological breakthroughs but rather assumed historical rates of technical change. We also assumed that people would not be fundamentally any different than they are now but that the environments (both physical and social) that they lived in would be very different.

Without you actually using the system and visiting the future virtual world yourself, it is, of course, difficult for me to describe. Like a real world, our simulated future was rich in detail. What follows is an attempt to convey some of that richness and texture by describing my own experiences in our simulated future world. These experiences covered a lot of different ground, but, taken together, they allow a fairly clear image of the future world we created. We agreed on a rough target date of 2050.

What really struck me about this future world was the overriding sense of calm and peacefulness but without any tinge of boredom. The best way to describe it is the difference between adolescence and mature adulthood. Our current society is adolescent — fixated on physical growth, changing so fast it is difficult to adjust — frenetic, self-absorbed, self-conscious, irresponsible, insecure, taking. Our envisioned future world was mature — not growing physically and therefore able to focus on development — improving quality not quantity, secure, invested in long-term relationships, responsible, nurturing, giving. For example, the average work week was 20 h but the distinction between work, learning, and leisure had become pretty blurred, so it is difficult to make this comparison directly, as you will see. But the bottom line is that life was not so hectic and people had more time for their families, each other, and the things that really interested them. That is where the calm and peacefulness came from. Since people could pursue what really interested them, they were not bored and their mental health and sense of satisfaction with life were excellent.

Susan was the first person I met in the simulation. I would wandered into a coffee shop near what was almost certainly a university campus (lattes were still on the menu). We struck up a casual conversation about the weather (very warm), and I innocently asked her, "What do you do?" I got a very quizzical expression. I quickly explained that I was visiting from another country and just wanted to know what kind of work she did. She said, "Oh, you must be on a travel sabbatical." (I later found out this was a common practice in 2050, where people exchange places for periods of a month to a year instead of taking vacations in the traditional sense.) She told me she worked as a researcher and teacher at the university, but it quickly became apparent that people in 2050 did not define themselves by their jobs to the extent they do today and, at the same time, that their lives and their work were more fully integrated. For example, Susan explained that all of her current research projects were also courses that she was teaching. Teaching had become much more problem based — learning by doing — rather than lecture based. Students and faculty participated in research projects together, and everyone learned while attacking real problems. When I asked what department Susan was in at the university, I got that quizzical expression again. She explained that the university had become transdisciplinary. There were research (and learning) centers focused on particular problems, but the traditional academic departments had disappeared. She suggested that I come along to a seminar on the *State of the World 2050* report that had just been released by the Worldwatch Institute.

As we walked through the campus, I noticed that the age distribution of the people we saw was much different than I am used to seeing on university campuses. Instead of a mass of young faces punctuated by a few older professors, the population looked much more evenly spread over the full range of ages. Susan said that people in 2050 considered learning a lifelong activity and had the time to actually implement that idea.

The seminar room was packed, and we arrived just in time to get seats at the back as things got under way. I asked Susan how long the Worldwatch Institute had been around, and she said at least 70 years or so. It was one of the first nongovernmental organizations (NGOs) formed at the end of the 20th century. Many of these had survived, grown, and diversified to the point of being equally if not more important than formal governments in the actual governance of society. They represented one of the many forms of the "strong democracy" that seemed to be the buzzword to describe the way society was now governed. More on that later.

The seminar began, and the speaker spent about an hour summarizing the report. It covered an awful lot of ground, and I started taking notes before I remembered that any notes I took would only be holograms that would disappear when I returned to the real world. These are some of the things I can remember:

- Global human population was stable at about eight billion people. This was due to better education everywhere, excellent elder care at the community level so that people no longer thought they needed many children to take care of them in old age, and a tacit multicultural norm of "replacement only." There was still quite a bit of international migration but not so much as to stress national borders, and, in fact, national borders were now for the most part open.
- The "material throughput" of national and global economies was decreasing slightly but not nearly as fast as in the past (obviously, the

speaker thought we could do better here). At the same time, the quality of life (QOL) index was going up at about 2% per year on average. The QOL measure was assessed annually using a global Internet survey that asked people to rank how well their needs in nine key areas (subsistence, protection, affection, understanding, participation, leisure, creation, identity, and freedom) were being met. The United States ranked near the top in subsistence, protection, and freedom but was below average in the other areas. Its overall QOL rank fell somewhere just above the median (but this had been improving in recent years). The real efficiency of the economy was now computed as the ratio of QOL to material throughput, and this was also increasing.

- Gaps in income were decreasing both between countries and within countries, and this contributed to building strong social capital, the solution to many recalcitrant social problems, and increasing QOL without increasing material throughput.

- Global biodiversity was making a comeback. Since the human population had stabilized and throughput was decreasing, pressure on the environment had also stabilized and there were concerted and well-funded efforts to protect and enhance biodiversity.

- The biggest problem seemed to be dealing with the continuing effects of climate change. Global CO_2 emissions were decreasing, but they had a long way to go before we were back to preindustrial levels. New Orleans had already disappeared and the Netherlands was under constant threat. But cautious optimism seemed to be the message here.

As we left the seminar, I asked Susan about the "strong democracy" concept that had been mentioned. The puzzled look again — where had I been? She said it was nothing really new, just the idea that everyone should participate directly in decision making at all levels rather than delegating that authority to elected representatives. When I expressed some skepticism that this could ever be practical, she just waved her hand and said, "Well look around — it is working." I never got the full answer, but I think it was a combination of people having more time for participation in politics, a better communications infrastructure that uses the advanced version of the Internet they had by then, a deep culture of participation that was inculcated from a very young age, and the general maturity of the whole system that I mentioned before.

Susan invited me to come over for dinner and meet her husband and children. I gladly accepted this chance to see how domestic life worked in 2050. Her house was an easy 10-min bus ride and 5-min walk from campus. It was clustered in a group of about 50 houses, along with some shops and small businesses, in what she referred to as a village (even though it was in a large urban area). The village shared common green space, gardens, bike and foot paths, and a few other resources. All transport within the village was by bike or foot. She explained that (like most villages) they used an internal LETS (labor-equivalent trading system) to keep track of shared labor services. For example, if I spent some of my free time helping paint somebody's house, I would rack up "hours" that I could cash in to get help on some project of mine. Again, an overriding sense of calm and peacefulness pervaded the place (probably due to the lack of car noise — replaced by the sounds of birds chirping and children playing in the shared green space).

Susan's husband, Paul, and their two young daughters, Lisa and Jennifer, shared a three-bedroom house that seemed to be about average by today's standards. In fact, Susan mentioned that the house had been originally built in 2001 and retrofitted with the latest in energy technologies so that it actually produced more electricity than it consumed. By making almost all buildings part of the energy-production grid, and drastically reducing the need for transportation, the whole economy was now able to run on renewable, sustainable resources.

Susan had to back up Paul in his decision not to let the girls spend the night at a friend's, and I inspected the books on their bookshelf while the girls threw a tantrum over this injustice (some things never change). After things settled down, we all sat down to dinner. I explained to the girls that I was on a "travel sabbatical" and was wondering what people did for fun in this part of the world. The answers were not dissimilar from what you might hear today, including movies, dances, parties, and concerts. The only difference I noticed was that most of the activities mentioned were social — people seemed to spend more time interacting with each other than staying at home watching TV — and "shopping at the mall" did not come up as a favorite activity, even among teenage girls. In fact, I think malls had all but disappeared — replaced by a combination of Internet shopping, local village shops, and a general lowering of consumption levels. The dinner, for example, was almost all food grown in the village gardens (the avid gardeners in the village were racking up a lot of LETS hours), and the rest came from the village shop, which was a 5-min walk from the house. I asked if there were any big problems in the village and got a litany of typical neighbor complaints — one was drinking too much, another had too many loud parties, and so on. But in general, these problems were solved by talking with people at village events rather than by calling the police (come to think of it, I do not think I saw a policeman or heard a siren the whole time I was there). People had not changed, it seemed, but the "system" had — and this allowed them to solve their inevitable problems in more mature, friendly, and productive ways.

As I left Susan and Paul's house, I was thinking that it just could not be this simple. There must be a catch. Would not all this social serenity require a suppression of creativity and initiative? How could people be happy and productive in an economy that was not growing? But after thinking it through, it was clear that, in fact, it could easily work. Just like an individual organism that goes through a stage of early rapid physical growth followed by later "development" without further growth, a whole socioeconomic system could do the same. And from personal experience, I can attest that the teenage years are often difficult and not as happy as later years when growth has stopped and one can concentrate on the joys of development. I found that I really liked being an adult in this adult society. And as I was thinking this, the simulation ended and I returned to the present.

10

Reflections on a Life Lived Well and Wisely

Joshua Farley

By 2055, the 92-year-old man lay ill and dying, but fairly comfortable, in his bed. He had a choice to make: should he go to the hospital, where superb medical care might prolong his life for a year or so, probably doubling his lifetime health-care costs in the process? Or should he die in the comfort of his home, well attended by family and America's national health-care service? Health care was a right, but with it came the responsibility to take care of one's health and to use the care system judiciously. Struggling with the decision, he reflected on the present and the past.

His granddaughter was due to begin her mandatory two years of national defense duty and had to choose between working in the area of food, water, energy, or ecosystem security. The most exciting security work was now taking place in sub-Saharan Africa, one of the regions suffering the worst from climate chaos. In much of the world, the new green revolution had proven successful at combining local and scientific expertise to build agroecosystems based on perennial polyculture that were resilient to extreme weather events. In addition to producing food, fiber, and fuel, these agroecosystems were designed to increase biodiversity, sequester carbon, purify water, and regulate the microclimate, all without external inputs. Extreme weather brought serious technical challenges, many best addressed at global research centers, but the system relied mostly on a bottom–up approach, spreading from farmer to farmer, with extension workers facilitating the process. Dissemination throughout Africa was complicated by tensions between neighboring ethnic groups who not long ago had been engaged in bloody wars triggered by food and resource scarcity. It helped that the nations historically responsible for excessive atmospheric carbon stocks shouldered the cost and risks of transition.

The old man's son had been in the first wave of recruits for the new defense service, but his work had been here in the United States, first dealing with the aftermath of the crisis decade — a seemingly endless bout of droughts, floods, and hurricanes that had finally woken people up to the reality of climate chaos. Food production plunged, people starved, infrastructure was destroyed. Many thought that the end had come, but that decade's events turned out to be unusual even for the new weather regime. Food prices increased 10-fold in response to a 10% drop in supply. There would have been enough to go around, but the market economy allocated food to those willing to pay the most. The rich kept eating their steaks and fueling their cars with ethanol, while the poor suffered serious malnutrition.

It turned out that the crisis years had a silver lining. First, the weather events totally changed the prevailing paradigm — people around the world realized that continued economic growth on a finite planet was impossible and that the ecological costs of continued growth outweighed the economic benefits. Something had to be done. Second, the extreme inequality and ecological degradation changed his nation's goals. People realized that maximizing monetary value, growing GNP (gross national product), was perverse. The contribution of agriculture to GNP had skyrocketed when food output plunged, which made no sense whatsoever — less food made society worse off, not better. Furthermore, converting corn to ethanol to run a limousine for a rich person while the penniless masses starved was unethical, even if markets deemed it efficient. People made it through the crisis by helping each other. Society realized that it had to

> *Society realized that it had to prioritize community over the individual and ecological sustainability and social justice over consumption.*

prioritize community over the individual and ecological sustainability and social justice over consumption. The government redefined recession as increasing levels of misery, poverty, and unemployment.

His country almost did not make it through the crisis. Rioting was serious. Out of control mobs even lynched many politicians, bankers, and other wealthy people who they blamed for our problems. With their monopoly of the airwaves, the corporate-controlled media called for mobilizing the military to protect the wealthy. Fortunately, the federal government took over many radio and TV stations, as did local governments and even citizen groups, broadcasting the message that we had to help each other to get through crisis times and coordinating people to do so. As the situation gradually got under control, corporations demanded back their ownership of the airwaves, which launched a national debate about why they had been given ownership to begin with. In the end, rights to the airwaves were restored to the public sector and civil society at the local, state, and national levels. Some of the airwaves were then leased out to the private sector, with revenue used to fund public/civic media. Better programming on commercial-free channels proved critically important in reducing consumerism and promoting civic duty. The Great Transition would have been impossible without it.

Reclaiming the airwaves raised a larger debate about the private ownership of wealth produced by nature or by society as a whole, leading eventually to the rebirth of the commons. In 2030, the Commons Act was passed, which declared all resources created by nature or society as a whole to be the shared wealth of society, including future generations. No more windfall profits for oil companies. This made it illegal to use natural resources faster than they could regenerate, to emit pollution faster than ecosystems could absorb it, or to deplete nonrenewable resources faster than we could develop renewable substitutes. Erosion of farmland was now treated as theft from future genera-

> *Erosion of farmland was now treated as theft from future generations.*

tions. It took some time, of course, to transition to better farming practices and agriculture based primarily on perennials. Now, however, throughout most of the landscape, carbon sequestration was rapidly rebuilding the soils.

Anyone who used common property for private gain was now forced to compensate the rest of society through taxes and cap-and-auction systems for natural capital, including waste-absorption capacity.

It also proved critically important to restore the monetary system to the commons. The old man still remembered when he had first taken out a mortgage. Most people back then thought that banks simply loaned out the money that others had deposited, not realizing that banking laws required deposits to back less than 10% of actual loans. The bank had written him a check, which created US$150,000 out of thin air, with an interest rate much higher than economic growth. He had paid back more than US$300,000 before he owned his house. When businesses back then had borrowed money for productive investments based on hard work, interest payments had siphoned away much of their profits. This practice ensured a steady transfer of wealth to the financial sector, away from productive sectors, and virtually guaranteed economic collapse as debt grew faster than the economy. Now only governments — through municipal, state, and national currencies — had the right to create money, and they mostly spent it into existence for public goods or loaned it interest-free for socially important activities such as farming. As the market economy began to shrink, taxes were kept higher than money creation, to control inflation. Progressive income tax rates now gradually approached 100% on the last dollars earned by the richest citizens, with additional taxes on speculation. Those who earned a lot stilled consumed a fair bit more than others, but because of the support they provided the public sector they were no longer ostracized.

The ostracism of the selfish was another key component of the Great Transition. Early in the 21st century, people had glorified the wealthy, but the images of the wealthy wasting food while the poor went hungry made people see such behavior as sociopathic. They began to scorn the rich, or worse, which made it possible to dramatically increase taxes on the rich. It also made it decidedly unpleasant to be wealthy, at least in respectable society.

The other major element of the Great Transition had been putting the market in its place. The crisis made people realize that for essential resources with no substitutes — such as food, water, energy, health care — small changes in quantity led to huge fluctuations in price. Furthermore, in the swine flu epidemic of 2018, monopoly profits had made vaccines too expensive for the poor, ensuring the spread of the disease and facilitating its evolution into forms that even killed many of the vaccinated. It turned out that making access to basic needs a human right had enormous stabilizing effects on the economy, which made it much easier for businesses and households to plan ahead. People liked stability. Markets were well designed for managing surplus production and nonessential commodities, but not for basic needs.

During the crisis years, other countries had been in similar turmoil. Environmental refugees were everywhere. Small wars were breaking out. Large wars were imminent. Far-sighted thinkers in the military had realized that there was no military solution to a problem like this. If people could not meet their basic needs, they would get violent. If others helped them meet their basic needs, they would be allies and friends. The government thus redefined national defense and national security. Mandatory service guaranteed employment for the young. The old man's son had first worked on the production of long-shelf-life staple crops in the plains states and their perennialization. He had then reenlisted to focus on the short-shelf-life fruits and vegetables once imported from abroad, now fertilized by humanure (sterilized first in biogas generators) in 80 million victory gardens around the country. The old man remembered the joy he had experienced growing bumper crops in his own backyard and the social prestige of sharing the surplus with the less fortunate. He had even won the neighborhood award for carbon sequestration in his garden plots several times. In his older years, however, he had let more of his yard return to native ecosystems, habitat for pest predators, food for his honeybees, and a pleasure for his eyes.

He had had an eventful and awarding life. His small home was a bit crowded with his wife, two children with spouses, and two grandchildren, but they brought him immense pleasure, especially in his illness. It was better to stay here and die in their company. He knew his body would nurture the garden, build its carbon. With his help, his son might even win the surplus production prize next year.

11

The Great Turnaround: How Natural Capital Entered the Economy?

Ronald Colman

What if the crisis of 2008 represents something much more fundamental than a deep recession? What if it's telling us that the whole growth model we created over the last 50 years is simply unsustainable economically and ecologically and that 2008 was when we hit the wall — when Mother Nature and the market both said: "No more."

Thomas Friedman, *The New York Times*, 7 March 2009

It is 2055, and the world is heaving one huge sigh of relief as scientists announce that — for the first time since the Industrial Revolution — atmospheric greenhouse gas concentrations have finally stabilized. Massive emission reductions in the last four decades have at last staved off impending catastrophe for life on earth.

Credit for what is now called The Great Turnaround is being universally given to the new sustainability-based economic paradigm globally adopted at the historic Bhutan Woods conference of 2013, where it was agreed that the benefits of early preventive action to avoid the worst of the damage wrought by climate change far outweighed the short-term economic costs of such action.

By 2018, natural capital values had been fully and properly incorporated into national income accounting worldwide. Finally, politicians had the tools and evidence they needed to reverse the calamitous global warming and resource depletion trends that constituted the greatest challenges humankind has ever faced.

Now, in 2055, as we celebrate this remarkable victory, let us take a look back at that critical Turnaround period in human history, when natural capital and ecosystem service values were finally taken into account, when the world adopted a new economic paradigm based on proper national income and wealth accounting, and when our leaders began to chart a sane and sustainable path into the future.

Sadly, as too often happens, the impulse to change was precipitated by disaster, which began in 2008.

It was not that nature's warnings were suddenly heeded. Indeed those warnings — of melting icecaps and receding glaciers, resource depletion, species extinction, and more — had become so familiar that they were barely news in 2008. Even the extraordinarily comprehensive UN Millennium Ecosystem Assessment, which was based on the best scientific evidence and demonstrated that two-thirds of the world's ecosystem services were in serious decline, was barely a blip on the radar screen of policymakers.

No. What unraveled in 2008 with dramatic abruptness was the economic system itself. Major banks failed, iconic symbols of American prosperity such as General Motors went bankrupt, the stock market collapsed, life savings disappeared, the ranks of the unemployed swelled, and 15 years of sustained economic growth suddenly morphed — seemingly overnight — into the worst economic downturn since the Great Depression.

But the real moment of truth came when Alan Greenspan, former head of the US Federal Reserve and chief of all bankers, went before Congress to beat his breast, to confess that he had been fatally wrong in his prescriptions for the economy, and that he, economic guru of gurus, had no inkling of the impending financial catastrophe. What proved bankrupt in 2008 was not only a failed economic paradigm but its most eminent theorists and practitioners and the accounting system that sent them the wrong messages.

And yet, as so often happens when things fall apart, those with the greatest stake mustered their troops for one last stand. With critically flawed accounts and progress measures and an armory correspondingly bereft of ideas, the defenders could only fight fire with fire, combating a collapse spurred by debt-fueled growth with yet more debt-fueled growth. It was a recipe for disaster.

Deeper problems in 2011

Not only had President Obama's proposed US$1.5 trillion fiscal stimulus package of 2008–2009 predictably failed to stimulate, but the next recession of 2011–2012 (or was it a depression?) was ushered in with a 9% unemployment rate and a US$1.8 trillion deficit in the United States. No more stimulus or bailouts now. The clarion call had changed from "stimulus" to "deficit reduction."

There was social unrest, unsurprisingly. Even during the prior two decades of apparent prosperity, young people lost ground, saw their median incomes drop and their debt loads increase, and even voted less — a sure warning sign of growing alienation from the established order.

On the sidelines, analysts like George Monbiot noted that "climate breakdown, peak oil, and resource depletion will all dwarf the current financial crisis, in both financial and humanitarian terms." In fact, the very measures taken in 2008 and 2009 to get the economy back to where it was — infinite growth on a finite planet — were a recipe for ecological disaster. And, wrote Monbiot in the *Guardian*, "When the world's ecological debt comes due, no World Bank or International Monetary Fund (IMF) bailout package will save the day." For the first time since the

> *The very measures taken in 2008 and 2009 to get the economy back to where it was — infinite growth on a finite planet — were a recipe for ecological disaster.*

Industrial Revolution, it was clear that the next generation would not be better off than previous ones — economically, socially, or ecologically.

So now, at last, in 2011–2012, with the global economy in free fall and governments themselves deeply indebted and teetering on bankruptcy, the world was searching for a genuine cure. And, at last, leaders were ready to listen. In the midst of the 2008–2009 emergency rescue packages — approved with stunning rapidity by an almost global consensus — that openness to a sane path forward did not exist. But in 2011–2012, the world was ready at last to explore other solutions.

But where to look? Theory was not enough now. The world needed a real example of what could work, a country somewhere that was not spiraling downward into depression and fear, a country whose people lived prosperously, with satisfaction, and in harmony with nature, and who were — dare we say it — happy.

A beacon of light

In 2012, a little Himalayan country was blessed with relative insignificance, just remote enough not to be entirely hooked to the materialist bandwagon and small enough, with a population of less than a million, to put the new paradigm into action. It was a country with a strong spiritual tradition and an ancient culture of respect for all living beings, with strong communities and social bonds, with its old-growth forests still intact, with half the country under complete environmental protection, and with a policy to grow all of its food organically. It was a country that had vowed to remain a net carbon sink in perpetuity and whose king had famously declared three decades earlier that "Gross National Happiness is more important than Gross National Product."

And yet, remarkable and rare as those qualities were, they drew only marginal interest from a frightened world spiraling into insecurity, conflict, and disarray. No, what changed in 2012 was that once secure and reliable global food and energy supply lines were suddenly cut as fearful leaders worldwide threw up protective barriers and citizens hoarded diminishing supplies.

So what really began to garner increasing global attention was that the economy of this little land of Bhutan was thriving on its own resources, that it had no food shortages and was feeding its people, that it exuded a palpable quality of peace and security, seemingly immune from the chaos surrounding it. And while the world shuddered and "hunkered down" in "fear," "panic," "gloom," "despair," and "resignation," gripped by unfolding "threat" and "disaster" (all actual phrases culled from a single day's London newspaper in 2008), the leaders of Bhutan spoke in calm and measured tones and its people smiled warmly.

How could this be? And could this remote little country really have something practical and useful to offer the world? Might even the formerly rich and powerful, who arrogantly held sway over the globe for so long with impunity, learn something from this seemingly insignificant nation?

Fortunately for the world, the leaders and people of Bhutan did not remain smugly secure in their little cocoon of well-being. In this globalized world, bound together by television, Internet, and trade, they were not so remote as to be unaware and unaffected by the unfolding pain and suffering all around them, and their hearts ached at what they saw.

The new Bretton Woods

Kindly, in the winter of 2013, the Prime Minister of Bhutan called and hosted a global gathering on a "new Bretton Woods" to build a consensus on a new, sane, global economic paradigm based on actual scientific and expert knowledge of the world, with new measures of progress, and new global institutions to manage and regulate the system.

The Bretton Woods system of 1944, he noted, enshrined gross domestic product (GDP) as the global measure of progress and prosperity and created the World Bank and the IMF to manage a system predicated on limitless growth. This system was constructed before the world had any awareness that its natural resources were finite and before even the most brilliant scientists were aware that human activity could change the climate of the planet Earth. "And," he added somberly, "that system was based on untenable, self-defeating economic premises."

In the presence of some of the world's most renowned economists, the prime minister's 2013 opening conference address was broadcast live worldwide. His simple words galvanized the world, sparked a ray of hope, and marked a new beginning. Very straightforwardly, he humbly described what Bhutan was doing:

"Our economy," he said, "is not based on economic activity fueled by endless desire, but on what our people genuinely need in order to achieve decent living standards and to fulfill their human potential. We're not interested in producing more stuff. Actually, we already have enough in aggregate. In fact, we have plenty! What we care about is how to distribute that wealth fairly to ensure no one is deprived."

"And so," he added, "when this new global depression hit and our markets dried up and our economy shrank, our first concern was to make sure no one got unduly hurt. Our full-cost national accounts, which account fully and properly for the value of our natural, human, and social capital, show that unemployment produces huge illness, crime, addiction, and other costs. And so, we haven't laid off anyone! Instead we've redistributed our work so all our people now work shorter hours. And they *like* it! They've got more time with family and friends and more time to contemplate, picnic, volunteer, and enjoy themselves."

"Maybe most importantly," said the prime minister, "our full-cost national accounts show us clearly that our economy is only as healthy as the natural resources that sustain our life on earth and that we need to power our economy. If we destroy our soils, forests, water, and other natural wealth, which provide hugely valuable services to our people, our economy and our people will die. And so, we've created an economy in full harmony with nature."

"One key feature of that economy is that it's basically local in scale. We grow enough food to feed ourselves, and it's healthy and nutritious because we grow nearly all of it organically. We can provide all our basic energy and necessities domestically from renewable sources, and we're proud to be a true 'zero waste' society. Most of our people walk to work, and we provide free public transport and van pools for those who need a ride. And so, we didn't hurt when food supply and energy lines were cut. Our economy is healthy and self-reliant."

The big leap

And then the Prime Minister of Bhutan made a big leap. Carefully gauging his audience, feeling them come around to his side, and deeply wanting to calm the palpable global panic and uncertainty, the leader of this little country now dared to offer advice to a desperate world.

"You have nothing to fear," he said. "Even in the midst of this great depression, you have plenty of resources and you are already producing enough to feed and supply everyone in this world. You don't have to grow. In fact, we can actually welcome this global economic slowdown as a tremendous opportunity, a chance to give nature a rest, to consume less energy and fewer resources, to emit less greenhouse gas, to reduce stress, to have more free time, to become more secure and self-reliant, and to improve the quality of our lives."

"Our full-cost national accounts very clearly show that the global economy had grown too large and that we were already globally consuming resources at a rate too fast to allow them to regenerate. In fact, shrinking the global economy creatively is essential for human survival on the planet."

"And this is good news from a human point of view. Our measures of progress clearly show that producing and consuming more stuff doesn't make people happier. On the contrary, when they overwork to buy more stuff and pay the bills, they mostly get more stressed. Renowned economist Dr John Helliwell at University of British Columbia showed that the strongest correlate of happiness is not income but strong social bonds. So, working, producing, and consuming less is not only good for nature but gives us more time to enjoy each other's company."

The prime minister concluded, "Together, let's use these next two weeks to create a healthy new global economic system based on caring for nature and for each other. We'll need new measures of progress that count the value of *all* our wealth — natural, social, human, and economic. And we'll need global regulatory mechanisms to replace the institutions like the IMF and World Bank that have failed us so badly — systems of fair trade, of rewards and incentives for sustainable behaviors, of penalties for pollution and resource degradation, and of protection and support for the world's most vulnerable peoples."

"And those new measures and systems will protect us from the kind of fear, despair, and crisis that is now roiling the world. Because we use a *net* rather than a *gross* accounting system, our new measures will properly assess the costs of production and provide early warning signals that allow timely remedial action. For instance, if our natural capital accounts show a decline in fish stocks, we'll take preventive action before the resource collapses."

"Indeed, we in Bhutan were not at all surprised by the present global economic slowdown because, unlike GDP that counts only gross income, production, and consumption, our net accounting mechanisms showed that debt was growing globally at a much faster rate than income. Sooner or later, as the subprime mortgage crisis that precipitated the present global collapse showed, it was obvious debtors would default on their payments. And when governments went deeply into debt to try to fuel more growth, our accounts clearly predicted the present disaster of national defaults."

"We, as human beings, are smarter than that, and we can do better — much better — in creating a secure, sustainable, harmonious, peaceful, and happy economy and society. Let's take this shaky moment in human history as a tremendous opportunity to forge a sane path forward together."

And so it was that in 2013, a historic meeting officially dismantled the 1944 Bretton Woods consensus, which had ruled the world for nearly 70 years, and replaced it with what became known in the history books as the Bhutan Accord. This accord paved the way for our present 2055 victory in finally stemming the tide of climate change and formed the basis for a good human society based on sufficiency, equity, sustainability, and dignity.

Author's note

This chapter reflects options open to both Bhutan and the world and — while it builds on present plans and policies that make those options possible — does not claim to reflect actual current realities in either Bhutan or the world at large. To give one example: While it is the official policy of the Bhutanese government to become 100% organic in food production and to increase food self-sufficiency, neither objective has yet been achieved, though the chapter implies they have been. Thus, all views, opinions, statements, and errors in the chapter are the sole responsibility of the author and have not been vetted in any way by any official of the Government of Bhutan. Nevertheless, the author believes that the foundation of what is described here does exist in practice and that the scenario outlined can be achieved.

12

How New Zealand Became a Green Leader?

John Peet

From New Zealand's position now in the year 2050, in a state of strong sustainability, it is clear that its citizens were quite unready in 2009 to embrace the concept of sustainable living and the changes required to achieve it. Modern historians have marveled at the fact that the 2008 general election scarcely mentioned the subject, despite the substantial evidence of imminent, unprecedented change. The drivers of major change that had been identified soon appeared in 2008, some with much more severity than had been envisaged.

The world economy fell into a deep recession. This recession was triggered initially by the turmoil in the money and credit system that began in 2007 and 2008, then snowballed into major declines in aggregate demand and international trade. Political unrest in several major nations and blocs spurred recession further and resulted in multiple regional conflicts. The economic forces supporting globalization weakened markedly.

As this happened, some of the basic assumptions about global economics began to change. Investors realized that they could not expect global economic growth to resume and, hence, that the prices of securities would in the future have little or no growth component. In the mid-2020s, money supply processes became regulated when commercial banks lost the privilege of creating the national currency and money supply as profit-making loans. This function reverted to the reserve bank, which acted in the national interest, and money itself reverted to its traditional role of facilitating the exchange of goods and services. Driven by the imperative to follow the requirements of a steady-state economy, fiscal and other legislative changes were well under way by 2025 to impose substantial taxes on the use of nonrenewable resources and, at the same time, to reduce the rates of direct sales, income, and company taxation. These changes were the first major steps in the shift to the new economics.

Through all of these events and continuing thereafter, sensible decisions were made in New Zealand whenever they were needed. With the benefit of hindsight, we now know that if any of the key actions had not been taken or had been unduly delayed, our recent history would have been one of much greater confusion, chaos, and hardship. There would have been a substantial collapse of human well-being in this country together with irreparable damage to our ecological systems.

New Zealand's economic output fell markedly and its dependence on international trade was drastically reduced. Consequently, principles of regional and local self-sufficiency were introduced. The years between 2009 and 2020 were very difficult — globally and in New Zealand — as the entrenched economic and governance systems struggled to cope, with deteriorating degrees of success.

As the severe inadequacy of the traditional approaches to economics and governance became apparent, movements in civil society began to question, with rapidly strengthening influence, the viability of the institutions involved, and the validity of the principles upon which they were based. Advanced development of the Internet had (and still has) great power in ensuring the connectivity of people who were now more physically separated. The Internet facilitated the rapid spread of transformational initiatives that began in civil society, then acquired strong political interpretations in northern Europe, and germinated quickly in New Zealand. The relative simplicity of government in this small country made the changes easier to implement.

In this gradual but insistent process, the traditional ideologies and institutions of economics and governance were rejected because they were failing and were replaced by alternatives. The people who led these changes are now greatly respected. At the time, the chaotic global situation did not support optimism, but these people had hope and vision, together with personal resilience and a commitment to find a path through the morass. Of course, those who were still engaged with the traditional approaches tried strenuously to maintain them, but the evolving changes eventually prevailed. They were quite different from any previous approaches to political economy.

As a result of the reforms brought about by this movement, New Zealand is now strongly sustainable within its sovereign territory and possesses substantial influence in other countries that are on a similar path. New Zealand achieved these results because the country embraced the following six enabling conditions[1]:

1. New Zealand limits emissions into the atmosphere, discharges into waterways and the ocean, and chemicals in the soil to levels within the assimilative capacities of the relevant ecosystems.
2. New Zealand regenerates and grows natural and social capital to sustain the health and resilience of its people, their institutions, and the whole of nature.
3. New Zealand substitutes renewable resources for nonrenewable resources wherever feasible, and uses these as efficiently as possible. Nonrenewable material resources are stewarded within closed cycles that maintain their quality, and nonrenewable energy resources are used at a rate that is no greater than the rate of investment in their replacement by renewable energy sources.
4. New Zealanders are broadly and deeply eco-literate and have a strong human–Earth relationship. Through education, they know that people are part of nature and ecosystems and understand that what they do to nature they do to themselves.
5. Strong sustainability understanding is deeply embedded in all of New Zealand's governance, economic, legal, and educational systems, and in all applications of these systems.
6. New Zealand imports only from countries and regions that have produced goods according to strongly sustainable criteria and refuses to benefit materially from unsustainable practices offshore. All of New Zealand's exports are produced by strongly sustainable processes and practices.

Alas, the way to full global sustainability is still very much in the balance. Scientists believe that catastrophic global warming tipping points and runaway climate change have been averted, but they are not certain. Global ecosystem degradation has been huge. Very turbulent climatic patterns persist and will do so for decades to come. New Zealanders have shaped their communities and lifestyles to adjust to this situation.

As we felt the painful impact of economic and ecological meltdown on a day-to-day basis, we were finally able to see what had gone wrong. It was not our good intentions and it was not that we did not have enough information. Maybe there was too much denial and complacency. But our biggest problem was a lack of imagination. Our public and private institutions were too busy keeping the economy going and never really tried to address the environmental crisis. There were true leaders — creative artists, inspiring teachers, visionary thinkers, innovative engineers, forward-looking people in business and government, young activists — but they could not, by themselves, bring about the necessary change.

When the citizens of New Zealand realized that their institutions lacked the necessary imagination and leadership, they decided to make changes themselves. That made all the difference! Institutions are like ecosystems, living systems with forces of stability and forces of change. If institutions follow short-term, economic interests, they will emphasize competition, stability, and material growth. If they follow long-term, ecological interests, they will emphasize cooperation and change.

Governance structures needed to reflect the strong sustainability model: economy nested within society and society nested within ecology. We identified issues-based units and associated governance structures with regional, river basin, and local layers of governance.

However, the way forward remained unclear, even after New Zealanders widely accepted the necessity of sustainability. The democratic institutions — governments, political parties, the media — remained fixated on economic growth and, as a result, sustainable development had not been accepted as part of the global market ideology. The market had displaced both democracy and sustainability.

Fortunately, we in New Zealand strongly felt that both concepts were absolutely indispensable and that one could not be realized without the other. The concept of democracy had to be reformulated and grounded in commonly accepted principles of freedom, equity, and justice. To these principles, we added strong sustainability. Our efforts pointed to the blind spot of democratic decision making: our political leaders accepted responsibility only for the here and now, not for the there and then.

As the various governments of the day had no sense of urgency and never admitted their own ineffectiveness, it was left largely to civil society to initiate and organize change. In New Zealand — as in most other countries — citizens, not governments, took charge. As a consequence, far-reaching governance reform became inevitable.

Within this new political context, the long-term issues relating to the Māori — especially the settlement of historical treaty claims and issues relating to lands, foreshore, and seabed — were resolved to the satisfaction of all citizens.

Once we asked the question about how democracy and sustainability could go together, we had a healthy debate on fundamental values. While some people were only ever concerned with increasing their wealth, most New Zealanders knew that market ideology had profoundly failed us and looked for a new arrangement between the public, the state, and the economy. Given the fundamental importance of sustainability, it became increasingly clear that any such arrangement had to be based on values and principles.

Reference

1. Peet, J (2009). *Strong Sustainability for New Zealand: Principles and Scenario. SANZ (Phase2) Report.* New Zealand: Nakedize Limited.

13

The New New York: 2050

Barbara Elizabeth Stewart

It seems impossible, until it is done.

Nelson Mandela

In 2050, it is a pleasure to breathe. The air is fresh, even in the biggest cities. Commuters do not reach home frazzled after being tied up in bad traffic.

The world is simpler in 2050. There are fewer consumer goods but there is more time, more conversation, and more contentment. The most threatening crises of 40 years earlier have been quelled or, at least, are being addressed. The air, water, and soil are no longer poisoned. The clean water, fresh air, and fertile soil that were once the birthright of all beings are on their way to being restored.

By 2050, great changes have taken place in nearly every aspect of life, but first and foremost in attitudes, values, and actions.

> *By 2050, great changes have taken place in nearly every aspect of life, but first and foremost in attitudes, values, and finally, actions.*

Things got bad before they got better. After superstorms and droughts in 2012 caused enormous damage. The gap between the rich and everybody else became unendurable. Economic collapse, endemic unemployment,

99

glaring injustice, and deepening and expanding suffering goaded people into riots and rebellion — and political action. Effective grassroots leadership arose throughout the world, and the changes began to take root.

> *Economic collapse, endemic unemployment, glaring injustice, and deepening and expanding suffering goaded people into riots and rebellion — and political action.*

By 2020, the primacy of profit and growth had been thoroughly discredited. Like smoking, the culture of greed and "profit first" had become repugnant. So had pollution, economic inequity, and overwork to earn more. Legislation to stem pollution, environmental destruction, and the systemic economic injustices of capitalism was passed in nearly every nation. Thousands and thousands of people joined together to bring about change.

By 2050, the bad old days seemed, quite frankly, insane and sad. Life has vastly improved. The land, air, and waters are cleaner, scrubbed of pollutants and poisons. The natural world is honored as a sacred trust for all, and damaging it for profit is a violation of local, national, and global law.

Cities have retained their character and vigor, but the noise and crush have been eliminated. Traffic jams have vanished and streets are now crowded with bicycles and pedicabs. Sidewalks are packed with pedestrians. Even more striking is the elimination of urban poverty. The streets are safe!

Their inhabitants live differently, too. In the midst of bustling cities, they have embraced community, calm, and the economic and social freedom to find an inner happiness that has nothing to do with materialism or moods.

In 2050, leisure time and contentment are like fresh, smoke-free air. Public policy measures have evened out income levels: the poor are richer and the rich have far less material wealth, but remarkably do not feel poorer. In 2050, the vast majority of people earn enough to live well — simply, but well. The big difference is in the definition of what *living well* means. In 2050 that means time with family and friends, time to relax, play, learn, and contemplate.

It is, in short, a sane world, where young people like Miriam, a New York college student, can choose a vocation without worrying if it will provide a decent living, where she has time for friends and neighbors and self-reflection, and is able to feel the inner contentment that is now the birthright of every citizen on earth.

New York city, 2050

Miriam has a lot in common with her mother. She lives in the same neighborhood in Queens, New York, the most multicultural place on earth. She speaks French nearly as well as her mother, Samira, who emigrated from Burkina Faso. But a lot has changed. Miriam's mother, Samira, had to work full-time waiting tables to cover her college tuition because her parents were too poor to contribute.

For Miriam, in 2050, it all sounds like the dark ages.

Her family's home is modest but well designed and is part of a cooperative housing group with communal green spaces and vegetable gardens. In cold weather and rain, she rides the renovated subway. But usually she bicycles on safe, segregated bike paths throughout the city.

Around 2015, the United States, like most nations around the world, at last began to take pollution and environmental degradation very seriously. Green candidates and those advocating for a new development paradigm were voted in around the world. Companies that polluted faced high fines and boycotts, while green innovators were awarded tax breaks and incentives. Plastic bags were banned everywhere. Fossil fuels were widely replaced with renewable energy.

Miriam chose her public college for its strong education department. College is free now. Like her mother, Miriam's days are full. But where her mother had a hard slog through college, Miriam dives lightly into her days and awakens to the prospect of learning, interesting work, and time for friends and family.

Miriam's life is simpler and easier than her mother's was. She spends a lot of time in her neighborhood, apprenticing at the local school and attending seminars with other local college students in her field. What is missing from her mother's time are tempting arrays of consumer goods of all kinds, the thousands of glitzy shops and manicure salons, the imported gourmet stores, the imported coffee shops with US$5 lattes, the cheap and gaudy fast-food burger joints.

In 2050, shopping is no longer a means of entertainment. Food, in particular, is rarely imported. Art and design and couture are displayed in museums, where people can enjoy without needing to own.

Technology and computers are now inexpensive, fast, and beautiful, and have opened up worlds of art, culture, and knowledge.

Looking back: two stories

Samira, Queens, New York

Samira, 59, knows how her college stories sound to her daughter: like tales from *Oliver Twist*. Her cramped family home. Her parents, quarrelling about money. Her evenings spent at menial jobs to cover the tuition.

It is a relief, really, that Miriam can not understand her past struggles. Samira worked hard to become a teacher and make a good life and is delighted that Miriam's life is so much better.

But Samira has a special source of pride shared by millions of others in her generation. It was they who made the changes happen. It was their collective work, inspiration, and energy, and their political action that created what in 2050 had come to be known as the Great Transition to a cleaner, more just, and more harmonious world.

Samira's efforts to get through college 40 years earlier had been typical of many from low-to-moderate income families. She attended classes in the mornings and afterwards worked full-time as a minimum-wage waitress in the local diner. She was on the subway to class by 7:30 a.m. and worked from 4 to 10 p.m. She was overworked and stressed, which took a toll on her schoolwork. When she was tired, she felt she would forever be running from class to work to home to study, and never climb out of the hole.

That despair drove her to take part in the protests and political action that swept the country and the world. Social networks brought it to far corners. She and her generation had actually changed the world!

Evan, Westchester County, New York

Almost 40 years ago, Evan, now a graying editor, had thought his future was made when he got into Columbia University. Evan, a child of wealth, had been groomed for the Ivy League since childhood. His college days had been nothing like Samira's. He lived on Columbia's leafy campus with his expenses and tuition paid in full by his parents. There, he befriended two young men from super-rich families, which made him feel inferior and resentful, a fault line of an entitled life. The satisfaction of knowing he had the most and the best faltered when he encountered others even more privileged. He began to augment his allowance by selling marijuana to dorm mates.

His grades dropped and he became depressed. His parents spent a good chunk of his trust fund on a private rehab center, which helped him quit drugs and enabled him to graduate. But he gradually realized that his youthful recovery had not addressed his feelings of entitlement based on his wealth, which was handicapping him. Fortunately, however, he had a reservoir of openness and was troubled by the destruction of the environment and glaring economic inequities. He took part in the protests that heralded the Great Transition. He adjusted to his diminished wealth, learned to appreciate new neighborliness and a slower pace, and, by 2050, took almost as much pride as Samira in helping to bring them about.

What was wrong: in a nutshell

In 2012, the richest 20% consumed 86% of the world's goods, while the poorest 20% consumed only 1.3%. Their incomes had grown by 150% over a period of three years, while the wages of the bottom 90% had grown by only 15%. The effects of this growing inequity included health problems related to stress, overwork, and junk food.

2050: a new world view

Samira, Evan, and others came of age in a world that was teetering on the brink of collapse. But the seemingly intractable problems and ineffective leadership actually created a new openness to alternatives. In 2014, at the United Nations, the global community embraced a New Development Paradigm that began to change the world.

Therefore, Miriam came of age in a world that was more balanced. The economic inequality and craving for more had been curbed. What people now wanted were deeper satisfactions: camaraderie, knowledge, and fun. They did not have to fear poverty anymore or worry about being left behind.

The overriding global goals of 2050 were genuine well-being and a happiness dependent not on mood or possessions, but on harmony and generosity. Nobody was allowed to profit at the expense of the community, a conviction that underlay individual and policy changes, like the near elimination of private cars, bans on advertising to children, and the removal of tax breaks on all other advertisements.

Ecological sustainability: Climate change created great suffering before global leaders finally responded, instituting effective policies and getting tough with polluters. Greenhouse gas emissions were eventually cut back to just 20% of 2012 levels, as back-breaking fines forced polluters and heavy fossil fuel users to switch technologies or go bankrupt. The monolithic power of Big Oil and Big Chem had been decisively undercut, never to return.

Living standards: In 2050, most countries had instituted a guaranteed minimum income (GMI) that could cover people's basic material needs and a 15-h workweek. By the time Miriam was in college, it was regarded as a basic right for all. The result was a flowering of volunteerism and creativity by a populace freed from the fear of want.

Housing: In 2012, the low-income apartments in Miriam's Queens, Evan's upscale New York suburbs, and places like the slums of Delhi all exemplified the extremes of housing in that era as well as the inequities of what, in 2050, was called the "Degenerate Age."

By 2050, the Queens, New York, neighborhood had been transformed, with co-housing communities throughout with many common spaces. Co-housing was popular because it cost less, was convenient, and gave residents amenities they could not otherwise afford. Most importantly, it created community while still providing family privacy.

In Delhi, like other global cities with high numbers of slum dwellers, the co-housing transition was first based on a major anti-poverty effort and the renewed popularity of Gandhian values. Indeed, a major national education reform in 2015 had dispelled the system inherited from colonial times and rooted Indian education in that country's rich, ancient wisdom traditions.

The solitary splendor of Evan's home created a more stubborn challenge, but the high costs of petrol and property taxes forced the family to act by leasing their yard to organic farmers and taking in an elderly boarder.

Transportation: By 2050 most urban traffic nightmares had been tamed. Metros, buses, and shuttle vans were the norm and private cars rarely seen. Most cities were organized into urban nodes with accessible work, housing, and shopping sections, and with excellent walking and bicycling paths. High-speed electric trains zoomed travelers comfortably and quickly from city to city.

Food: By 2050, nearly all food was local. It was not heavily processed or mass produced, nor was it junk. Nearly everybody gardened, in co-housing areas and terraces and window boxes, proudly consuming their produce. Of course, local gardening could not produce enough food to live on. In 2050, most crops were grown on small- and medium-sized farms within a 100-km radius of their market. Meat, by 2050, was universally organic. The shrinking number of carnivores ate it once or twice a week, and in relatively small amounts.

By 2050, food had become highly nutritious and was not wasted. These trends have improved health worldwide. People often share meals within co-housing communities, and the resultant savings more than make up for higher grocery costs. Even ordinary meals are something of an occasion for family and friends to gather and talk.

Work and leisure: Work in 2012 was too often a stressful business. Those with jobs worked too many hours for fear of failing and those without lived on the edge or over it, desperately sending out applications and trying to stave off despair. Many sank deeper into debt that they could not pay or service.

Eventually, starting in 2011–2012, the unemployed protested and rioted. The well employed drove themselves to stay on top, neglecting their families and health. The underemployed often worked at two or more jobs to make the rent. Small business owners struggled and often failed to hold on, while corporate employees felt like replaceable cogs.

By 2050, work had become something else altogether. The few major corporations that remained had downsized. Most companies were local and directly responsible to the communities they served. They manufactured and sold their wares and services in their local communities and gave back to the communities that supported them. Worker-owned companies, shops, and cooperatives flourished and increasingly became the norm.

Shorter work hours meant more jobs and job-sharing was common, so unemployment was no longer an issue. People no longer lived to work — it is tough to be a hard-driving chief executive officer (CEO) on a 20-h workweek! Instead, once-ambitious people found fulfillment in their families, friends, and their particular interests and talents. These were characterized by remarkable diversity: reviving of ancient cooking techniques, the study of indigenous languages, creative math, and science, among many others.

Education and culture: By 2050, school was held in workplaces where young people apprenticed, in museums, in community centers where knowledgeable parents volunteered as tutors. A lot of learning is hands-on and takes place in real-world settings: in the Hudson River science center in New York and at Delhi's National Museum, for instance. Technology connects children directly with people from distant lands and enables them to practice foreign languages and engage virtually in cultural exchanges.

In addition, there is enormous encouragement for children to read in all formats — e-books, print, and multimedia. Through investigating, debating, reading and discussion, children learn to learn, to question, to research, and to study their world. They gain confidence in their own abilities to learn and come up with solutions themselves, attitudes that will mold them for the rest of their lives.

The content and quality of education has changed, as well. History studies, for instance, emphasize leaders who have produced groundbreaking change, rather than those who simply held power. These include the following:

- Vaclav Havel, who peacefully led the Velvet Revolution and willingly gave up half of Slovakia, his homeland.

- F.W. de Klerk and Nelson Mandela, who dismantled apartheid in South Africa and avoided what could have been a bloody war.
- The Fourth King of Bhutan, who dismantled an absolute monarchy, willingly abdicated the throne, and introduced democracy.

These leaders are among those who let go of power and helped create better societies, a paradigm that is analyzed in the new learning centers. While the New Development Paradigm adopted by the United Nations in 2014 ushered in the Great Transition, education embedded its principles into the marrow of society.

Epilogue: can it happen?

This vision of life in the Era of the New Development Paradigm might seem utopian. But history has shown that dramatic changes can occur — and quickly. What statesmen, like Gorbechav, Mandela, and Havel, did was recognize reality, acknowledge the coming change, and act skillfully, preventing violence.

In 2013, the world stands at such a turning point. It may seem that our problems are too big to overcome. But history has demonstrated that major leaps into new civilizations are possible. In short, this vision narrative is not fantasy. On the contrary, from the saner perspective of the 2050s, our present lifestyle is the crazy one.

From the perspective of the New Development Paradigm, this vision narrative is attainable. If we agree on that, then our task of sketching out the New Development Paradigm should not be too daunting: our job is to elucidate the clearest and most straightforward path to our shared vision.

Part 3

Pieces of the Puzzle: Elements of the World We Want

14

Sustainability and Happiness: A Development Philosophy for Bhutan and the World

Jigmi Y. Thinley

Thirty years ago, the fourth king of Bhutan famously proclaimed that "Gross National Happiness is more important than Gross National Product," setting the country on a development path that seeks to integrate sustainable and equitable socioeconomic development with environmental conservation, cultural promotion, and good governance.

This "happiness" has nothing to do with the common use of that word to denote an ephemeral, passing mood — happy today or unhappy tomorrow due to some temporary external condition like praise or blame, gain or loss. Rather, it refers to the deep, abiding happiness that comes from living life in full harmony with the natural world, with our communities and fellow beings, and with our culture and spiritual heritage — in short, from feeling totally connected with our world.

And yet our modern world, and particularly its economic system, promote precisely the reverse — a profound sense of alienation from the natural world and from each other. Cherishing self-interest and material gain, we destroy nature, degrade our natural and cultural heritage, disrespect indigenous knowledge, overwork, get stressed out, and no longer have time to enjoy each other's company, let alone to contemplate and meditate on life's deeper meaning. Myriad scholarly studies now show that massive gains in gross national product (GNP) and income have not made us happier. On the contrary, respected economists have demonstrated empirically that deep social networks are a far better predictor of satisfaction and well-being than income and material gain.

It is significant that the term "Gross National Happiness" was first coined in direct contrast with GNP — as a sharp critique of our current materialist obsession and growth-based economic system. And it is even more significant that the statement was not made in relation to Bhutan alone but as a universal proclamation true for the world and for all beings. The universal chord it struck explains why 68 nations joined Bhutan in cosponsoring the UN General Assembly resolution in July 2011 on "Happiness: Towards a Holistic Approach to Development," which was adopted by consensus by the 193-member United Nations.

And yet, despite valiant efforts made by individuals, communities, and certain nations, human society will continue to hurtle toward self-annihilation unless we act together. The time has come for a global effort to build a new economic system no longer based on the dangerous illusions that irresponsible growth is possible on our finite planet and that endless material gain promotes well-being. Instead, it will be a system that promotes harmony and respect for nature and for each other, that respects our ancient wisdom traditions and protects our most vulnerable people as our own family, and that gives us time to live and enjoy our lives and to appreciate rather than destroy our world.

Sustainability is the essential basis and precondition of such a sane economic system. An economy exists not for mere survival but to provide the enabling conditions for human happiness and the well-being of all life forms. The new economy will be based on a genuine vision of life's ultimate meaning and purpose — an economy that does not cut us off from nature and community but fosters true human potential, fulfillment, and happiness.

> *The new economy will be based on a genuine vision of life's ultimate meaning and purpose — an economy that does not cut us off from nature and community but fosters true human potential, fulfillment, and happiness.*

15

Flourishing as a Goal of International Policy

Martin Seligman

The discipline of positive psychology studies what free people choose when they are not oppressed. I call these desiderata the elements of "well-being," and when an individual or nation has them in abundance, I say it is "flourishing."

Governments continue to organize their politics and economics around the relief of suffering, and I cannot confidently predict that the planet's future will be bright with nonoppressed peoples freely choosing the elements of well-being. But if there is to be a "positive human future," and not just a "nonnegative human future," it is necessary to discover what the elements of well-being are and how to build them.

Well-being has the following five measurable elements that count toward it:

1. Positive Emotion (of which happiness and life satisfaction are aspects).
2. Engagement (being in flow, being one with the music).
3. Good Relationships.
4. Meaning and Purpose (belonging to and serving something you believe is bigger than you are).
5. Accomplishment, Achievement, and Mastery.

A handy acronym for these five elements is PERMA. My book *Flourish*[1] discusses in further depth many arguments for and against different conceptions of what the elements of well-being might be.

Well-being theory is plural: it is a dashboard theory and not a final-common-path, monistic approach to human flourishing. Positive emotion alone is only a subjective variable; what you think and feel is dispositive. The other elements have both subjective and objective indicators. Engagement, meaning, relationships, and accomplishment have both subjective and objective components. The upshot of this is that well-being cannot exist just in your own head: well-being is a combination of feeling good as well as actually having meaning, engagement, good relationships, and accomplishment.

This plurality of well-being is why economist Richard Layard's important argument that "happiness" is the final common path and the gold-standard measure for all policy decisions does not work.[2] Layard's theory sensibly departs from the typical economist's view of wealth — that the purpose of wealth is to produce more wealth. For Layard, the rationale for increasing wealth is to increase happiness, and so he promotes happiness as the single-outcome measure that should inform public policy. While I welcome this development, I disagree with the idea that happiness is the be-all and end-all of well-being and its best measure. Happiness and life satisfaction are useful subjective measures, and they belong on the dashboard. Truly useful measurement of well-being for public policy will need to include subjective measures of life satisfaction along with both subjective and objective measures of engagement, meaning, good relationships, and positive accomplishment.

This suggests that increasing the well-being of a nation is a plausible goal of international policy, and I call this goal the "new prosperity." Wealth contributes substantially to life satisfaction, but above providing a certain safety net, it has rapidly diminishing returns on happiness and good mood. At the average income levels of the developed world, there is a huge disparity between gross domestic product (GDP) — a measure of wealth — and well-being.[3] Building more jails and lawyering more divorces increases GDP but subtracts from well-being. Prosperity in the traditional way of keeping score equals the volume of goods and services utilized. I want to suggest now a better goal and a better way of keeping score that tracks well-being and regards wealth only as a means to well-being.

When nations are poor, at war, in famine, in plague, or in civil discord, it is natural that their first concerns should be about containing damage and building defenses. These distressing straits describe most nations through most of human history. Under these conditions, GDP has a palpable influence on how well things will turn out. In those few instances when nations are rich, at peace, well-fed, healthy, and in civic harmony, something very different happens. Their eyes turn upward.

Florence of the mid-15th century is a beacon. She became very rich by 1450, largely through the Medici banking genius. She was at peace, well-fed, healthy, and harmonious — at least relative to her past and to the rest of Europe. She considered and debated what to do with her wealth. The generals proposed conquest. Cosimo the Elder, however, won the day and Florence invested its surplus in beauty. She gave us what 200 years later was called the Renaissance.

Could our Renaissance be the building of international well-being?

History, in the hands of the post-modernists, is taught as "one damn thing after another." I believe the post-

> *Could our Renaissance be the building of international well-being?*

modernists are misguided and misguiding. I believe that history is the account of *human progress* and that you have to be blinded by ideology not to see the reality of this progress. Balky, with fits and starts and gut-wrenching downturns, the moral and economic trajectory of recorded history is, nevertheless, upward. As a grandchild of the Great Depression and a child of the Holocaust, I am clear-eyed about the terrible obstacles that remain. I am clear-eyed about the fragility of prosperity, and I am clear-eyed about the billions of human beings who do not yet enjoy the fruits of human progress. But it cannot be gainsaid that even in the 20th century, the bloodiest of all of our centuries, we defeated fascism and communism, we learned how to feed six billion people, and we created universal education and universal medical care. We raised real purchasing power more than fivefold. We almost doubled our life spans. We began to curb pollution, we began to care for the planet, and we made huge inroads into racial, sexual, and ethnic injustice. Violence decreased markedly.[4]

The age of the tyrant is coming to an end and the age of democracy has taken firm root.

These economic, military, and moral victories are civilization's proud heritage of the 20th century. What gift will the 21st century pass on to its posterity?

Much higher well-being across this planet.

References

1. Seligman, M (2011). *Flourish*. New York: Free Press.
2. Layard, R (2005). *Happiness: Lessons from a New Science*. New York: Penguin.
3. Diener, E and M Seligman (2004). Beyond money: Toward an economy of well-being. *Psychological Science in the Public Interest*, 5(1), 1–31.
4. Pinker, S (2011). *The Better Angels of Our Nature*. New York: Viking.

16

What Else?

Wendell Berry

For more than 100 years, the coal-producing counties of eastern Kentucky have been dependent on the coal industry, which has dominated them politically and, submitting only to the limits of technology, has come near to ruining them. The legacy of the coal economy in the Kentucky mountains will be immense and lasting damage to the land and to the people. Much of the damage to the land and the streams, and to water quality downstream, will be irreparable within historical time. The lastingness of the damage to the people will, to a considerable extent, be determined by the people.

A Vision

by Wendell Berry

If we will have the wisdom to survive,
to stand like slow-growing trees
on a ruined place, renewing, enriching it,
if we will make our seasons welcome here,
asking not too much of earth or heaven,
then a long time after we are dead

(*Continued*)

(Continued)

the lives our lives prepare will live
there, their houses strongly placed
upon the valley sides, fields and gardens
rich in the windows. The river will run
clear, as we will never know it,
and over it, birdsong like a canopy.
On the levels of the hills will be
green meadows, stock bells in noon shade.
On the steeps where greed and ignorance cut down
the old forest, an old forest will stand,
its rich leaf-fall drifting on its roots.
The veins of forgotten springs will have opened.
Families will be singing in the fields.
In their voices they will hear a music
risen out of the ground. They will take
nothing from the ground they will not return,
whatever the grief at parting. Memory,
native to this valley, will spread over it
like a grove, and memory will grow
into legend, legend into song, song
into sacrament. The abundance of this place,
the songs of its people and its birds,
will be health and wisdom and indwelling
light. This is no paradisal dream.
Its hardship is its possibility.

The future of the people will, in turn, be determined by the kind of economy that may come to supplement and finally to replace the economy of coal. Contrary to my own prejudice and sense of caution, I am going to yield here, briefly, to the temptation to talk about the future.

In talking about the future, wishes have a certain standing. My wish for eastern Kentucky, as for the rest of the state, is that the economies of the future might originate in the local use of local intelligence. The coal economy, by contrast, has been an *imposed* economy, coming in from the outside and also coming down from the high perches of wealth and power. It is the product of an abstracting industrial and mercenary intelligence, alien both to the nature of the land and to the minds and lives of the people. But as we humans seem always to have known, though we have often needed to be reminded, freedom is founded upon the land and upon the free use of local intelligence in husbanding the land. Disfranchisement approaches the absolute when powerful outsiders do your thinking for you. This can happen only when local intelligence is degraded and disvalued and when, as a consequence, political responsibility is sold out.

The local use of local intelligence must start with the local landscape. And so, as a necessary discipline for any wishing, we must ask what, besides coal, the landscape of eastern Kentucky offers to its people. The answer is that the other great natural resource of the region is its forest. Though the forest has a long history of abuse, and though huge parcels have been and are being destroyed outright by surface mining, forestry and the economy of forest products offer the greatest opportunities to local intelligence. And whereas the coal economy is an economy based upon the exhaustion of the resource, the forest, by good use, can be made sustainable.

The other important resource of the region is a significant, if limited, capacity for sustainable food production. The landscape is predominately steep and most of it is obviously best suited for forestry, but there are some bottomlands, gentler slopes, and ridges that can be used without damage as pastures or croplands or gardens. This is made thinkable as a prospect by the numerous people of the region who, as any observant traveler will notice, are excellent gardeners, who practice other arts of subsistence such as beekeeping, and who by such means have kept alive the spirit of self-sufficiency and independence.

I do not know how many such people there are. Nor do I know the number of acres that might properly be used to produce food. I do not know how near the region might come to feeding itself. But common sense and mere caution require that every region should become as self-sufficient as possible in food production, just as every community should sustain itself as far as possible by the good use of its land.

As in the rest of the state, the forestry and farming of eastern Kentucky have been wasteful, and the coal companies have made the topsoil and the forest as temporary as coal. But if the region is to replace, or survive, the coal economy, it must develop sustainable ways of using its forest ecosystems and productive soils.

We might like to suppose that it would be better for eastern Kentucky, and for the whole state, if university and government experts should ever become inclined to think about a coal-less future for the region. *Maybe* so. But we should be extremely uneasy about supposing so.

If these experts ever begin to dare to think beyond their long addiction to coal power, coal money, and such fantasies as "clean coal," then we should expect and prepare for a noisy tumult of central planning, summoning of outside experts, grant-proposing, visions of high-tech development, souping up of technical education, economic incentives, tax breaks, "job creation," and marketing of cheap labor. The result, in sum, would be yet another imposed economy for the region, making light (again) of the local economic potential of the local landscape, of local intelligence, local history, and local culture. Industrial intellectuals, as we know, do not hesitate to "apply" ideas and technologies to places they do not live in and know nothing about. They are recognizable by their contempt for everything they regard as "provincial" and their inability to tolerate anything modest or local. They will run in headlong panic from whatever is small in scale, low in cost, or "old-fashioned."

We are not confronting the question of whether or not another exploitive economy *will* try to fasten itself upon the region. That is happening already, most noticeably in the appearance of timber industries that operate, expectably, without regard for forest ecology. It is horrible to think that the coal economy might be replaced by an economy that would in effect mine, and thus destroy, the forest.

And so I wish that in the face of continuing industrial destruction, and despite the official sound and fury of "economic development," the people of eastern Kentucky will recognize in their own minds and places the powers of economic, political, and ecological self-defense and local self-determination.

17

Let Us Envision Gender Equality: Nothing Else is Working

Jane Roberts

At the 2007 Women Deliver conference in London, *The Lancet* put out a special edition with this message on the cover: "Since the human race began, women have delivered for society. It is time now for the world to deliver for women."

I envision a world where people, men and women together, will DELIVER for women, who will climb over the barricades in a nonviolent struggle for enormous change. We have to make it happen. We need a peaceful, purposeful, stubborn, and obstinate revolution.

Gender inequality is the greatest moral challenge of our age. There has been a willful denial of girls' and women's full humanity by individuals, governments, religions, cultures, and customs.

On page 4 of my book *34 Million Friends of the Women of the World*, I say: "We have to imagine a world where all people, men and women together, in equal partnership, with no artificial legal, cultural, religious, or economic barriers, work together for the greater good. We must imagine a world where all people, regardless of their gender, are judged, as Dr Martin Luther King might have said, only by the content of their character."

Nothing else is working. To be pessimistic about the future is to be realistic. With food, water, energy, environmental, conflict, and climate

121

crises present and looming, we need all human beings to be educated and motivated to demand long-term solutions that will not be sacrificed on the altar of short-term and private gain. Wow, would not that be revolutionary!

Envision a world where all girl babies were welcomed as much as their male counterparts. This would mean an end to sex-selective abortion, female infanticide, and neglect of the girl child. This cultural shift would have enormous implications for both people and planet.

Envision a world where the education of all their citizens might be the first priority of governments. Universal education as encompassed by Millennium Development Goals 2 and 3 would affect many more girls and women than men and boys. The whole world is saying that girls' education is crucial. Educated, literate girls value themselves, marry later, marry "better," have fewer children, educate their children, and keep them healthy. Educated girls become educated women who participate in their communities and are empowered to earn both income and respect. Country-specific budgets must prioritize quality education for girls. If this is done for girls, boys will benefit too.

In important ways, education leads to health. What if every girl and woman on the planet were given access to health? For instance, what if every baby were guaranteed to have a birth weight of 7 to 8 pounds and to be AIDS free? That would give every baby a good start. Imagine the revolution in health that this guarantee would imply. It would imply a world commitment to every aspect of reproductive health. It would imply that early marriage might disappear. It would mean the end of female genital mutilation. It would probably mean that every pregnancy was wanted, that prenatal care was universal, that every birth was safe, that obstetric fistula and maternal morbidity and mortality would disappear. It would mean that family planning would be universally available, as promised in human rights documents — particularly at the International Conference on Population and Development in Cairo, Egypt, in 1994.

The health benefits of family planning are so vast as to be almost invisible. A total of 200 million women lack access to family planning. The underlying cause of this dereliction of duty is gender inequality. The Cairo Consensus has been more honored in the breach than in the implementation.

Fulfilling the Cairo Consensus to the letter would mean that the huge toll of unsafe abortion (70,000 deaths and 5 million injuries, hemorrhages, and infections every year) would disappear. The acronym PAC (post-abortion care) would disappear. The fact that abortion remains illegal and that family planning remains controversial, especially in the developing world, results from gender inequality, from women's disempowerment politically and culturally, from enormous hypocrisy on the part of power structures, and from, in my view, the pernicious influence of certain religious persuasions. When the world takes care of women, women take care of the world. We have to envision a world that takes care of women.

Let us be honest — for once! Africa is on a path toward a humanitarian disaster. Its population, if present predictions hold true, will nearly double by 2050, from one billion to two billion people. Women do most of the work in Africa and men make most of the decisions. About 40% of Africa's children are undernourished. If maternal mortality is a measure of the African continent's well-being, then Africa fails. If infant and child mortality are measures of health or lack thereof, then Africa fails. Africa does not take care of its women. Gender equality is on a very distant horizon.

Beyond Africa, the countries of the world that are the most unstable and have the highest misery index, and whose people are the most poverty-stricken, the least educated, and the least healthy, are those where women's status is low.

On 28 February 2010, on the eve of the two-week session of the 45-member UN Commission on the Status of Women, Thoraya Obaid, Executive Director of the United Nations Population Fund (UNFPA), said: "We can't continue to pay lip service to gender equality ... World leaders should not just say they are committed, but must prove their commitment with tangible allocations of budgets and people ... When men and women have a respectful relationship in which they recognize each other as equal partners, men will benefit as much as women." That is the whole point. Gender equality would achieve enormous tangible benefits for people, the planet, and peace.

I do not believe that change will come from the top without pressure from the bottom, from the grassroots, from both women and men. Media attention to this profound issue is the key to mobilizing world opinion.

Come on, CNN! Stop twittering and dithering. Come on, Bono. Write us a song. Come on, peoples of the world! Ponder the prophetic words of Stephen Lewis: "I challenge you … to enter the fray against gender inequality. There is no more honorable or productive calling. There is nothing of greater import in this world. All roads lead from women to social change."

And those of the late Dr Allan Rosenfield, a world-renowned champion of women: "It is not enough to know for the sake of knowing. We have the responsibility to act on what we know. Acting on knowledge is an imperative. And that imperative we can truly delight in."

At 3 a.m. on the morning of 23 July 2002, I lay in my bed lamenting how Colin Powell had sold his soul the day before by announcing that the George W. Bush administration was not going to release US$34 million to the UNFPA — for what I knew to be totally spurious reasons. After all, the whole world knows that UNFPA takes care of the world's women.

My thought was to ask for US$1 from 34 million Americans. It was time for me to take a stand. I envisioned, and still do envision, that 34 million people — not only Americans but also people from around the world who hear about 34 Million Friends — would eagerly comply. Grassroots at its purest and finest!

The world is out of balance, careening toward an uncontrollable unknown. Gender equality in education, health, and the opportunity to contribute to family, community, and world is at the very core of any acceptable future. So I repeat: We need people, men and women together, who will DELIVER for women, who will climb over the barricades in a nonviolent struggle for enormous change. We need a peaceful, purposeful, stubborn, and obstinate REVOLUTION.

Envision gender equality. Make it happen.

18

Another World: Finally Her(e)

Kavita N. Ramdas and Jamie Querubin

The year is 2100 and I am attending the annual meeting of the Global Council of Peoples in the newly regenerated Amazon basin. Inspired by Costa Rica, the first nation in the world to dismantle its military and redirect public investments toward human development and conserving natural resources, the indigenous peoples of Latin America were early implementers of sweeping social changes that included laws ensuring the full and equal participation of women and freedom and equality for gay and transgender people.

We are celebrating the 25th anniversary of Gender Justice and Equality, a global pact that guaranteed women's liberation and fundamentally altered human relationships and their underlying structures and systems. Delegations of youth and elders, women, men, gays, lesbians, and transgender individuals are present to celebrate the first quarter century in the world's history in which all human beings have experienced peace and freedom and have taken joint responsibility for leading, governing, and caring for future generations. This annual gathering is more than a celebration — it is a reminder to the global community of what it took to achieve these outcomes and how we cannot afford to be complacent.

Dancers, musicians, and acrobats dramatically retell the story of how the planet and her human beings faced dire threats and then engineered the remarkable breakthroughs that made it possible to avert the ultimate catastrophe. Homage is paid to women in this story — the peace and prosperity evident in our world today are thanks to defenders of women's rights, working in concert with social justice and ecological movements.

The audience gasps in response to the litany of problems that were present in 2010:

- Wars and conflict were entrenched. Well, over a million lives were lost in Afghanistan and Iraq, and "lesser" wars plagued Congo and Somalia — women and children were the majority of civilian casualties and refugees.
- Climate change disproportionately affected women, the primary gatherers of water and firewood, and they were forced to become global migrants in search of economic survival.
- Women and girls in both rich and poor nations did two-thirds of the world's labor but owned less than 1% of the world's assets.
- More than two-thirds of the world's illiterate were girls and close to 500,000 women died each year in childbirth or of related causes, while millions had limited or no access to contraception.
- Worldwide, one in three women experienced sexual assault, abuse, or violence in her lifetime.

These facts horrify us and are a reminder of how much human civilization has finally progressed. In this 22nd century world, women and men are free to make choices that allow them to participate equally in all aspects of our societies. It has been over 25 years since there has been any major incidence of violence against women or gay/transgender people.

At the societal level, all children are equally welcomed into societies across the globe. The practices of both female and male circumcision have disappeared, and indicators of health and vitality have improved. Girls and boys enjoy equal access to education, both at the primary and advanced levels. All genders enjoy equal access to the arts, music, and other recreational activities, including sports. Same-sex or different-gender partners share roles and responsibilities in the household, and local wisdom councils provide additional support for the raising of children, who are seen as the prime resource in our societies. Council elders interact with and provide grandparent care for all children in the community — with the belief that it "takes a village" to raise a healthy, happy, and peace-loving child.

Advancements in biology make it clear that male and female characteristics exist in all beings. Sexual health and well-being is prized in all communities, starting with children, who are taught to value and prize their bodies. The exploitation of human sexuality for profit is no longer tolerated, although society has matured to allow open exploration of sensuality, pleasure, and consensual sexual exchanges between adults. A woman's reproductive capacity is not only deeply respected but also recognized as only one aspect of her whole body. The widespread, voluntary use of sophisticated forms of contraception has made abortions exceedingly rare. Women's bodies and minds are valued not only for their ability to create and sustain life but also for the many other ways in which they contribute to the well-being of the planet.

The decision-making power women now wield over their own bodies ripples in transformative waves into other aspects of society. Women's leadership in village councils and civil-society organizations has led to the gradual irrelevance of nation states, while power has simultaneously devolved away from central governments toward local wisdom circles. Representatives to the Council of Peoples are elected from these wisdom circles, which are local associations that are inclusive and representative of their own communities. The Council of Peoples has replaced the United Nations. The term "secretary-general" became obsolete when military titles were discontinued. Traditional political borders common in the early part of the 21st century have long since ceased to be used to separate people from one another. Few resources are expended on military defense. Instead, the Council of Peoples invests in a collective and limited use of force that is mainly focused on countering unexpected environmental disasters, planetary shifts, or atmospheric changes. The council also oversees a quick-reaction, nonviolent communication peace force that can be swiftly deployed to address conflict between and among peoples. There has been no war in over 15 years.

Valuing gender equality has shifted our economic systems as well — now that all human and intellectual resources can be tapped, innovation has allowed new forms of growth. People are no longer prevented from moving across borders, except as restricted by energy consumption levels. People have reorganized themselves, both within and across those old borders, according to environment, culture, and resources in ways that maximize free trade, the exchange of ideas, and the movement of people and investments, and this fuels robust and sustainable economic systems. There is plenty of room in our societies for women to explore rich and fulfilling careers in a variety of fields, including those seen as being traditionally masculine, while men who are drawn to nurturing, care-taking roles are valued and held in high esteem.

The storytellers at this Global Council of Peoples delve deeper into our history and remind us that we did not get here without paying a high price. Women paid the highest price of all — literally with their bodies. Yet they refused to resort to violence or despair. Instead, they patiently built and strengthened social change movements around the globe. Their collective actions sparked a series of tipping points, beginning in 2011, that helped alleviate and shift paradigms at the personal, political, ecological, and societal levels:

- The UN Gender Agency was established, led by Michelle Bachelet, the single mother, doctor, and former president of Chile. During her 10 years at the agency, violations of women's rights were systematically addressed and publicized, and nations failing to protect women's rights were penalized in terms of access to trade and diplomatic relations with other countries and the United Nations. Bachelet worked closely with former Irish president Mary Robinson and the Council of Leaders on Reproductive Health to influence key leaders, especially in the world's poorest nations, convincing them that advancing access to contraception and strengthening women's leadership at all levels could ensure economic growth and stabilize world population.

- In 2012, as the United States prepared for elections, women political leaders around the world — including Sonia Gandhi, Cristina Fernández, Dilma Rousseff, Angela Merkel, and Tarja Halonen — established a Council of Wise Women as a space for women leaders to share what they would do differently if they could publicly embrace the feminine and stop acting "macho." Among the council's first acts was a pact to rid the world of nuclear weapons by 2020 and to advance a climate change action plan. Over the years, the council expanded to include feminists of all genders, including Carlos Zapatero and Rafael Correa.

- In 2012, President Obama survived a serious right-wing challenge to win the US election. More than 90% of eligible women voted, determining the outcome. In his second term, Obama used his mandate to pass sweeping legislation ending all practices that discriminate on the basis of gender. Major challenges to the US economy and pressures created by growing social activism in other parts of the world, particularly by BRIC (Brazil, Russia, India, and China), also moved the US government to make major cuts in its defense expenditures, ending the wars in Iraq and Afghanistan and closing nearly 1000 US military bases around the globe. Finally, US taxes were used to invest in education, health, and developing some of the most innovative carbon-neutral energy sources on the planet.

- In 2014, a massive grassroots mobilization of women — aided by communication via cell phone — resulted in a global Freedom from Violence March led by African women. More than 100,000 women converged on the borders of the Congo. They formed a human chain around mining operations, government buildings, and UN peacekeeper camps and refused to leave. International activists from Greenpeace, Amnesty, Oxfam, and the Global Fund for Women joined their cause and succeeded in pressuring the Congolese government, the United Nations, the Rwandan government, major mining companies, cell phone corporations, and rebel groups to hammer out an agreement to end violence. Social movements across the globe realized that people power and not national governments or corporate actors has to move social change on a global scale. Women then led the move to reconstitute the United Nations into the Global Council of Peoples, using Virginia Woolf's famous lines as their motto, "As a woman my country is the whole world."

- The following year, in 2015, Nobel Prize winner Shirin Ebadi and Iraqi freedom fighter Yanar Mohammed held an unprecedented summit of Iraqi and Iranian women on the border of the two countries, calling for an end to the repressive laws limiting the freedom of women in the name of Islam. State forces on both sides attacked the women, and hundreds were killed, many more injured. The leaders of the effort were publicly flogged and jailed for life. The incident, however, sparked a massive movement for change among women in

Muslim communities worldwide, from Afghanistan to Senegal. Using civil disobedience campaigns, women disrupted the status quo in Saudi Arabia and brought about new governments in both Egypt and Yemen, made up of 50% women.

Watching this reenactment, and knowing how far we have come, I am smiling. The drums are growing louder, and hundreds of children run onto the open playing field to sing praise to Pachamama, our mother earth, our living planet. We have survived because we remembered that women and girls are among our earth's most precious resources. We let them speak, their energy and power fueled a new way of seeing, a new way of being — and their liberation liberated us all.

19

Policy Reform to 350

Bill McKibben

Editor's Note:

These two stories, told from the perspective of the year 2100, explain how we got to 350 parts per million CO_2 in the atmosphere. They are quite different stories; both are plausible. They are presented here to help us envision the range of paths we might take into the future. One involves policy reforms and a difficult, century-long transition, the other focuses on more far-reaching social and cultural changes that could lead to a brighter century. As a society, we need to think much more creatively about our possible futures so that we can build the future we really want.

Let us imagine for a moment that we are at 2100, and the atmospheric CO_2 level is slowly subsiding back toward 350, and the worst is over. Let us try to figure out how we got there — reverse-engineer a century of halting but ultimately decisive progress.

The first decision, clearly, was the most important. In 2011, after 22 years of hemming and hawing and circling, the world's governments — moved by a series of devastating floods on every continent that galvanized the already growing climate movement around the globe — grudgingly took the initial steps toward imposing a cap on carbon emissions. The fight was by no means easy: developing countries insisted, with reason, that the cap could not hit them yet, and China insisted that it was still a developing country. Still, the climactic political battle with big oil and bigger coal ended decisively — it would be many years before they ceased to be powerful parts of the economy, but the fossil fuel era began to end on that day when the parties signed on at the Nairobi conference center.

A few things happened, and more quickly than anyone but the economists had dared hope. For one, anyone looking at a spreadsheet quickly figured out that future investment had better be green — that coal-fired power was going to get steadily more expensive until it made no sense at all. And so the trajectory of the future began to shift: money started to fall in the direction of the new economic gravity. It started to pool around railroads, and insulation manufacturers, and all the other businesses that featured relatively low energy cost as a selling point.

The effect on consumers was not quite as strong, since few households had Chief Financial Officers (CFOs) charged with plotting the bottom line return of future expenditures. Still, every family was now getting a rebate check each month for its share of the permits for putting CO_2 into the atmosphere, which meant a steady flow of capital. Some of it went for flat-screen TVs, but a nontrivial amount ended up buying solar hot-water heaters, plug-in hybrids, and local tomatoes.

Meanwhile, governments started figuring out where the future was headed too, and the political demand for greater investment in basic research began to grow. Helpfully, with each passing legislative session, the pockets of the wind and solar barons got a little deeper, and they began to exert more and more pressure for switching subsidies away from the "technologies of the past."

None of it, though, happened anywhere near fast enough to slow down the momentum of the heating. Year after year saw catastrophe after catastrophe. Human-caused temperature change, barely 1° when the decade began, edged toward 2°, and the toll of damage steadily mounted. Some of it was insidious and daily — like the steady drip-drip of lost agricultural yield as temperatures climbed and water evaporated and the continuing spread of disease-bearing mosquitoes, which damaged not only ever-larger populations but also the development budgets of one nation after another.

As time went on, it became increasingly clear that there was no way simply to pull the internal combustion engine out of the world's economy, toss in a few solar panels, and continue on as before. Not only was the drag on old economies from changes in the weather creating real friction, but the logic of renewable energy began to assert itself. Sun and wind were everywhere, but diffuse. And so a new kind of power grid began to grow — based on many million rooftops, not a few thousand centralized power stations. Other commodities began to go in the same direction. After a century of agricultural consolidation, for instance, local food networks were spreading fast, replacing much of the oil-starved, monocultural, industrial food system that had dominated the planet since World War II.

If it sounds as if this happened smoothly, however — well, it did not. The immense gulf between the rich and poor worlds was the most intractable problem, as people across Asia, Africa, and South America felt themselves being denied the fruits of modern development. The outbreaks of chaos were ugly, as migrants from low-lying areas tried to move inland across India and China and refugees from newly formed African desert edged outward onto land already fully occupied. And there were always the floods, now a perennial feature of any wet part of a planet whose atmosphere was much moister — adding constantly to the woes of already stressed populations.

Europe, Japan, and America — and increasingly China and India — did at least a little to help, but the technology assistance and crisis aid never came close to matching the damage their carbon emissions had caused. Mortality rates climbed all over the planet, and life expectancy dropped. There was some of the Malthusian horror long predicted, and skirmishes and wars were constantly breaking out. But there was also a much more popular and general political uprising of people around the world who insisted that the push toward climatic stability go faster, no matter the cost. The iconic number 350 came to mean one thing above all: shutting down the coal mines and the tar sands, keeping the carbon in the ground. And within a few decades, this had — more or less — happened. The world was running rough, but still running, with the Internet providing the kind of links that jet planes had once allowed.

At last, the level of carbon in the atmosphere began to plateau. Smaller increases — measured at the station on the side of Mauna Loa where this science had begun in the 1950s — gave way to tiny decreases, as forests and oceans slowly began to suck some of the carbon back below the surface. This did not "make the problem go away," and, in fact, as the century wore on, researchers began to show that even 350 ppm of CO_2 was too much, that we needed to retreat closer to the 280 ppm level that prevailed in the days before the Industrial Revolution. There was no way to refreeze the Arctic, and ocean productivity continued to dwindle because of elevated levels of acid. But at a certain point, the volume of crises began to slowly diminish, both because temperatures had nearly stabilized and because society had been rebuilt in ways that made it more resilient, less easily vulnerable.

The most essential things — a culture, a civilization, some semblance of the natural world — had come through the bottleneck more or less intact. It had been a miserable century, but not, in the end, a completely impossible one.

That this is a good news scenario should give us pause. It would be easier, and perhaps more plausible, to write a much uglier forecast. A few things worth noting here: First, action to change the price of carbon comes very early in this scenario, in 2011. It is pretty clear we need to tip this system quickly in another direction. Second, the decisive interventions are not technological as much as political — in many ways, the outcome will be decided by whether people pull together or are pulled apart as a result of the forces we are unleashing in the atmosphere. There are many variables we cannot predict, including that one. But at least we can have an influence — by building a political movement right now, across borders, faiths, ideologies, and languages — that allows us to understand our novel global predicament.

20

The Great Transition to 350

Dylan Walsh and Tess Croner

Editor's Note:

These two stories, told from the perspective of the year 2100, explain how we got to 350 parts per million CO_2 in the atmosphere. They are quite different stories; both are plausible. They are presented here to help us envision the range of paths we might take into the future. One involves policy reforms and a difficult, century-long transition, the other focuses on more far-reaching social and cultural changes that could lead to a brighter century. As a society, we need to think much more creatively about our possible futures so that we can build the future we really want.

It is the year 2100, the atmospheric CO_2 level is subsiding back toward 350 parts per million (ppm), and the best is yet to come. Beset with a host of global problems just a century ago, our generation rose to the challenge. Here is our story.

It was 2010. We were young people wobbling on the edge of a new decade, and we felt almost crippled by the complexity of the challenges we faced: a warming climate; a rusted, intransigent political system; environmental deterioration on a massive scale; war; widespread corruption; and financial irresponsibility. It was easy to feel cynical: for 35 years, one president after another had promised energy independence and had failed to deliver it. Even as we came to know and care more about the environmental problems we faced, we worried that it was already too late

135

and that our individual contributions would be too small to matter. We felt disconnected from one another. Collective action was dismissed as uto-pian. We wanted to consume responsibly, but we stood in the grocery aisle feeling duped and distrustful. And time and again, we watched our increasingly partisan government bicker and stall over the tiniest increments of progress. Meaningful, large-scale change seemed the stuff of fantasy. Despite all this — because we were young and because we had to — we allowed ourselves a cautious optimism.

It was 2010, and it was difficult to know where to start. The *Deepwater Horizon* oil rig lay at the bottom of the Gulf of Mexico, and the well was belching untold barrels of oil into the ocean. The disaster exemplified so many of our global challenges, and yet we now remember it as the start of something better. The spill laid bare the huge social and economic costs of an extractive industry, which were embodied and externalized in the constant risk of ecological disaster. It also marked the beginning of a sharp rise in the price of oil, as blossoming demand in China and India began to outstrip global supply. These were the years of what historians now call the Great Energy Transition. During this time, the environmental move-ment, which had been grasping for purchase, found firmer footing, and young people across America began to demand and choose a different future.

Ours is a country founded on experimentation and innovation, and the Energy Transition presented another opportunity for revolution. After their overwhelming turnout in the 2008 presidential election, young peo-ple learned to be activists again. Our politicians were not representing us, and the answer lay not simply in elections but in a more ambitious reen-gineering. We used new technologies to expand democracy, to engage the public more directly, and to hold our representatives more strictly and bindingly accountable. Increased political engagement at the federal and state levels also began to nourish local activism, strengthening efforts against suburban sprawl and homogeneity. Small businesses were freed from the crushing competition of megastores, and vacant parking lots reverted to urban gardens as cities undertook new design initiatives geared toward public transportation and walkable downtowns. Amid tighter, more vibrant communities, town meetings emerged again as a vehicle for self-government. People gathered in community spaces to learn about and discuss national issues, and votes cast here became mandates for federal politicians. Those years marked the beginning of a transformation that restored a sense of place and character to our nation. The political landscape was forever altered.

After the oil crisis, a persistent public demand for transparency changed not only government but also business. Information labeling, overseen by independent review bodies, became ubiquitous both in the grocery store and on the campaign trail. Each product came with a variety of recognizable stickers, rating its social and environmental responsibility. (Items that scored below a certain point threshold carried something akin to a sin tax.) And politicians gave speeches and debated with corporate logos (and the dollar amount of each donation) emblazoned on their podiums and on viewers' computer or TV screens.

As the relative cost of renewable energy fell, a rising workforce of young entrepreneurs, scientists, and engineers established a network of green industries. Federal and private investment, previously timid, flooded the market. Talk of a green jobs movement was no longer undermined by halfhearted follow through. This was a large-scale, national, grassroots, and coordinated *movement*. The shift to renewables came along with a massive push for increased energy efficiency. The boom in green jobs and services made it possible to retrofit old homes with energy-saving appliances, and solar panels and green roofs became commonplace in every community. Power meters, informing each family about its energy usage, became standard in every home. And people were motivated to conserve energy — and to take other simple, everyday environmental steps — because they felt involved in a personal, community-based movement that had swept the nation.

The Energy Transition was, of course, also a global phenomenon, with global causes. In the early decades of the 21st century, following years of aggressive public investment, China had become the uncontested leader in green technology. This reality had unexpected, and ultimately positive, implications for the international effort to reduce carbon emissions. Driven by a desire to expand global demand for its technologies, China emerged as a leader at international climate talks, pushing aggressively for a strict global carbon-cap-and-auction plan. Using its financial leverage over the United States, and with the strong support of European Union leaders, China was eventually able to secure international agreement. The dividends from the sale of carbon credits went to developing nations to help fund their transition to clean energy. The cap was also accompanied by a large-scale carbon offset program, Reducing Emissions from Deforestation and Forest Degradation in Developing Countries (REDD), which created a strong financial incentive for forested nations in the developing world to conserve their native forests and to reforest stripped lands.

Though it took time, the staggering world economy regained its footing. By mid-century, unemployment crept down in lockstep with CO_2 emissions. A generation that had witnessed simultaneous economic and environmental collapse had found steadier ground upon which to rebuild. And once and for all, the supposed correlation between consumption and happiness was proven specious. As the economy recovered, people were happier; and they were happier without the crutch of lavish consumption. Back in the early decades of the 21st century, when unemployment had hit record levels, several governments in the Organisation for Economic Co-operation and Development (OECD) (including the United States) made a risky decision: they mandated a four-day work week. As a result, there were more jobs to go around, and housing breaks and decreased consumption made it possible for workers to invest their extra time in family, community involvement, civic engagement, and education.

This is the brief story of our transformation. Work remains to be done. But, knowing what we have accomplished already, our vision of the future is even grander and more hopeful than anything we could have imagined in 2010. And this is what remains most necessary — the vision — for, in the words of poet Czeslaw Milosz, "what is unpronounced tends to nonexistence."

21

On Baselines That Need Shifting

Daniel Pauly

A flurry of articles in recent years shows that loss of knowledge about the past may have contributed to an acceptance of other losses, such as declines in biodiversity. I first identified this form of collective amnesia in a 1995 article describing how fisheries biologists assess changes in biomass abundance. Every generation begins their conscious life by assessing the state of the world and society around them and using what they see as a baseline to evaluate changes that occur subsequently.[1]

However, the baselines of previous generations are commonly ignored, and thus the standard by which we assess change also changes. I called this phenomenon "shifting baselines."

For example, those studying wildlife today might be impressed by the abundance of large wild mammals (bears, wolves, various herbivores) in Alaska, while being unaware that such abundance was at one time prevalent in the lower 48. Therefore, they might not miss the large animals there and might look askance at efforts to (re)introduce previously abundant species.

The shifting baseline phenomenon has been well documented in marine science, including fisheries research. For example, there are many cases where the law mandates rebuilding of fish populations to the level prevailing, say, 20 years before, although populations were already depleted by then, at least as compared to 50 years earlier. Indeed, it is only by combining the declines noted by successive generations that we can get a full appreciation of the great loss of biodiversity that has occurred in the sea and on land due to the impact of humanity.

But shifting baselines need not be associated with losses. Indeed, forgetting can be a good thing, as any tree will testify that depends on squirrels to bury their seeds in various caches and then forget some of them (and if trees could testify to that, the squirrels would concur).

Forgotten and shifting baselines can be useful to people as well. For example, when people who have suffered under the load of a long, stifling tradition emigrate and thus are enabled to distance themselves, both geographically and emotionally, from the ancestral conflicts, which, in their home countries, confined them within balkanized camps, a positive shifting baseline occurs in the generations that follow.

Positive shifts in baselines also occur after social change. One example is smoking in enclosed public spaces, which was ubiquitous in the 1960s. At the time, change seemed impossible, and the stranglehold that the tobacco industry had on our legislators seemed unbreakable. Then, somehow, anti-tobacco activism, medical science, and common sense coalesced into an unstoppable force — let us call it the *Zeitgeist* — which overcame all resistance, first in the United States, then in Europe, including France (France!). Now we look back, and our baseline — and especially that of young people — has so shifted that we do not understand how we ever accepted smoking in tight public places. We have collectively forgotten how it felt (and smelt) and how we could even tolerate it — just as we have collectively forgotten how it was when the majority of people were farmers or, even earlier, hunter-gatherers surrounded by nature that teemed with a diverse animal and plant life.

Similarly, in our culture, it now seems impossible to even imagine that women and minorities could not vote, attend universities, or become elected politicians. In fact, in the West, the very act of questioning these social advances defines fringe culture, just as denying evolution or climate change defines fringe science. Similarly, our baselines have shifted so much that we have forgotten the once powerful notion that there are special people, kings and queens and their broods, which should rule us because a deity said so.

Getting back to earth: for baselines to shift is not always bad. There are stupid things that must be forgotten even if they have been the rule for thousands of years. Getting rid of these notions is similar to detoxifying oneself, freeing our minds to be able to concentrate on things that matter, including those "old" things that we should remember. One of these old things is that what we eat should be healthy. We do not need to eat the abject stuff that now passes for food, but would certainly not be recognized as such by our ancestors. Other old things are that we should not be surrounded by pollutants of various kinds, and that we should not accept that sprawl should eat up natural landscapes, and that we should not allow out-of-control fisheries to eat up the ocean.

Indeed, reversing the present destructive trends induced by large-scale, industrial fisheries — which is possible under a regime in which fuel energy costs its true price — would lead not only to more plentiful, larger fish for coastal, small-scale fisheries to catch, but to a world in which fisheries could coexist with whale watching and other forms of coastal tourism. It would be a world in which people could acquaint themselves with the sea as the wondrous habitat of the many life forms that we may eat as seafood or just enjoy for being there.

In other words, we want the bad old things to shift away and the good old things to shift back into focus.

Reference

1. Pauly, D (1995). Anecdotes and the shifting baseline syndrome of fisheries. *Trends in Ecology and Evolution*, 10, 430.

22

The Future of Roads: No Driving, No Emissions, Nature Reconnected

Richard T. T. Forman and Daniel Sperling

Suppose we could move gloriously and quietly along in our own comfortable car compartment some 20 feet high between the trees, yet with no engine running, no fossil fuel use, no greenhouse gas emissions, and no need to watch the road (Fig. 1). Or, we could zip along in channels dug just below ground level and topped with translucent covers. No unpredictable drivers to worry about or vehicles to crash into. No driver fatigue, indeed no driving. Barely any traffic noise. We watch nature around us, remember the bad old days of polluting traffic, play family games, work on the computer, or read. When ready to return to ground level, we simply take manual control of our fully charged battery "pod" car and drive off on local roads to our destination.

Why is this vision of travel, perhaps a generation ahead, so appealing and so important? In it, not only is nature restored on a massive scale, but both fossil fuel and greenhouse gas emissions are eliminated, mobility for people and goods is safer and more efficient, and there are significant benefits for food production and recreation near towns and cities.

Figure 1: The netway transportation system linked with the land. Large natural forest patches connected by major water-and-wildlife corridors and separated by agricultural land are traversed by an elevated way (lower right) and partially sunken earthway (lower center). Wildlife, streams, livestock, and people can cross beneath elevated and over sunken routes. A service center is located at the edge of town. Along the partially sunken earthway are solar collectors, low wildlife overpasses, a translucent cover, productive market-gardening plots, and, in the distance, wind-energy turbines. On the elevated way, medium to small wind-energy devices are visible. (*Credit*: Taco Iwashima Matthews.)

Two giants: transportation and nature in uneasy embrace

Roads slice the land into pieces yet also tie it together for us. For centuries, spreading roads have progressively degraded nature (Fig. 2). The direct ecological impacts of the road system have been estimated as affecting one-fifth of the US land surface, with indirect effects spreading much further.[1] A core objective of this chapter is to outline a transportation system that does not just slow or stop the degradation process but reverses the trajectory and restores our land. At first glance, the solution appears visionary, but a second look reveals a close-to-feasible transportation system.

The four million miles (6.25 million km) of public roads across the United States were largely built before Earth Day 1970 and the rise of

Figure 2: Cars speed by on the westbound and eastbound lanes of Interstate 630 in Little Rock, Arkansas. Our modern day transportation system has had a range of negative effects on both nature and human society, including habitat loss, deaths from traffic accidents, and harmful greenhouse gas emissions. (*Credit*: Greg Drzazgowski.)

modern ecology.[2,3] A quarter billion vehicles use this network, which penetrates almost everywhere. Beyond transporting people and goods, effects reverberate widely through society. But first, how does this massive system of roads and vehicles affect nature and its processes?[2,4-9]

Look at these impacts: (i) habitat loss (nearly 1.5% of the United States covered by road and roadside); (ii) roadkilled animals (millions hit each year); (iii) barriers blocking wildlife movement (especially busy roads); (iv) habitats fragmented (with population extinction and biodiversity loss); (v) traffic noise (creating unsuitable habitat for sensitive animals); (vi) degraded roadsides (disturbed and contaminated); (vii) altered wetlands (both drained and inundated areas); (viii) soil erosion (from cutbanks and fill-slopes); and (ix) sedimentation (degrading streams, rivers, ponds, lakes, and fish). Although "road ecology" emerged barely a decade ago,[2,6,7,9-11] few people have begun pondering solutions for such a broad set of issues.[12,13] Our vision for transportation eliminates, or noticeably mitigates, this entire array of problems.

Even more familiar are transportation's big problems for society.[3,7,14] Frequent headlines highlight fuel shortages and rising gasoline costs, greenhouse gas emissions, deteriorating roads, traffic jams with wasted time and frustrated drivers, stormwater flooding and pollution, communities split by highways, particles and aerosols from vehicles, deficient bridges, and accidents. The solution outlined here addresses these issues and also enhances local food production and recreational trail systems around cities and towns.

We focus on remote, rural, and outer suburban areas of the United States, where the benefits to nature are enormous, though the basic approach should then be extended to cities and regions worldwide. Specifically, the solution is targeted to large areas containing both busy highways and our most valuable nature. We initially focus on highways with more than 3000 vehicles per day passing any given point[15–19] and the posted safe speed limit is more than 50 miles per hour (80 kph)[20,21] (Fig. 3). The vision presented is no panacea, but it does enhance biodiversity, water, mobility, energy, atmosphere, food production, and recreation.

The netway system

Imagine starting a commute to work or trip to the city by walking to a nearby netway service center. The place is attractive, safe, and welcoming, with a small convenience store open. You step into a large public (or social) "pod," like a streamlined comfortable van or bus, which operates with a service attendant but no driver. The pod is carried along the netway until you decide to disembark at one of the frequent on/off stops, which may be another service center or simply a structure with stairs and ramp to ground level plus protection against weather.

Alternatively, at the small service center, an attendant provides you with a personal pod, which may be your own or may be rented for an hour or day or week or year. It has the feel of a ski gondola or a car compartment with comfortable seats. You enter and the pod moves smoothly ahead under automated control. No driving, no traffic jams, no accidents to worry about. Just time to relax, write, or even bird-watch. You depart the netway at another service center, usually located in a town, a village,

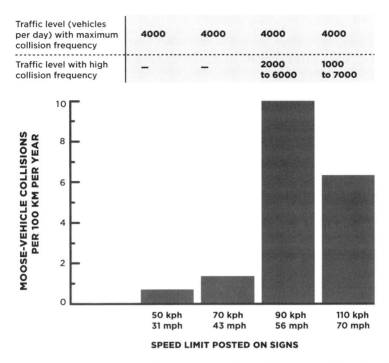

Traffic level (vehicles per day) with maximum collision frequency	4000	4000	4000	4000
Traffic level with high collision frequency	–	–	2000 to 6000	1000 to 7000

Figure 3:   This graph shows wildlife–vehicle collisions relative to speed limit, based on a 10-year data set of 2185 moose-vehicle collisions on unfenced roads of one or two lanes in a large area of south-central Sweden.[20] Above the histograms for speed limits are data for collisions relative to traffic level. The maximum number of collisions is always on roads with 4000 vehicles/day, but only at the higher speed limits are there many collisions (high collision frequency indicates traffic levels with greater than 85% probability of at least one moose-vehicle collision per kilometer in 10 years). Various studies suggest that traffic of greater than 3000 vehicles/day has "substantial" ecological impacts for all five major vertebrate wildlife groups, and that greater than 10,000 vehicles/day creates a severe barrier to wildlife movement.[19,42,43] (*Credit*: Richard Morin/*Solutions.*)

or at an intersection. Here you can either leave the personal pod or drive it away on local ground-level roads.

These comfort and safety benefits come from converting busy highways to netways elevated at various heights ("elevated ways"), or partially or fully sunken belowground ("earthways"), and replacing today's cars with simple, lightweight, aerodynamic vehicle-like pods. These pods provide space for personal comfort and a strong protective shell with doors and windows. The pod electronically "attaches" to the infrastructure using power embedded in the paved surface. Using automated controls, pods can be efficiently moved as a platoon close together, even inches apart, to minimize air drag, or can be far apart in sparse traffic.[22,23]

Pods, vehicles, and energy

As illustrated, netways are lined with solar panels, wind turbines, and other local energy sources designed to minimize effects on natural processes and bird populations. These predominantly renewable energies run netway machinery, which is spaced at intervals. Using inductive coupling, electricity from wires embedded in the netway surface crosses a small air gap to an electric motor in the pod.[22,24,25] Thus, pods holding people and goods are electronically guided smoothly and safely across the land by a netway control center. With a small battery, many pods can also store electricity for driving off the netway on ground-level local roads. At the numerous on/off small service locations, the netway energy supply charges batteries for a fleet of stored pod cars.

Three types of pods are carried along netways: (i) personal pods for up to, say, six people; (ii) long public pods for hyperefficient public transport; and (iii) freight pods for transporting goods. All are strong and lightweight to minimize electrical energy use as well as wear on the netway system. In outlining the netway system, we focus on personal pods — the next phase after walking, horse power, and cars — where individuals largely choose their timing and routes. Public pods are an important supplement to group transport in buses, electric streetcars, subways, light rail, fast trains, and airliners.[26] Freight pods when full are typically separated in the flow of pods to evenly distribute weight on elevated netways and to accommodate different destinations of goods carried. Also, freight pods carry lighter-weight goods, not dense material such as coal or grain shipped by rail.

While some lightweight pods, outfitted with a tiny battery or ultracapacitor, operate exclusively on the netway system, other pods with somewhat larger batteries (though much smaller than in today's electric cars) can move off the netway onto urban streets and low-traffic local roads. Compared with today's typical 2000–4000-pound car, personal pods moving only on netways might weigh about 1000 pounds. Pod cars that can also move on roads would be somewhat heavier (for the battery and for stronger structural integrity). Small netway-pod systems exist at London's Heathrow Airport, in Morgantown, West Virginia, and in Korea. In Masdar City, United Arab Emirates, a passenger enters a driverless pod, pushes a button for a destination, and is automatically carried there.

Although creative designs allow a rich array of forms, we envision all pods as aerodynamic and somewhat oval or elongate in form,[23] analogous to certain tropical coral-reef fish.[27] All have windows, doors, and comfortable seats. All are securely and easily linked electronically to the netway transport system. No driving. No oil consumption, greenhouse gas emissions, brake wear, or traffic accidents. When off the netway, drivers operate autonomously under their own control and with onboard energy storage.

Energy from the sun, wind, and earth's heat is plentiful, widespread, and permanent, unlike oil, which fuels current vehicles plus most road construction, maintenance, and repair and is in increasingly limited supply.[3,14,26,28] Renewable energy sources represent a flexible and dependable foundation for transportation, and they do not emit CO_2. In the system outlined, although these energies are fed locally into the netway system, energy transmission and storage is also required when the wind is not blowing and the sun is not shining. Excess energy production could support local communities and the electrical grid.

Solar collectors will doubtless become ubiquitous along netways. Power generated from wind is a function of the cube of wind speed (which increases with height aboveground) and, for turbines, the square of blade length.[29,30] Thus, tall and large turbines produce the most power, but even small turbines high above elevated netways can produce useful power, with little noise or visual intrusion. Considerable "high-temperature" geothermal energy is available with expensive deep drilling in certain areas, while inexpensive shallow drilling in many areas can produce small amounts of "low-temperature" geothermal energy.

Batteries in personal pods charged en route on the netway will provide flexibility by permitting local ground-level driving. Pod cars with a small battery could drive about 20 miles on the ground or longer distances when designed with a bigger, heavier, and more expensive battery. Still, as the netway system expands over time, off-netway vehicle use should noticeably decrease.

Structural characteristics common to all netways

In this system, pods of different types are relatively constant in width and move quietly both ways along a netway. Each lane is about 7 feet (2.1 m) wide for pods being transported along a fixed line and a strip 9 feet (2.7 m) wide down the center allows access for service and emergency use (Fig. 4). The total width of a netway is approximately 27 feet (8.5 m), which is slightly more than the width of a soccer goal or the goal posts in American football. Small service centers, where pods attach and detach from the main electric netway line, have a surface about twice the normal netway width.

The transport mechanism highlighted mainly uses renewable energy to produce electricity, which flows through wires embedded just below the netway surface (or other connector) to power electric motors in light-weight pods. The electric current in the wires is transferred to vehicles across air gaps of up to about 12 inches (30.5 cm) by inductive coupling,[24] a well-understood technique currently used experimentally. (Alternatively, vehicles might receive electricity conductively from a thin rail alongside the lanes, as used for electric subways.) No exposed shock or electrocution hazard exists with inductive coupling.

Netways in our system mostly have gradual turns reminiscent of railways. For sharp turns, a pod is gently slowed down and then gradually sped up in the changed direction. The system's regenerative braking captures energy from the slowing of a pod for a sharp curve or upon arrival at a service center.[23] At intersections where netways cross at different levels, a pod is moved to the outer lane at a bifurcation of the embedded electric wire, slowed down, gradually curved upward or downward to the new level, and gently accelerated into the mainline flow in the new direction.

The constant safe running speeds of pods might be in the range of 40 to 55 miles per hour (65–90 kph) in suburban areas, where on/off netway locations are frequent or many freight pods are present. However, the system outlined has few netways initially deployed in suburbia where priority natural areas are scarce and trips are diffuse. In more rural or remote country, pod speeds on netways would normally be higher.

Netways are a traffic engineer's dream. With no traffic jams, no speed-up-and-wait driving, no cross-traffic, no crashes, and no speeding "crazy

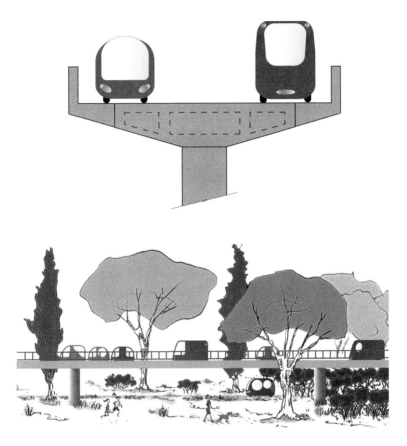

Figure 4: Elevated way with pods in cross-section and side view. The netway illustrated is 27 feet (8.5 m) wide. Pillars are 100 feet (30 m) apart, and clearance under netway is 13 feet (4 m). *Cross-section* (*top*): a personal pod (left) and public pod (right) move in fixed lines powered by electric wires embedded in netway surface; some only move on netways, while others have small batteries charged en route and can be driven on local roads at ground level. There is a central lane for maintenance and emergency access. *Side view* (*bottom*): four personal pods (three close together) and two separated freight pods, all are electronically transported with automated controls on an elevated way. There is also a battery-powered pod vehicle driving on a small, unpaved service road below, as well as a vegetation corridor crossing under the netway on the right. (*Credit*: Taco Iwashima Matthews.)

drivers" (indeed no drivers at all), pods moving safely at a good, constant speed reach destinations very quickly. Travel time is noticeably reduced, less stressful, and productively used, so passengers arrive relaxed — a huge benefit.

A safe, secure netway system for people is achievable and sustainable. Sleek, narrow, fast emergency "vehicles" (perhaps with autonomous hydrogen-powered fuel-cell electric engines)[31] can streak down the emergency lane of a netway. Wires and sensors embedded in the netway structure automatically pinpoint the presence of a tree branch, person, or debris. Trips are made safer with locked pods with good visibility, individual control over where to enter/exit, personal communications to service centers at frequent intervals, and real-time system communications to pods, plus lights, video cameras where appropriate, service-center attendants, and patrol officers.

Today's busy road surfaces are designed to be repaved about every 3–10 years, depending on levels and types of traffic. We anticipate that design and construction of netways will be for some 50-plus years (the same as for most houses and small bridges built today), depending mainly on the structural material used and the amount of freight pod usage.

Negligible air pollution will be produced by moving pods compared with that from today's vehicles on roads. No fossil fuel use means no greenhouse gas emissions. The wide range of polluting particulates, aerosols, and gases emitted from our roads and vehicles can be sharply reduced by using small electric motors for lightweight pods, centralized electricity-generating machinery, and tires constrained to narrow strips of netway surface designed for low wear, low pollution, low noise, and long life (without the diverse road conditions facing today's drivers). Relatively little maintenance is required. The limited pollutants from elevated netway usage will be dispersed in the wind or channeled in stormwater to small retention ponds or basins beneath the netway for treatment.

In case of a system breakdown, such as loss of power, a pod's driving apparatus and tiny battery would be automatically enabled and sufficient to drive slowly to the next service center. In case of a pod breakdown, the pod would be automatically moved into the central emergency strip for servicing or removal.

Points along the main transport line where people can get on and off, and where system personnel work, are also keys to the netway system's success. Numerous on/off pedestrian access locations function like bus stops or for emergency use. Frequent small service centers include lifts/

elevators for personal pods and people, attractive maintained toilets, storage space for personal pods, electric charging of batteries, and attendants assisting people entering/exiting pods and netways. Less frequent large service centers can provide the same services for people but also can contain sections like bus terminals and truck distribution centers; thus everything is larger — shopping areas, lifts, pod storage areas, and so forth — and freight pods with goods are efficiently transferred for different local and long-distance destinations. Infrequent netway machinery and maintenance centers, not open to the public, will contain the large electric engines running the transport system, the stockpiles of netway replacement components, and the service personnel for the netway system.

Elevated ways

Although no netway as described exists, a lot of related transport systems currently carry people, vehicles, or trains above ground level.[3,11,12,25,32] Think of monorails, as in Sydney or Seattle, or high-mountain gondolas and tramways on cables. Small gondolas moving in opposite directions, one above the other, reduce the width of damage to a rainforest canopy, as in Costa Rica. Other elevated examples include causeways with raised roadbeds and viaducts on rows of pillars, like long horizontal bridges over land (occasionally used to protect farmland in China).[32] Consider suspension and many other types of bridges, including bridges with traffic in opposite directions on one level over another, as in Rio de Janeiro. Walkways and bikeways cross over highways. Wildlife overpasses, from massive[2,11,33] to lightweight,[10,34] facilitate movement of many species across highways.

Unlike today's large cars, buses, and trucks, the pods described are relatively lightweight, are separated at intervals, and move in two opposite direction lanes. Consequently, the elevated way itself, using strong durable pillars beneath a narrow netway surface structure, is relatively lightweight, like a hybrid between a walkway and a small road bridge over a highway. Netway sections might be supported by single (or paired) pillars, perhaps 4.5–5 feet (1.37–1.52 m) in diameter to provide extra solidity. Pillars might be 80 to 110 feet (25–35 m) apart, or more, with some variability to fit topography.

We expect clearance under the netway to be typically only about 13 feet (4 m), suitable for all North American wildlife to easily pass, though awkward for giraffes. In places, clearance rises to 16–20 feet or more (4.88–6.09 m), for small roads to cross and for streams/rivers and their floods to flow. Thus the supported surface sections of netways, some 13–17 feet (3.96–5.18 m) aboveground, are roughly at the height of second-story windows or the tops of apple trees. In moist climates, trees existing or planted along elevated netways visually screen the structures in a landscape and may provide some shade and wind reduction for moving pods.

Pillars and surface sections of elevated ways could be made of familiar inexpensive, long-lasting concrete. Or they could be made of well-tested, lightweight composite material (e.g., fiberglass-like carbon fiber), potentially with structural and chemical integrity for 50-plus years. Bridges made of recycled plastic (fiber-reinforced polymer composites) may be very strong and long lasting, requiring little maintenance and repair.[10]

A netway surface section may be a "spanner" (girder or box beam spanning the distance between pillars), with L-shaped "wings" attached on each side (Fig. 4). Spanners can be efficiently lowered into place by small- or medium-sized cranes on the service road alongside. In this way, components such as a damaged pillar, spanner, or wing are readily removed and replaced with relatively little disruption to pod flows.

In short, the compact elevated ways carrying lightweight pods are somewhat narrower than two-lane highways and lower than highway bridges. Elevated structures are simple, modular, and flexible, composed only of pillars, spanners, and wings. Construction time and cost, as well as environmental damage, is reduced. Spanners contain embedded electric wires to power the system as well as slots for channeling stormwater and snow to ground-level depressions below. The simple design also facilitates automated control of many maintenance activities.

Very little traffic noise is generated on elevated netways. Lighting on netways is easily shielded to minimize impacts on migrating birds and on the people below. Fallen branches or trees on netways — for example, in high winds — rarely occur because of the height of elevated ways. Grounding everything against lightning is standard. Snow and ice (which do not affect the electric induction drive system)[22] are mainly eliminated through designed openings in the netway, or possibly electric heating in spots, and service personnel. Finally, although farmland under four-lane highway viaducts doubtless has lower crop production due to limited light and rain, plant growth under netways that are 27 feet (8.23 m) wide would be only slightly affected.

Large portions of today's road infrastructure are in need of repair or replacement, including 30% of America's bridges, plus numerous culverts functioning as major bottlenecks for surface-water flow and fish movement.[2] Netways require no culverts for water flow, and they largely avoid the need for massive highway bridges, which are continually pounded by traffic and require frequent maintenance and repair. Pods zipping across streams and rivers on lightweight netways have less impact on river flows, stream habitats, and fish.

Where highways are replaced by netways, both water quantity and quality should noticeably improve in streams, rivers, lakes, ponds, vernal pools, and wetlands.[2,6,12,33,35] Roads significantly alter hydrologic flows and water bodies, such as those upstream and downstream of bridges and culverts. Wetlands by roads are commonly drained or inundated. Pollutants from road systems, including sediment, heavy metals, hydrocarbons, and salt, widely degrade water bodies and their aquatic ecosystems and fish. In contrast, stormwater pollution from netways will be minimal and contained, as water is channeled into retention ponds or basins at ground level for treatment or removal. Also, drinking water from wells and other water supplies would become cleaner.

Another attraction of elevated netways is that they eliminate almost all traffic collisions and animal-vehicle crashes. Consequently, human fatalities, injury, medical treatments, and time lost are avoided. Auto insurance costs should plummet. Elevated aerodynamic pods moving at efficient, constant speeds also virtually eliminate roadkilled wildlife.

Earthways

In addition to elevated ways, the system includes covered U-shaped troughs called earthways below, at, or somewhat above ground level (Fig. 5). Essentially invisible from a distance, these partially or entirely sunken earthways may be particularly useful in dry open landscapes such as desert and grassland, perhaps in outer suburban areas and elsewhere. Earthways burrow below streams and major gullies.

Figure 5: Buried earthway in cross-section and side view. *Top*: a buried earthway is covered with a foot of soil, in which meadow plants (center) and shrubs take root, with trees alongside. There is a path for walking along the earthway. *Bottom*: A wildlife corridor, walking path, stream and fish, all cross over a buried earthway. (*Credit*: Taco Iwashima Matthews.)

Cut-and-cover construction (digging and covering a trough) is relatively simple through sandy, unconsolidated earth or soft rock such as limestone and shale.[11,12] Like highway tunnels and subway systems, the trough can be composed of impervious concrete with polymeric (plastic) and/or bituminous membrane layers to prevent groundwater from entering. Many types of cover, including translucent ones, keep precipitation out. An added foot of light sandy soil can permit drought-resistant shrubs to cover the earthway.

Typically, the trough would only extend 6–8 feet (1.83–2.44 m) belowground and have its covering 6–8 feet aboveground (Fig. 6). Open air or clear windows could be used in places, providing light, ventilation, and views for travelers. Frequent low, vegetated wildlife overpasses would facilitate the free flow of animals across these raised earthway covers[2,10,11] (Figs. 1 and 6). A relatively constant earthway microclimate will minimize maintenance and repair costs, and will please people who dislike weather variations.

Features at ground level along netways

Ecological and other features on the ground surface, under elevated and over sunken netways, are key elements for the netway system. Plenty of design options and flexibility exist.[36–38] In place of a multilane highway, the netway would use less than half of the current right of way, so considerable area would be restored to nature or other uses, a large gain for society.

Most important in this system is reasonably continuous vegetation or natural habitat so that wildlife can cross from one side of a netway to the other (Figs. 4–6). In moist climates, both tree and shrub vegetation is optimal. In drier areas shrubs are important, with certain trees a local option. In this manner, habitats on opposite sides of a netway are effectively connected for virtually all wildlife species. In addition, streams and rivers crossing a netway flow in relatively unaltered natural condition, with negligible netway-caused pollution, scouring, or blockage of fish movement. Frequent convenient crossings are also present for local residents and farmers and their livestock. In essence, replacing highways with netways reconnects our land.

Yet the linear characteristic of netways offers another huge benefit to nature and wildlife, especially in much-altered and habitat-fragmented landscapes. At present very few species move efficiently along either highways or their roadsides.[2] Vegetation strips of shrubs with or without

Figure 6: Partially sunken earthway in cross section and side view. *Top*: the earthway has a raised translucent cover that lets in sunlight and windows on upper sides for views and natural air flows. To the left, a pod vehicle drives on a service road. *Bottom*: the translucent cover and windows can be seen on the left, with a wildlife-crossing overpass in the center, and an array of solar panels on the cover to the right. (*Credit*: Taco Iwashima Matthews.)

trees along a netway would form wildlife corridors, helping to reconnect fragmented habitat patches to sustain wildlife populations.[37,39]

A narrow, unpaved slow-traffic road, sometimes with limited access, along one side of the netway would provide maintenance and repair access. Various infrastructure pipelines and conduits serving society would parallel these dirt roads (such infrastructure would probably not be incorporated in the netway structure, where easy repair/replacement of modular components is important). Buried pipes could include water supply, sewer and electrical conduits, even potentially supercooled long-distance energy transmission from huge wind- or solar-energy farms.

Recreational (leisure) use of netways at ground level, especially near cities and towns, is a distinct bonus of this system. Walkers, hikers, and bicyclists can easily cross netways, in contrast to hazardous highways. Furthermore, the linear form of netways and their interconnection in a network provides a new, immensely valuable trail system for local residents, walkers, and hikers. In places, service roads along netways would be useful for cyclists in recreation or commuting to work. Also, the elimination of highways means greatly improved water bodies and fish populations near netways, and more happy fishermen.

Various types of food production may prosper along netways, including community gardens (allotments), greenhouse production, poultry production, narrow livestock pastures, and long, thin crop fields with tractors (Fig. 1). Market gardening or truck farming along netways would be an especially valuable mode of food production near cities and towns.[40] With little transportation cost, fresh vegetables and fruits would be readily provided to markets and restaurants.

We anticipate that many specific land uses will also be associated with netways. Arrays of solar panels and wind-energy-capturing devices will power the netway system. Small neighborhood parks bordering the netways would generate public support, plus stewardship. Any of these land uses must be compatible with a core rationale for the netway system: to eliminate traffic disturbance effects and to reconnect natural flows and movements between opposite sides of a netway.

Fitting netways to the land for nature

The broadest objective of the netway system is to restore and sustain nature on our planet, especially biodiversity, wildlife habitat, and aquatic ecosystems. This requires converting our widely permeating heavy-imprint road system to a light-imprint transportation system that dovetails with nature's major patterns and processes. Simply removing a road from an important natural area is the ecologically best and most cost-effective strategy. However, where road removal seems to be impossible, the net-way system is an effective alternative that also provides for transportation.

Three habitat types encompass our most valuable nature.[21,36–41] (i) Large natural areas or "emeralds" can sustain unpolluted aquifers, lakes, and major clean-water supplies; animals with large home ranges; viable populations of many interior-habitat species; connected natural stream networks; and sources of rich biodiversity that can then spread across our human-imprinted land. Major natural areas exist at many scales, from extensive remote forests/woodlands and deserts/grasslands to local large woodland and wetland patches. (ii) Wildlife and water corridors connecting these large green areas facilitate the movement of species and also enhance biodiversity in the large natural areas. Protect the emeralds first, and then connect them, to restore our highway-disrupted emerald network.[2] (iii) Vegetation protecting streams and rivers, ponds and lakes, vernal pools and reservoirs, and diverse wetlands provides numerous benefits to nature, and to us. These benefits include clean water supply, unpolluted water bodies, natural flood control, diverse aquatic habitats, natural fish populations, commercial fish harvest, and a wide array of recreational opportunities.

Combining busy highways (greater than 3000 vehicles per day[42,43] and with a posted speed limit of 50 mph/80 kph[20,21] (Fig. 3)) with these most valuable types of nature leads to the following priority areas where netways should have the greatest benefit in replacing highways (Fig. 7).[2,40,44]

Extensive forest, woodland, grassland, or desert areas. Busy highways bisecting or dissecting these natural areas degrade nearby habitat and also form a barrier or filter against movement of certain key species, thus partially fragmenting the natural landscape. Netways here restore our last best nature. Where an extensive natural landscape has many large cropland or built patches present, the natural habitat between them is especially valuable and hence a priority area for replacing highways with netways.

Large cropland areas. In cultivated landscapes, the few remaining large natural-vegetation patches are of central ecological importance, so

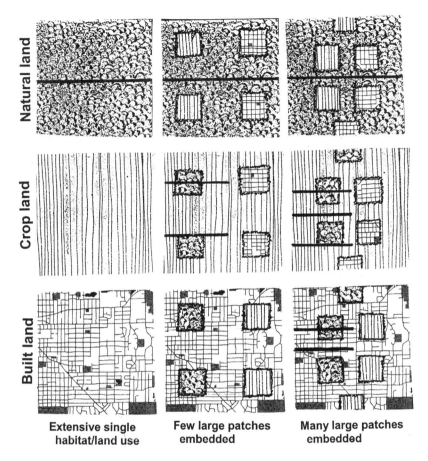

Figure 7:   Priority locations for converting highways to netways to restore and reconnect nature. Three land types are shown: natural land (i.e., extensive forest, woodland, grassland, or desert areas) with patches of built land and cropland; cropland with patches of natural land and built land; and built land (i.e., cities and suburbs) with patches of natural land and cropland. The dark horizontal lines indicate priority locations for netways. In the landscapes with both patches and dark lines, busy highways crossing or alongside wetlands, lakes, rivers, and major streams are also priorities for replacement by netways. (*Credit*: R. Forman and D. Sperling.)

highways cutting through or alongside them are priorities for conversion to netways. Where large natural patches are close together in cropland, highways disrupt the flows of wildlife and water between them and thus should be replaced by netways.

Suburban/sprawl landscapes and cities. In suburban and sprawl areas, continued urbanization renders long-term protection of rare species and natural aquatic ecosystems unlikely. Thus the only priority netway site in such areas is a highway bisecting a scarce large natural patch or passing between two nearby ones. In cities, where only shreds of nature persist, netways for nature protection are normally unnecessary.

Consider an example of netway-like structures in Florida. Around 23 98-foot-wide underpasses were constructed in 1986–1993 under a 76-mile (122 km) multilane highway (Alligator Alley, Interstate 75) to increase surface-water flow for the adjoining Everglades Park, reduce roadkills of the threatened Florida panther (*Puma concolor coryi*), and provide limited public recreational access.[2,10] Each goal was achieved, and in addition seemingly all appropriate vertebrate species moved through the underpasses. In the next phase, one mile of the road is currently being elevated, with nine more miles of elevated highway scheduled. This new phase should achieve even more success, specifically the reversal of habitat loss, habitat degradation, and habitat fragmentation due to the highway, thus effectively restoring the land. Still, the large new elevated highway will have little of the mobility, energy, and emissions-reduction benefits provided by the netway system.

Maps of busy highways are now laid over maps of priority nature patterns. In almost exactly this manner, the Dutch Ministry of Transport and the Florida Department of Transportation have identified key conflict or bottleneck locations, where cost-effective mitigation/compensation efforts and resources can be concentrated to eliminate the conflicts.[2,7,12]

Similarly, using this map overlay process in planning the netway system will pinpoint the priority conflict locations in every state or regional planning area. The highway segments and areas identified will be the highest priorities for replacement with netways. The system of elevated ways and earthways in these areas will provide the greatest benefit, indeed will restore nature, for society's future.

Timing, costs, and opportunity

The last transformation of US transportation happened in a mere 25 years. In about 1900, almost all passenger transport was by rail or was horse powered on roads, with people traveling by horseback and in buggies and carriages.[45] Roads outside cities were muddy and dusty. By 1925, motorcars and trucks powered by fossil fuel were widespread, and roads were rapidly transformed to black strips of asphalt.

Today's transformation to a netway system can begin promptly. For example, in years one to five, we can create a plan to (i) review the ecological goals and proposed solutions; (ii) review the diverse engineering dimensions; (iii) map the major ecological network of large natural patches, major wildlife-and-water corridors, and highest-priority water bodies, and map traffic levels on busy roads in remote, rural, and outer-suburban areas; (iv) identify existing and potential renewable (and other) energy sources; (v) identify potential materials, manufacturers, and contractors in each region; (vi) consider frontier technologies, for example, that mimic how nature makes things and works;[46,47] (vii) identify large pilot-project areas in all regions; (viii) build local public interest and support in the pilot-project areas; (ix) generate policymaker support at federal, state, and local levels; and (x) conduct cost/benefit analyses.

During years 5–10, we can build, monitor, and test the pilot projects. From approximately year 10 onward, we can then expand the pilot projects and construct the netway system in all nature priority areas, beginning with those regions and corridors where interest and funding are strongest. Early in this final phase, large numbers of people are likely to use pods on netways and many may have, or may want to have, their own pod car. This is likely to quickly generate interest in extending the netway system into other areas, for example, into lower-traffic areas (1000 vehicles a day), suburban areas, and as fingers into the city so that everyone has ready access to the netway system. Over time, perhaps like the horse-power-to-fossil-fuel conversion, our land transportation system will be transformed.

Understanding costs, private as well as social and environmental, and benefits is key for netway-system implementation. Planning, construction, energy generation, pods, and conversion of highways to green corridors are explicit, obvious costs to estimate. Benefits to nature's biodiversity, to wildlife and their movement, and to diverse water bodies and aquatic ecosystems are equally obvious, though they will be more difficult to specify. There will be further benefits from recycling today's vehicles, highway asphalt (gravel and fossil fuel), guardrails, signs, and sandy roadbed fill. Reducing oil and energy consumption will be a major gain. Significant benefits should result from flood reduction, meeting increasingly urgent clean-water needs, reduced air pollution and climate change, fewer polluted aquatic ecosystems and less loss of fish, enhanced food production and transport near population centers, and valuable trail-recreation opportunities. Pursuit of these nonmarket and market benefits will stimulate further gains.

Financing for the netway system could come mostly from netway users, similar to how the massive US interstate highway program launched in 1956 was financed. A share of today's national transportation trust fund could be invested in the netway system. Today the trust fund is fed mostly by user fees in the form of gasoline and diesel fuel taxes, but in the future the user fee might be based on vehicle miles traveled (a more appropriate fee for financing infrastructure, especially as gasoline consumption plummets). Concern over reallocation of public funding would be mitigated by the huge cost savings of a netway system, which eliminates extensive and expensive maintenance and rebuilding of roads and bridges. Sale of considerable unneeded land, for example, from multilane highways, provides revenue. Also, ongoing revenue from the sale of renewable energy and from food products and recreation fees on netway land near cities and towns would offset many costs.

The netway system promises a boon for industry and jobs. Vast new fields of research and development would be energized; automotive manufacturers would build new types of vehicles; a new industry for manufacture of netway components would be launched, including for pillars, spanner sections with wings, large engines, and earthway covers. Construction of elevated ways, earthways, and netway service centers would boom. Energy investments in solar- and wind-energy devices, geothermal (including low-temperature) production, and batteries would rapidly expand.[14,48]

Here we have focused on creating an entirely new netway system. Yet many incremental approaches can facilitate the transition phase. Constructing an elevated way with pillars on an existing road shoulder, and providing 16 feet (4.88 m) of clearance beneath, would permit concurrent use of the existing highway during a transition phase, and thus minimize traffic disruption. Fossil fuel can be a significant energy component at the outset of the netway system and then be rapidly phased out as renewable energy sources are linked to the system. Sections of an existing road can be removed at different rates, for example, beginning where streams/rivers cross and between major wildlife areas. Perhaps elevated netways could also be used as demonstration projects in high-visibility corridors — such as Boston to Washington, Milwaukee to Chicago to Detroit, and San Francisco to San Diego — to accelerate public usage and support for netways and pods.

A future for transportation and our land

A system of low-impact elevated and sunken infrastructure with light-weight, automated electric vehicles promises solutions for several major issues facing society. As tomorrow's netway system replaces today's high-way system, the litany of environmental problems highlighted at the out-set of this chapter disappear, virtually eliminating the pervasive conflict between transportation and natural systems. Nature would be dramatically reconnected and rejuvenated across our land.

Indeed netway system benefits would reverberate through society. Safer and more efficient movement of people and goods would occur. Eliminating fossil fuel use in favor of renewable sources would be a major energy ben-efit. Eliminating greenhouse gas emissions from the transportation system would provide major atmospheric and other values. New food-production sites and recreation resources (market-gardened fresh vegetables and fruits, plus trail systems) would noticeably expand near cities and towns, provid-ing important benefits for our increasingly urbanized world.

The netway system promises to reverse centuries of environmental degradation by road systems and humans. A key to transforming transpor-tation in this way is flexibility — thinking beyond our cities; building on engineers' creative design of new cost-effective technologies; using mar-ketplace competition; and meshing solutions with ecological patterns and processes. Such solutions — building from vision to imminent feasibility, and reversing rather than slowing or stopping downward spirals — are far too rare. Weaving the threads together for recovering our planet's natural processes produces synergisms, which in turn can lead to a cornucopia of other major societal benefits. Certainly a far brighter future for both nature and us can lie ahead.

No single solution or recipe will solve our long accumulation of issues related to transportation and the environment. But we can now outline the theater, and even parts of the stage. Leaders with bold ideas, new alliances, and novel solutions will play primary roles in the rapidly unfolding play ahead. Success will be a land and road system where both nature and people thrive long term.

Note: *For a more-detailed description of the netway system and its benefits, please see our extended online article on the* Solutions *website (www.thesolutionsjournal.com).*

Acknowledgments

We warmly thank Heim van Bohemen, Lawrence Buell, Anthony P. Clevenger, Barbara L. Forman, Jochen Jaeger, Michael B. McElroy, Joe Roman, Daniel Schodek, Daniel P. Schrag, and Andreas Seiler for valuable insights and Taco Iwashima Matthews for wonderful graphics.

References

1. Forman, RTT (2000). Estimate of the area affected ecologically by the road system in the United States. *Conservation Biology*, 14, 31–35.
2. Forman, RTT *et al.* (2003). *Road Ecology: Science and Solutions.* Washington, DC: Island Press.
3. Sperling, D and D Gordon (2009). *Two Billion Cars: Driving toward Sustainability.* Washington, DC: Island Press.
4. Rajvanshi, A, VB Mathur, GC Teleki and SK Mukherjee (2001). *Roads, Sensitive Habitats and Wildlife: Environmental Guideline for India and South Asia.* Dehradun: Wildlife Institute of India.
5. Clevenger, AP, B Chruszcz and KE Gunson (2003). Spatial patterns and factors influencing small vertebrate fauna road-kill aggregations. *Biological Conservation*, 109, 15–26.
6. National Research Council (2005). *Assessing and Managing the Ecological Impacts of Paved Roads.* Washington, DC: National Academies Press.
7. Davenport, J and JL Davenport (eds.) (2006). *The Ecology of Transportation: Managing Mobility for the Environment.* New York: Springer.

8. Searchinger, T *et al.* (2008). Use of U.S. croplands for biofuels increases greenhouse gases through emissions from land use change. *Science*, 319, 1238–1240.

9. Mao, W (2009). *Road Ecology.* Beijing: China Communications Press (in Chinese).

10. Beckmann, JP, AP Clevenger, M Huijser and JA Hilty (eds.) (2010). *Safe Passages: Highways, Wildlife, and Habitat Connectivity.* Washington, DC: Island Press.

11. Iuell, B *et al.* (2003). *Habitat Fragmentation due to Transportation Infrastructure: Wildlife and Traffic; A European Handbook for Identifying Conflicts and Designing Solutions.* Brussels: KNNV Publishers.

12. van Bohemen, H. (2005). *Ecological Engineering: Bridging between Ecology and Civil Engineering.* Boxtel, Netherlands: Aeneas Publishers.

13. Dolan, LMJ *et al.* (2006). Towards the sustainable development of modern road systems. In *The Ecology of Transportation: Managing Mobility for the Environment*, J Davenport and JL Davenport (eds.), New York: Springer, pp. 275–331.

14. Jacobson, MZ and MA Delucchi (2011). Providing all global energy with wind, water, and solar power. Part I: Technologies, energy resources, quantities and areas of infrastructure, and materials. *Energy Policy*, 39, 1154–1169.

15. Fahrig, L *et al.* (1995). Effect of road traffic on amphibian density. *Biological Conservation*, 73, 177–182.

16. Reijnen, R, R Foppen and H Meeuwsen (1996). The effects of car traffic on the density of breeding birds in Dutch agricultural grasslands. *Biological Conservation*, 75, 255–260.

17. Forman, RTT, B Reineking and AM Hersperger (2002). Road traffic and nearby grassland bird patterns in a suburbanizing landscape. *Environmental Management*, 29, 782–800.

18. Jaeger, JA *et al.* (2005). Predicting when animal populations are at risk from roads: An interactive model of road avoidance behavior. *Ecological Modeling*, 185, 329–348.

19. Charry, B and J Jones (2009). Traffic volume as a primary road characteristic impacting wildlife: A tool for land use and transportation planning. In *International Conference on Ecology and Transportation Proceedings*, PJ Wagner, D Nelson and E Murray (eds.), North Carolina

State University, Raleigh: Center for Transportation and the Environment, pp. 159–172.

20. Seiler, A (2003). The toll of the automobile: Wildlife and roads in Sweden. Doctoral thesis, Swedish University of Agricultural Sciences, Uppsala.

21. Trocme, M *et al.* (eds.) (2003). *Habitat Fragmentation due to Transportation Infrastructure: The European Review.* Brussels: COST Action 341, European Commission.

22. Gustafsson, J (2009). Vectus — intelligent transport. *Proceedings of the IEEE*, 97, 1856–1863.

23. Thornton, RD (2009). Efficient and affordable maglev opportunities in the United States. *Proceedings of the IEEE*, 97, 1901–1921.

24. Nesbitt, K, D Sperling and M Delucchi (1990). Initial assessment of roadway-powered electric vehicles. *Transportation Research Record*, 1267, 41–55.

25. Vuchic, VR (2007). *Urban Transit Systems and Technology.* New York: John Wiley.

26. Gilbert, R and A Perl (2010). Transport revolutions will be needed to keep ahead of oil depletion. In *The Post Carbon Reader: Managing the 21st Century's Sustainability Crises*, R Heinberg and D Lerch (eds.), Berkeley: University of California Press.

27. Benyus, JM (2009). Personal communication.

28. Delucchi, MA and MZ Jacobson (2011). Providing all global energy with wind, water, and solar power. Part II: Reliability, system and transmission costs, and policies. *Energy Policy*, 39, 1170–1190.

29. Burton, T (ed.) (2001). *Wind Energy Handbook.* New York: John Wiley.

30. Gipe, P. (2004). *Wind Power.* White River Junction, VT: Chelsea Green Publishing.

31. Sperling, D (2008). *New Transportation Fuels: A Strategic Approach to Technological Change.* Berkeley: University of California Press.

32. Morelli, E (2005). *Disegnare linee nel paesaggio: Metodologie di progettazione paesistica delle grandi infrastrutture viarie.* Firenze, Italy: Firenze University Press.

33. Bekker, H, B van den Hengel, H van Bohemen and H van der Sluijs (1995). *Natuur over Wegen* [Nature across motorways]. Delft, Netherlands: Ministry of Transport, Public Works and Water Management.

34. Michael Van Valkenburgh Associates [online]. Available at www.mvvainc.com. [accessed on 8 August 2013].

35. *International Conference on Ecology and Transportation Proceedings* 6 vols (1996–2009). North Carolina State University, Raleigh: Center for Transportation and the Environment.

36. Forman, RTT (1995). *Land Mosaics: The Ecology of Landscapes and Regions*. New York: Cambridge University Press.

37. van der Grift, E and R Pouwels (2006). Restoring habitat connectivity across transport corridors: Identifying high-priority locations for de-fragmentation with the use of an expert-based model. In *The Ecology of Transportation: Managing Mobility for the Environment*, J Davenport and JL Davenport (eds.), New York: Springer, pp. 205–231.

38. Lindenmayer, DB and J Fischer (2006). *Habitat Fragmentation and Landscape Change: An Ecological and Conservation Synthesis*. Washington, DC: Island Press.

39. Collinge, SK (2008). *Ecology of Fragmented Landscapes*. Baltimore, MD: Johns Hopkins University Press.

40. Forman, RTT (2008). *Urban Regions: Ecology and Planning Beyond the City*. New York: Cambridge University Press.

41. Findlay, CS and J Houlahan (1997). Anthropogenic correlates of species richness in southeastern Ontario wetlands. *Conservation Biology*, 11, 1000–1009.

42. Seiler, A and J-O Helldin (2006). Mortality in wildlife due to transportation. In *The Ecology of Transportation: Managing Mobility for the Environment*, J Davenport and JL Davenport (eds.), New York: Springer, pp. 165–189.

43. Reijnen, R and R Foppen (2006). Impact of road traffic on breeding bird populations. In *The Ecology of Transportation: Managing Mobility for the Environment*, J Davenport and JL Davenport (eds.), New York: Springer, pp. 255–274.

44. Forman, RTT and RD Deblinger (2000). The ecological road-effect zone of a Massachusetts (USA) suburban highway. *Conservation Biology*, 14, 36–46.

45. Lay, MG (1992). *Ways of the World*. New Brunswick, NJ: Rutgers University Press.

46. Benyus, JM (2002). *Biomimicry: Innovation Inspired by Nature*. New York: Harper Perennial.

47. Aizenberg, J (2010). New nanofabrication strategies: Inspired by biomineralization. *MRS Bulletin*, 35, 323–330.

48. McElroy, MB (2011). Time to electrify: Reducing our dependence on imported oil — while addressing the threat of climate change. *Harvard Magazine*, 113, 36–39.

23

The New Security

Gary Hart

The old security, defined by the Cold War, was based on containment of communism. It was almost always described in military terms — the size of the defense budget, the range of nuclear missiles, the numbers of planes, ships, and tanks. And during that period, that definition made some sense.

But even during the Cold War, those with a broader perspective defined national security as security of our borders, a sound dollar, and the confidence of the people in their government. If we apply that definition to the United States in 2011, we are profoundly insecure. Our borders are not secure. The dollar is weak. And too many Americans have lost confidence in their government.

Replacing containment of communism with "war on terrorism" too narrowly defined America's role in the new world of the 21st century. It was a way to avoid the new realities of globalization, the information revolution, the failure of states, and the changing nature of conflict. To deal with this new world, and to define a greater and more positive role for our nation in this revolutionary age, we must create a new security framework.

> *Replacing containment of communism with "war on terrorism" too narrowly defined America's role in the new world of the 21st century.*

Our future security must be based first and foremost on the most capable military forces in the world, military forces shaped, sized, equipped, and trained for an era where conflict will more likely involve stateless nations, nonstate actors, and unconventional warfare. There are institutional structures seeking to perpetuate a Cold War military. But those who have experienced combat in Afghanistan and Iraq know our military structures must be adapted to the conflicts of the 21st century, which more closely resemble 11th century combat with the Assassins than 20th century conflict involving the massed armies of nation-states.

But the new security acknowledges that this transformed military capability depends on a productive economy. We cannot continue to borrow money from the Chinese and others to pay our troops. We must become much less dependent on debt and borrowing and more dependent on our own productivity. Today, however, we cannot have a productive economy without an educated and healthy work force.

> *We must become much less dependent on debt and borrowing and more dependent on our own productivity.*

Several years ago, the US Commission on National Security/21st Century stated that, "Aside from a weapon of mass destruction detonating in an American city, we can think of nothing more dangerous to our national security than the failure properly to manage investment in education, especially in science, math, and technology."

Likewise, a work force that is unhealthy is a danger to our economy and our national security. Proper health care for all is not only an obligation of a humanitarian nation but it is also critical to that nation's security.

The new security will also recognize, as senior retired military officers have reported, that significant climate change can become a genuine threat to global stability and therefore to our security and the security of our allies. The consequences of climate change — tens of millions of coastal inhabitants migrating to higher ground, the disruption of crop yields worldwide — must be prevented in the interest of our new security.

It is in no one's interest to spread weapons of mass destruction further. This is not just a concern for the United States. This is a concern for every nation that values peace and its own survival. We have a start with the International Atomic Energy Agency. But nations of good will must expand its inspection and sanction powers and support its efforts more uniformly. Curbing the spread of these catastrophic weapons and preventing their proliferation will be central to our new security agenda.

The new security will deal with the threat of viral pandemics, the possibility of the loss of millions of lives at home and abroad from rampant viruses. Neither we nor other nations are prepared to prevent this. Our security interest requires us to immediately network the public health systems of advanced nations to quarantine outbreaks, distribute mass inoculations speedily, and develop systems of instant global communication and data sharing.

Stable nations of the world must have better shared capabilities to stabilize fragile nations or to properly manage their reorganization in our collective security interest. Collapsing nation-states endanger the stability and security of entire regions, especially where ethnic identities reach across national boundaries and ties of race, culture, and religion draw people from multiple countries into conflict.

The US security will also depend on our ability to use skilled diplomacy to engage emerging regional powers in addressing shared security threats. China has a profound interest in curbing a North Korean nuclear capability. India has a strong interest in Pakistan's stability, especially since they both have nuclear arsenals. Russia can play a larger role in constraining Iran's ambitions and shares other security concerns, such as combating terrorism, with us.

Diplomacy will also provide an essential security tool as we must persuade oil-importing nations to share the burden with us of guaranteeing the security of oil distribution systems. Here again, the US has almost exclusively assumed a security burden that should be and could be shared with others who have an equivalent interest in the free flow of oil. At least, a half dozen nations, if not more, are substantial importers of foreign oil and have more than adequate military forces to contribute to its secure distribution.

A new diplomacy is necessary, one based on principle, not Cold War expediency. Expediency says: the enemy of our enemy (regardless of his policies) is our friend. The new diplomacy must be transparent and principled. Among our principles are the following:

1. The use of force is a last resort — not a first resort.
2. We should anticipate crises rather than react to them.
3. Globalization requires international cooperation.
4. Where we have interests in common with friendly nations, we will seek their help in promoting and protecting those interests.

5. While respecting national security, all facts will be revealed to Congress and the people regarding our dealings with other nations.
6. Our foreign policy will be consistent with our constitutional principles and values.
7. Our interests should not deviate from our principles.
8. We are a republic — not an empire.

Additional factors in a definition of the new security could be listed, but the point is clear. Our security is no longer one-dimensional. It cannot be guaranteed by military means alone. And it requires cooperation with other nations that share our values and share our security concerns.

Our military will require resetting, rebuilding, and reform to address a 21st century security environment. But we must also include the productivity of our economy, the education and health of our work force, repair of a damaged climate, prevention of the proliferation of weapons of mass destruction, prevention of the spread of dangerous diseases, management of failed and failing states, and burden-sharing of security concerns in our understanding of the new security in a new century. If we continue to rely on old security thinking and programs, we will be weaker rather than stronger, at greater rather than less risk.

24

Green Accounting: Balancing Environment and Economy

Peter Bartelmus

The High-Level Meeting on Happiness and Well-Being at the United Nations on 2 April 2012, called for "realizing the world we all want." But what is it we *all* want? Is it maximum well-being or happiness, or is it just meeting our needs, as proclaimed by the popular definition of sustainable development?[1] Happiness, needs, and development goals are holistic and, to a great extent, nonmaterial. They are also hard to define, measure, and implement.

The commonly used national accounts, therefore, focus narrowly on observable market activities and economic growth. Indicators of sustainable development, well-being, human development, quality of life, or environmental sustainability seek to show that such a focus is misleading. They combine selected concerns and statistics, deemed to be representative of our broader goals in life. All these indicators are proxy measures for something bigger than what the underlying statistics suggest. Their meaning and validity need careful examination before they can be used in policy and decision making.[2] Some indicators give equal weight to unequal issues when calculating averages of, for instance, health, education, or pollution data. Other measures apply controversial money values when pricing "priceless" environmental services like waste disposal and the supply of natural resources.

It is not surprising that national statistical offices are reluctant to include these indicators in their regular data collection programs. Nor is it a surprise that policymakers continue to focus on the economy and its established statistics and accounts. The national accounts provide the standard indicators of economic performance and — over time — economic growth. Gross domestic product (GDP) is just one of many accounting indicators, but has been the focus of economic analysis and policy. It has also been accused of being a misleading measure of well-being.

GDP-bashing is not the solution

The popular Genuine Progress Indicator (GPI) — supposedly a measure of national welfare — famously asked: "why is America down, when GDP is up?"[3] Dismissing GDP out of hand might jump the gun, though:

- GDP was never designed as a measure of human well-being or national welfare. It is simply the total economic value of goods and services produced in a country during one year. The final use of goods and services by households, enterprises, and other countries balances their supply. GDP is thus not only a measure of national output but also of the uses of national output for consumption, capital formation, and net exports (minus imports). As pointed out by the Stiglitz Commission: "GDP is not wrong *as such*, but wrongly used."[4]
- The worldwide-adopted System of National Accounts[5] defines and measures, among others, economic production, national income, consumption, and capital formation. Accounting equations and the use of market prices provide transparent and consistent tools for adding up the results of different economic activities, notably for the calculation of GDP. Showing the accounting results for different economic sectors (households, industries, government) makes it possible to assess production and consumption patterns and the distribution of income and wealth.
- GDP-bashing might throw the baby out with the bathwater — the baby being the national accounts and GDP the bathwater. There is indeed no other place where standardized measures of economic activities can be

found and presented to policymakers in a meaningful "nutshell." Individuals, corporations, and trade unions also find information on their economic situation and prospects, which they can compare with those of their own country and other nations.

Seeing that the national accounts will not go away, why not go right into the accounts and adjust them? Policymakers should find it easier to accept a need for reorienting the economy when their main source of information tells them to do so. The price for this is, however, limited coverage: the national accounts include only those issues that can be readily observed, measured, and valued. This includes the interaction between the economy and the environment, but excludes less well-documented social, cultural, or institutional concerns.

The System of integrated Environmental and Economic Accounting (SEEA) has been designed to assess the environment–economy interaction and, at least originally, to adjust the key economic indicators of GDP, capital, and income. The 1992 Rio Earth Summit endorsed the original SEEA.[6] When measuring economic activity, the SEEA accounts additionally for the costs of hitherto ignored environmental impacts. It adjusts the standard economic indicators by further deducting these new environmental costs. Note, however, that the SEEA has now been twice revised. The latest 2012 version of the SEEA appears to reject the full adjustment of accounting aggregates as a matter of research and experimentation.[7] The SEEA thus avoids being drawn into controversial measurement of well-being, happiness, the quality of life, or sustainable development. Compatibility with the national accounts should appeal to policymakers who wish to compare the conventionally measured and "greened" performance of the economy.

Accounting for sustainability: a practical step toward redesigning the economy

At the heart of greening the national accounts is measuring the sustainability of economic activity and its use of the natural environment. The idea is to consider nature and its services to the economy as natural capital. The services of natural capital include, in particular, the provision of raw materials to the economy and the absorption of wastes and pollutants by environmental sinks. This allows treating the depletion of natural resources (e.g., by deforestation, mining, or overfishing) and the degradation of the environment (notably, by pollution) as capital consumption. The idea is to apply the accounting concepts of produced capital (such as roads, buildings, or machines) and their wear and tear to natural capital and its depletion and degradation.

The purpose of accounting for the *costs* of both produced and natural capital consumption is to retain funds for replacing used-up capital goods. Produced and natural capital maintenance is the accounting definition of the sustainability of future production and consumption, in other words, of economic growth. Measuring the costs of sustainability as capital consumption allows their deduction from *gross* indicators of economic activity, including value added, domestic product, and capital formation. The results are an environmentally adjusted *net* domestic product (EDP) and environmentally adjusted *net* capital formation (ECF) (Fig. 1).

Figure 1: Pricing the priceless: A 1990 green accounting study estimated that the environmental costs in West Germany were equal to 60 billion Deutschmark, about 3% of net domestic product. (*Credit*: VisLab/Wuppertal Institute for Climate, environment and Energy.)

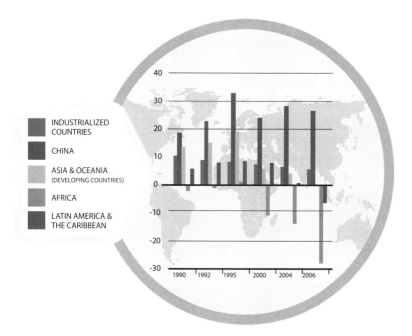

Figure 2: Environmentally adjusted net capital formation (percent of environmentally adjusted net domestic product, or EDP). The world economy and industrialized countries are — weakly — sustainable. The economic performance of most African countries has not been sustainable. (*Credit*: Richard Morin/*Solutions*.)

Source: Bartelmus, 2009.

A global application of the SEEA can illustrate the meaning of these adjustments and their results. Data gaps and different cost concepts in the available data make this a rough first study of global sustainability.[8] Global

> *Global environmental depletion and degradation costs amounted to about US$3 trillion or 6% of world GDP in 2006.*

environmental depletion and degradation costs amounted to about US$3 trillion or 6% of world GDP in 2006. During 1990–2006, the world economy showed similar growth rates for GDP and EDP. For such short time periods, ECF paints, however, a better picture of the *potential* sustainability of economic activity: it indicates the capacity to produce new capital after accounting for the loss of produced and natural capital. Figure 2 shows large differences in the sustainability of economic growth for the world's major regions and countries. Positive ECF in industrialized countries and China shows sustainable economic growth. Negative ECF in developing countries indicates that these countries have been living off their natural and produced capital base. Overall, the world economy appears to be sustainable, at least in terms of *weak* economic sustainability.

Weak sustainability maintains the overall monetary value of produced and natural capital. It implies that the different capital categories can be substituted in reinvesting for capital maintenance. This is the reason why some ecological economists prefer physical sustainability measures such as the carrying capacity of territories or the resilience of ecosystems to perturbations. The complexity and large variety of ecosystems make it difficult to apply such "ecological sustainability" at national or international levels.[9]

Produced and natural capital maintenance is a narrow but operational definition of the sustainability of economic growth. It ignores other less tangible human, social, and institutional capital categories. Measurement and conceptual problems — e.g., what is capital consumption — have so far prevented accounting for human capital (health and skills) and social/institutional capital (networking, social cohesion, law and order). Nonetheless, all these capitals have been called forth as pillars of sustainable development.

International organizations use the multiple-pillar argument to explain the connections between sustainable economic growth and development. The United Nations Environment Programme's green-economy report suggests that sustainable development can be easily translated into economic well-being: maintaining the use of all capital categories supposedly maintains economic welfare, "now and tomorrow."[10] The Organisation for Economic Co-operation and Development's green growth strategy is more concrete: greened economic growth, which maintains produced and natural capital, cannot replace sustainable development but is a "measurable … subset" of such development.[11] In both cases, sustainability, in terms of capital maintenance, looks like the anchor that prevents us from drifting off into difficult-to-measure realms of well-being or development.

The next step of actually redesigning the economy requires the allocation of the environmental sustainability cost to those households and enterprises that contributed to nonsustainability, in particular, by their environmental impacts. Well-known market instruments such as eco-taxes or pollution permits can prompt economic agents to internalize

Figure 3: Finding the balance: What are the trade-offs between economic production and environmental quality? (*Credit*: Arik Bartelmus.)

Source: Bartelmus, forthcoming.

these costs in their plans and budgets. The purpose is to make them change their environmentally harmful production and consumption styles. Delayed and weak responses might make it necessary to supplement market instruments with governmental rules and regulations. Integrated environmental-economic accounts can provide the benchmarks for setting the level of market instruments and for evaluating the efficiency of sustainability policies. Greening the national accounts could unleash the greening of the economy — the leitmotiv of the forthcoming Rio+20 Earth Summit (Fig. 3).

Further work

A number of open questions remain, including the following:

- *The valuation of environmental services.* Many stocks of natural resources and most sinks for pollutants are not traded in markets. They do not obtain a market price, and their economic value has to be imputed with the help of different valuation techniques. Contrary to the original SEEA, the latest revision relegates environmental degradation — mostly from pollution — and its monetary valuation to future research and experimental ecosystem accounting. Allowing only for the depletion of economic natural resources, which are already part of the national asset accounts, looks like omitting the environment from environmental-economic accounting.

- *Satellite accounts.* Agenda 21 of the 1992 Rio Earth Summit recommended implementing the SEEA "as a supplement to, rather than a substitute for, traditional national accounting."[6] Satellite accounts leave the conventional national accounts untouched, even if they ignore running down economic resource stocks of minerals, timber, or fish. Should the conventional accounts adjust their economic indicators for natural resource depletion? Do we need a satellite of the satellite accounts to include environmental degradation in the SEEA? Will satellite accounts continue to be ignored by policymakers? These are some of the questions that will determine the adoption of the SEEA by the official statistical services of countries.

- *Strong versus weak sustainability.* What is the significance of ignoring critical (i.e., essential and nonsubstitutable) natural capital in weak-sustainability accounting and policy? How can critical capital be identified in the greened physical and monetary national accounts?

- *Corporate accounting.* Corporations have shied away from environmental "full-cost accounting" for their environmental impacts. Obviously, they prefer showing what they have done for the environment (i.e., their expenses for environmental protection). Can the national environmental-economic accounts serve as a model for corporate accounting? Can such linkage improve corporate social responsibility?

- *Coverage of human, social, and institutional capital.* Capital consumption of these intangible categories is difficult to imagine and even harder to measure. Can nonmonetary indicator sets adequately describe the use of intangible capital? Can these indicators be used for aggregating all capitals into holistic measures of sustainable development, well-being, or happiness? This is an important area of further research. As we all know: noncountables count.

The first 1992 Earth Summit in Rio de Janeiro called for establishing the SEEA in all member states "at the earliest date."[6] The Johannesburg Summit in 2002 ignored green accounting and encouraged instead further work on indicators of sustainable development. One of the two main themes of the forthcoming Rio+20 Summit is "a green economy in the context of sustainable development."[12] Hopefully, this will put comprehensive environmental-economic accounting back on the international agenda of monitoring and implementing sustainable growth and development.

References

1. World Commission on Environment and Development (WCED) (1987). *Our Common Future*. Oxford: Oxford University Press.
2. Bartelmus, P (2008). *Quantitative Eco–nomics: How Sustainable Are Our Economies?* Dordrecht: Springer.
3. Cobb, C, T Halstead and J Rowe (1995). If the GDP is up, why is America down? *The Atlantic Monthly*. Available at http://www.theatlantic.com/past/politics/ecbig/gdp.htm [accessed on 8 August 2013].
4. Report by the Stiglitz Commission on the Measurement of Economic Performance and Social Progress: Executive Summary [online] (14 September 2009). Available at www.stat.si/doc/drzstat/Stiglitz%20report.pdf [accessed on 8 August 2013].
5. European Commission, International Monetary Fund, Organisation for Economic Co-operation and Development, United Nations, and World Bank (2009). *System of National Accounts 2008* [online]. New York: United Nations. Available at unstats.un.org/unsd/nationalaccount/docs/SNA2008.pdf [accessed on 8 August 2013].
6. United Nations Sustainable Development (1992). United Nations Conference on Environment & Development. Agenda 21, Ch. 8 [online]. Brazil: Rio de Janeiro, June 3–14, 1992. Available at www.un.org/esa/sustdev/documents/agenda21/english/Agenda21.pdf [accessed on 8 August 2013].

7. The different versions of the SEEA are available on the website of the United Nations Statistics Division [online]. Available at unstats.un.org/unsd/envaccounting/seea.asp [accessed on 8 August 2013].

8. Bartelmus, P (2009). The cost of natural capital consumption: Accounting for a sustainable world economy. *Ecological Economics*, 68, 1850–1857.

9. Bartelmus, P (2012). *Sustainability Economics: An Introduction*. London and New York: Routledge.

10. United Nations Environment Programme (UNEP) (2011). *Towards a Green Economy: Pathways to Sustainable Development and Poverty Eradication* [online]. Available at www.unep.org/greeneconomy/GreenEconomyReport/tabid/29846/Default.aspx [accessed on 8 August 2013].

11. Organisation for Economic Co-operation and Development (OECD) (2011). *Towards Green Growth* [online]. Available at www.oecd.org/dataoecd/62/59/48302542.pdf [accessed on 8 August 2013].

12. Rio+20: United Nations Conference on Sustainable Development [online] (20–22 June 2012). Available at www.uncsd2012.org/rio20/objectiveandthemes.html [accessed on 8 August 2013].

25

A Vision of America the Possible

James Gustave Speth

The following is an excerpt from a new book by James G. Speth, America the Possible: Manifesto for a New Economy *(Yale University Press, 2012). Speth envisions a future America in which citizens have created a sustainable and desirable society, and lived up to our present challenges. The vision is focused on America, but the lessons are relevant for many parts of the modern world.*

If we manage well, we can achieve a higher quality of life both individually and socially. Life in America the Possible will tend strongly in these directions:

Relocalization. Economic and social life will be rooted in the community and the region. More production will be local and regional, with shorter, less-complex supply chains, especially but not only in food supply. Enterprises will be more committed to the long-term well-being of employees and the viability of their communities and will be supported by local, complementary currencies and local financial institutions. People will live closer to work, walk more, and travel less. Energy production will be distributed and decentralized, and predominantly renewable. Socially, community bonds will be strong; connections to neighbours are genuine, unpretentious connections important; civic associations and community service groups plentiful; support for teachers and caregivers high. Personal security, tolerance of difference, and empathy will be high. Local governance will stress participatory, direct, and deliberative democracy. Citizens will be seized with the responsibility to manage and extend the commons — the valuable assets that belong to everyone — through community land trusts and otherwise.

New business models. Locally owned businesses, including worker-, customer-, and community-owned firms, will be prominent. So, too, will hybrid business models such as profit/nonprofit and public/private hybrids. Cooperation will moderate competition. Investments will promote import substitution. Business incubators will help entrepreneurs with arranging finance, technical assistance, and other support. Enterprises of all types will stress environmental and social responsibility.

Plenitude. Consumerism will be supplanted by the search for abundance in things that truly bring happiness and joy — family, friends, the natural world, meaningful work. Status and recognition will go to those who earn trust and provide needed services to the community. Individuals and communities will enjoy a strong rebirth of re-skilling, crafts, and self-provisioning. Overconsumption will be considered vulgar and will be

> *Status and recognition will go to those who earn trust and provide needed services to the community.*

replaced by new investment in civic culture, natural amenities, ecological restoration, education, and community development.

More equality. Because large inequalities are at the root of so many social and environmental problems, measures will be implemented to ensure much greater equality, not only of opportunity, but also of outcomes. Because life is simpler, more caring, and less grasping, and people are less status-conscious, a fairer sharing of economic resources will be possible. Livelihoods will be secure.

Time regained. Formal work hours will be cut back, freeing up time for family, friends, hobbies, household productions, continuing education, skills development, caregiving, volunteering, sports, outdoor recreation, and participating in the arts. Life will be less frenetic. Frugality and thrift will be prized and wastefulness shunned. Mindfulness and living simply with less clutter will carry the day. As a result, social bonds will strengthen. The overlapping webs of encounter and participation that were once hallmarks of America, a nation of joiners, will have been rebuilt. Trust in each other will be high.

New goods and services. Products will be more durable, versatile, and easy to repair, with components that can be reused or recycled. Applying the principles of industrial ecology, the negative impacts of products throughout their life cycles will be minimized, and production systems will be designed to mimic biological ones, with waste eliminated or becoming a useful input elsewhere. The provision of services will replace the purchase of many goods, and sharing, collaborative consumption, and community ownership will be commonplace. Fewer people will own, and more will prefer to lend and lease.

Resonance with nature. Energy will be used with maximum efficiency. Zero discharge of traditional pollutants, toxics, and greenhouse gases will be the norm. Green chemistry will replace the use of toxics and hazardous substances. Organic farming will eliminate pesticide and herbicide use. Prices will reflect the true environmental costs of the products we consume. Schools will stress environmental education and pursue "no child left inside" programs. Nearby natural areas and zones of high ecological significance will be protected. Environmental restoration and cleanup programs will be focuses of community concerns. There will be a palpable sense that all economic and social activity is nested in the natural world. Biophilic design will bring nature into our buildings and our communities.

Growth off the pedestal, children on. Growth in gross domestic product (GDP) and its local and regional variants will not be seen as a priority, and GDP will be seen as a misleading measure of well-being and progress. Instead, indicators of community wealth creation, including measures of social and natural capital, will be closely watched. Special attention will be given to children and young people. Their education and receipt of loving care, shelter, good nutrition, and health care, and an environment free of toxins and violence will be our measures of how well we're doing as a nation.

Resilience. Society and economy and the enterprises within them will not be too big to understand, appreciate, or manage successfully. A key motivation will be to maintain resilience, the capacity to absorb disturbance and outside shocks without disastrous consequences.

Glocalism. Despite the many ways life will be more local, and in defiance of the resulting temptation to parochialism, Americans will feel a sense of citizenship at larger levels of social and political organization, even at the global level. In particular, there will be a deep appreciation of the need to bring political accountability and democratic control to the many things that can be done only at national and international levels.

I cannot do better than to close with a quote from the remarkable John Maynard Keynes. He was also thinking about possible futures in his 1933 essay "Economic Possibilities for Our Grandchildren." There, he envisioned the day not unlike today when the "economic problem" was solved, at least for the affluent countries. He wrote,

> For the first time since his creation, man will be faced with his real, his permanent problem — how to use his freedom from pressing economic cares, how to occupy [his] leisure . . . how to live wisely and agreeably and well. . . .
>
> When the accumulation of wealth is no longer of high social importance, there will be great changes in the code of morals. The love of money as a possession . . . will be recognized for what it is, a somewhat disgusting morbidity, one of those semi-criminal, semi-pathological propensities which one hands over with a shudder to the specialists. . . .
>
> I see us free, therefore, to return to some of the most sure and certain principles of religion and traditional virtue — that avarice is a vice, that the exaction of usury is a misdemeanor, and the love of money is detestable, that those walk most truly in the paths of virtue and sane wisdom who take least thought for the morrow. We shall once more value ends above means and prefer the good to the useful. We shall honor those who can teach us how to pluck the hour and the day virtuously and well, the delightful people who are capable of taking direct enjoyment in things. . . .
>
> Chiefly, do not let us overestimate the importance of the economic problem, or sacrifice to its supposed necessities other matters of greater and more permanent significance.

Chiefly, do not let us overestimate the importance of the economic problem, or sacrifice to its supposed necessities other matters of greater and more permanent significance.

To most, the life depicted here will seem like a corner of paradise. Others may find the local focus a bit confining. But I believe we can rest assured that Americans will always find ways to keep things exciting, interesting, and amusing. There will be no shortage of challenges in America the Possible.

As e. e. cummings almost said, there's a hell of a good country next door: let's go!

Part 4
Getting There

26

The Way Forward: Survival 2100

William E. Rees

Industrialised world reductions in material throughput, energy use, and environmental degradation of over 90% will be required by 2040 to meet the needs of a growing world population fairly within the planet's ecological means.

Business Council for Sustainable Development[1]

It is not as if we are unaware of the problem. Symptoms were already so persistent two decades ago that a proclamation by many of the world's top scientists warned that "a great change in our stewardship of the earth and the life on it is required if vast human misery is to be avoided and our global home on this planet is not to be irretrievably mutilated."[2] This assertion was echoed a dozen years later by the Millennium Ecosystem Assessment's no less urgent warning that "human activity is putting such a strain on the natural functions of the Earth that the ability of the planet's ecosystems to sustain future generations can no longer be taken for granted."[3]

One might think that humanity's best science would be enough to stimulate a decisive policy response, but the feeble effort so far has done little to stem the cumulative cascade of dismal data. No national government, no prominent international agency, no corporate leader anywhere has begun to advocate in public, let alone implement, the kind of evidence-based, visionary, morally coherent policy responses that are called forth by the best science available today.

On the climate front, the first six months of 2010 were the warmest ever recorded, and 2010 tied with 2005 and 2008 for hottest year in the instrumental record. (This while we should have been experiencing modest cooling — the world is just emerging from the longest solar minimum in decades.) Glikson posits that the world may be experiencing the fastest climate change in 34 million years. Atmospheric CO_2 concentrations are rising at 2+ parts per million by volume per year (ppmv/yr) and the rate is increasing. Already, at 392 ppmv CO_2 and 470 ppmv CO_2 equivalent (CO_2e) (read: a level of greenhouse gases equivalent in climate forcing to 47 ppmv of CO_2), the atmosphere/ocean system is just below the 500 ppmv CO_2e upper stability limit for the Antarctic ice sheet.[4]

Some climate scientists are now stepping into the policy arena. Anderson and Bows argue that the world will be hard-pressed to stabilize greenhouse gases at 650 ppmv CO_2e, which implies a 50% chance of a catastrophic 4°C increase in mean global temperature, the desertification of much of the world's habitable land mass, dramatically rising sea levels, and hundreds of millions of climate refugees by the end of the century. Indeed, unless we can reconcile economic growth with unprecedented rates of decarbonization (in excess of 6% per year), avoiding this increase will require a "planned economic recession."[5]

Of course, climate change is just one symptom of generalized human ecological dysfunction. A virtual tsunami of evidence suggests that the global community is living beyond its ecological means. By one measure, the human "ecological footprint" is about 2.7 global average hectares per person (gha/capita), yet there are only 1.8 gha/capita on earth. The human enterprise has already overshot global carrying capacity by about 50% and is living, in part, by depleting natural capital and overfilling waste sinks.[6,7]

Coming to grips with reality

In theory, *Homo sapiens* is uniquely equipped to confront this self-made crisis. Four critical intellectual and emotional qualities distinguish people from other advanced vertebrates. Humans have

- an unequaled capacity for evidence-based reasoning and logical analysis;
- the unique ability to engage in long-term forward planning;
- the capacity to exercise moral judgment; and
- an ability to feel compassion for other individuals and other species.

As noted above, despite decades of hardening evidence, mainstream global society nevertheless remains in policy paralysis, stymied by cognitive and behavioral barriers to change that have deep roots in both human nature and global society's culturally constructed economic growth fetish.[8]

But what if mounting public pressure (think Occupy Wall Street) or a series of miniclimate catastrophes finally overwhelms these barriers? Assume the world community becomes fully motivated to deal effectively with biophysical reality. Now the question becomes, What would truly intelligent, forward-thinking, morally compassionate individuals do in response to available data, the historical record, and ongoing trends?

Survival 2100

In a more rational world, political leaders might come together in a special forum to acknowledge the nature and severity of the crisis and to establish the institutional and procedural basis for a worldwide "Survival 2100" project.[8] This initiative would formally recognize (i) that unsustainability is a global problem — no nation can achieve sustainability on its own; (ii) that unsustainability springs, in part, from the failure of a global development paradigm that is based on integration and consolidation of the world economy (globalization), deregulation, and unrelenting material growth; (iii) that the failed paradigm is a social construction, a product of the human mind; and (iv) that this is good — it means that the model can be deconstructed, analyzed, and replaced. In effect, the metagoal of Survival 2100 would be to rewrite global society's cultural narrative to achieve greater social equity and economic security in ways that reflect biophysical reality.

The major elements and themes of the new story are, in some respects, self-evident. The practical goal of Survival 2100 would be to engineer the creation of a dynamic, more equitable steady-state economy that can satisfy at least the basic needs of the entire human family within the means of nature. ("Steady-state" implies a more or less constant rate of energy and material throughput compatible with the productive and assimilative capacities of the ecosphere.[9] Contrary to simplistic criticisms, a steady state is anything but static. Innovation will be more necessary, and necessarily more creative, than ever.)

Clearly, the economic policy emphasis would have to shift from efficiency and quantitative growth (getting bigger faster) toward equity and qualitative development (getting truly better). Indeed, the steady-state economy would be a smaller economy. Eliminating overshoot requires a 50% reduction in global fossil energy and material throughput. And to address egregious inequity, wealthy countries will have to reduce their consumption by up to 80% to create the ecological space necessary for justifiable growth in developing countries. Implementing an equity-oriented planned economic contraction in turn requires that the underpinning values of society shift from competitive individualism, greed, and narrow self-interest — all sanctioned by the prevailing narrative — toward community, cooperation, and our *common interest in surviving with dignity*.

> *Implementing an equity-oriented planned economic contraction in turn requires that the underpinning values of society shift from competitive individualism, greed, and narrow self-interest — all sanctioned by the prevailing narrative — toward community, cooperation, and our common interest in surviving with dignity.*

The emotive rationale for such a developmental about-face is captured in the last phrase above. *Global change is a collective problem requiring collective solutions.* Individual actions produce inadequate, even trivial improvements; no individual, no region, no country can succeed on its own. Perhaps for the first time in history, individual and national interests have converged with the collective interests of humankind. Governments and international organizations must therefore work with ordinary citizens to devise and implement policies that serve the common good on both national and global levels. Evidence abounds that failure to act in ways that reflect humanity's shared interest in survival with dignity will ultimately lead to civil insurrection, geopolitical tension, resource wars, and ecological implosion.

The magnitude of the required value shift is daunting but manageable given sufficient resources. The world community will have to agree to fund worldwide social marketing programs to ameliorate "pushback" and bring the majority of citizens on board. Public reeducation is necessary both to inform ordinary citizens of the nature/severity of the crisis and to advance a positive vision for the future that will be more attractive than the future likely to unfold from maintaining the status quo. (Those who dismiss such broad-scale social learning as social engineering should remember that the denizens of today's consumer society already represent the most thoroughly socially engineered generation of humans ever to walk the planet, and billions are spent every year to ensure that they remain wedded to the status quo.)

Essential steps forward

One thing that has passed its "best before" date is the contemporary cult of consumerism. The material ethic is spiritually empty and ecologically destructive. A sustainable society, by contrast, will cultivate investment and conserver values over spending and consumption.

A sustainable conserver society would also abandon predatory capitalism with its unbridled confidence in markets as the wellspring and arbiter of all social value. Unsustainability is quintessential market failure. Society must relegitimize public planning at all levels of government. We need selective reregulation and comprehensive extramarket adaptation strategies for global change.

A necessary first step would be to acknowledge that globalization encourages the externalization of ecological and social costs (think climate change). Many goods and services are therefore underpriced in the marketplace and thus overconsumed. As any good economist will acknowledge, government intervention is legitimate and necessary to correct for gross market failure. Indeed, resistance to reform makes hypocrites of those who otherwise tout the virtues of market economies. Truly efficient markets require the internalization of heretofore hidden costs so that prices tell consumers the truth.

Consistent with the concept of true-cost economics, Survival 2100 would recognize the need to

- end perverse subsidies to the private sector (e.g., to the fossil fuel sector, the corn ethanol industry, and private banks "too big to fail");
- reregulate the private sector in the service of the public interest;
- introduce scheduled ecological fiscal reforms — tax the bads (depletion and pollution) not the goods (labor and capital) — which might require a combination of pollution charges/taxes on domestic production and import tariffs on underpriced trade goods; and
- tie development policy to the "strong sustainability" criterion (i.e., maintain constant, adequate per capita stocks of critical natural, manufactured, and human capital assets in separate accounts).

This final point requires that we learn to live on sustainable natural income, not natural capital liquidation. Society must therefore

- implement "cap-auction-trade" systems for critical resources such as fossil fuels (i.e., place sustainable limits on rates of resource exploitation, or waste discharges; auction off the exploitation rights to available capacity; and use the rents captured to address subsequent equity issues);
- revise systems of national accounts to include biophysical estimates of natural capital stocks and sinks in support of such a system; and
- replace or supplement gross domestic product with more comprehensive measures of human well-being.

Survival 2100 would also require that society unravel the increasingly unsustainable eco-economic entanglement of nations induced by globalization. Without becoming isolationist, nations should strive for greater self-reliance. In the service of "efficiency," unconstrained trade allows trading regions to exceed local carrying capacity with short-term impunity, while increasing the risk to all by accelerating waste generation and depleting remaining reserves of natural capital. In the process, this creates mutual dependencies that are vulnerable to accelerating global change, energy bottlenecks, and geopolitical instability. The world and individual nations should therefore revise or abandon World Trade Organization rules and similar regional trade treaties (e.g., North American Free Trade Agreement (NAFTA). In place of these agreements, we instead need economic plans and accords that also foster local economic diversity and resilience. "Trade if necessary, but not necessarily trade" is a suitable mantra. Nations should therefore

- develop deglobalization plans to reduce their dependence on foreign sources and sinks (i.e., reduce a nation's ecological footprint on other nations' ecosystems and on the global commons);
- simultaneously relocalize (i.e., reskill domestic populations and diversify local economies through import displacement);
- generally increase national self-reliance in food, energy, and other essential resources as a buffer against climate change, rising scarcity costs, and global strife; and
- invest in rebuilding local/regional natural capital stocks (e.g., fisheries, forests, soils, biodiversity reserves, etc.) using revenues collected from carbon taxes or resource quota auctions.

Economic contraction and massive structural change inevitably have adverse social effects. Consistent with the principles of community solidarity and cooperation, as well as society's shared interest in the peaceful resolution of the sustainability conundrum, Survival 2100 would explicitly renew the social contract and repair holes in the social safety net. This would include

- a return to more progressive taxation policies encompassing income, capital gains, and estate and corporate taxes;
- recognition that a negative income tax may be necessary to assist low-income families through the transition;
- using the tax system and related policies to promote a cultural shift from private capital accumulation to investment in public infrastructure (e.g., transit, community facilities) and human development;
- designing and implementing new forms of social safety nets to facilitate peoples' transition to the postcarbon economy in which

obsolete, unsustainable "sunset" industries are phased out (e.g., coal-based electricity generation);

- implementing job-training and job-placement programs to equip people for employment in emerging "sunrise" industries (e.g., solar energy technologies);
- capitalizing on the advantages of a shorter work week and job sharing to improve work–life balance (self-actualization); and
- implementing state-assisted family-planning programs everywhere to stabilize/reduce human populations.

Conclusions: can survival 2100 fly?

The forgoing is only an introduction to the kinds of policies implicit in a Survival 2100-type project, but it is sufficient to show that sustainability does, indeed, demand what many scientists (and even politicians) have been asserting for decades. We are engaged in a genuine paradigm shift — the abandonment of the beliefs, values, assumptions, and behaviors underpinning the status quo and their replacement by an alternative development paradigm. The good news, of course, is that the alternative offers a more economically secure, ecologically stable, and socially equitable future for all than does staying our present course.

The bad news is that there will be strident resistance from those with the greatest stake in the status quo, from people who reject global change science, from extreme libertarians, from those who worship at the altar of the marketplace, and from anyone who regards regulation and government — particularly in the international arena — as the spawn of the devil (e.g., factions of the US Republican and Tea Parties who "repudiate sustainable development and describe the global effort to achieve it as 'destructive and insidious'" and who regard UN agencies and various nongovernmental organizations (NGOs) as anti-American conspiracies).[10] More generally, planned economic contraction hardly resonates with the times. Indeed, if the basic science of global change is correct, resistance to change may well be the greatest threat to the future of global civilization and overcoming it a more difficult task than implementing the transformation itself.

And failure is possible. As Tainter reminds us, the most intriguing thing about complex societies is the frequency with which their ascent to greatness is interrupted by collapse.[11] Collapse on a global scale, however, would be unprecedented. Should *H. sapiens* fail in efforts to implement something like Survival 2100, evolution's great experiment with self-conscious intelligence will have finally succumbed to more primitive emotions and survival instincts abetted by cognitive dissonance, collective denial, and global political inertia.

But if we succeed ... !!

References

1. Business Council for Sustainable Development (BCSD) (1993). *Getting Eco-Efficient*. Report of the BCSD First Antwerp Eco-Efficiency Workshop, Geneva.

2. Union of Concerned Scientists (UCS) (1992). *World Scientists' Warning to Humanity* [online]. Cambridge, MA: UCS. Available at www.ucsusa.org/about/1992-world-scientists.html [accessed on 8 August 2013].

3. Millennium Ecosystem Assessment (2005). Living beyond our means: natural assets and human well-being (statement from the board) [online]. Available at www.maweb.org/en/BoardStatement.aspx [accessed on 8 August 2013].

4. Glikson, A (2011). Trends and tipping points in the climate system: portents for the 21st century (draft report) [online]. Available at www.countercurrents.org/glikson241111.pdf [accessed on 8 August 2013].

5. Anderson, K and A Bows (2008). Reframing the climate change challenge in light of post-2000 emission trends. *Philosophical Transactions of the Royal Society A* [online] 366, 3863–3882. doi:10.1098/rsta.2008.0138.

6. Rees, WE (2013). Ecological footprint, concept of. In *Encyclopedia of Biodiversity*, 2nd Ed., S Levin (ed.), San Diego: Academic Press.

7. WWF (2010). *Living Planet Report 2010*. Gland, Switzerland: World Wide Fund for Nature.

8. Rees, W (2010). What's blocking sustainability? Human nature, cognition, and denial. *Sustainability: Science, Practice, & Policy* [online] 6(2), 13–25. Available at http://sspp.proquest.com/static_content/vol6iss2/10001-12.rees.pdf [accessed on 8 August 2013].

9. Daly, HE (1991). *Steady-State Economics*, 2nd Ed. Washington: Island Press.
10. Roberts, N (2012). Paranoid GOP sees global conspiracy in U.N. and small nonprofit. *Care2* [online]. Available at www.care2.com/causes/paranoid-gop-sees-global-conspiracy-in-u-n-and-small-nonprofit.html [accessed on 8 August 2013].
11. Tainter, J (1988). *The Collapse of Complex Societies*. Cambridge: Cambridge University Press.

27

An Integrating Story for a Sustainable Future

Mary Evelyn Tucker and Brian Thomas Swimme

As we see our present interconnected global challenges of widespread environmental degradation, climate change, crippling poverty, social inequities, and unrestrained militarism, we know that the obstacles to the flourishing of life's ecosystems and to genuine sustainable development are considerable.

In the midst of these formidable challenges, in an era that Paul Crutzen has dubbed the Anthropocene,[1] we are being called to the next stage of evolutionary history. This new era requires a change of consciousness and values — an expansion of our worldviews and ethics. The evolutionary life impulse moves us forward from viewing ourselves as isolated individuals and competing nation states to realizing our collective presence as a species with a common origin story and shared destiny. The human community has the capacity now to realize our intrinsic unity in the midst of enormous diversity. And, most especially, we have the opportunity to see this unity as arising from the dynamics of the evolutionary process itself. In the 150 years since Darwin's *On the Origin of Species*, we have been developing — for the first time — a scientific story of the evolution of the universe and earth.[2,3] We are still discovering the larger meaning of the story, namely, our profound connectedness to this process.

With the first photograph of earth from space in 1966 came a new and emerging sense of belonging to the planet. In addition, our growing knowledge of evolution continues to give us an expanded sense of the whole. We are beginning to feel ourselves embraced by the evolutionary powers unfolding over time into forms of ever-greater complexity and consciousness. The elements of our bodies and of all life forms emerged from the explosions of supernovas. We are realizing, too, that evolution moves forward with transitions, such as the movement from inorganic matter to organic life and from single-celled organisms to plants and animals that sweep through the evolutionary unfolding of the universe, the earth, and humanity. All such transitions come at times of crisis, they involve tremendous cost, and they result in new forms of creativity. The central reality of our times is that we are in such a transition moment.

Surrounding this moment is an awakening to a new consciousness that is challenging older paradigms of the human as an isolated being in a random, purposeless universe. Paul Raskin of the Tellus Institute has called this the Great Transition,[4] while the deep ecologist and systems thinker Joanna Macy has named it the Great Turning.[5] Many such thinkers are suggesting that our consciousness is gradually shifting from valuing hyperindividualism and independence to embracing interdependence and kinship on a vast scale. This will take time, but the ecological sciences are showing us the interconnectedness of life systems. The Enlightenment values of life, liberty, and the pursuit of happiness are being reconfigured. Life now includes the larger life of the earth, individual freedom requires responsibility to community, and happiness is being defined as more than

> *The Enlightenment values of life, liberty, and the pursuit of happiness are being reconfigured.*

material goods.[6] A sense of a larger common good is emerging: the future of the planet and its fragile biosphere.

In this spirit, we are moving from an era dominated by competing nation states to one that is birthing a sustainable multicultural planetary civilization. Such a transition, while marked by struggle and conflict, is occurring within the context of our emerging understanding of the Journey of the Universe.[7] The thousands of organizations dedicated to reconfiguring sustainability are an indicator of this shift. And these organizations are coming into being at every level, from the international and national to the bioregional and local, as Paul Hawken describes in his book *Blessed Unrest*.[8]

The cosmological context: evolution and extinction

Over the past century, the various branches of science have begun to weave together the story of a historical cosmos that emerged some 13.7 billion years ago. This has been called the Epic of Evolution by E. O. Wilson[9] and Cosmic Evolution by Eric Chaisson.[10] The magnitude of this universe story is beginning to dawn on humans as we awaken to a realization of the vastness and complexity of this unfolding process.

At the same time that this story is becoming available to the human community, we are becoming conscious of the multidimensional environmental crisis and of the rapid species and habitat destruction taking place around the planet.[11] Just as we are realizing the vast expanse of time over which the universe has evolved, we are recognizing how late is our arrival in this stupendous process. Just as we are becoming conscious that earth took more than four billion years to bring forth this abundance of life, it is dawning on us how quickly we are foreshortening its future flourishing.

We need, then, to step back to assimilate our cosmological context. If scientific cosmology gives us an understanding of the origins and unfolding of the universe, philosophical reflection on scientific cosmology gives us a sense of our place in the universe. And if we are so radically affecting the story by extinguishing other life forms and destroying our own nest, what does this imply about our ethical sensibilities or our sense of the sacred? As science is revealing to us the particular intricacy of the web of life, we realize we are unraveling it, although unwittingly in part. Until recently we have not been fully conscious of the deleterious consequences of our drive toward economic progress and rapid industrialization.

As we begin to glimpse how deeply embedded we are in complex ecosystems, and how dependent on other life forms, we see we are destroying the very basis of our continuity as a species. As biology demonstrates a fuller picture of the unfolding of diverse species in evolution and the distinctive niche of species in ecosystems, we are questioning our own niche in the evolutionary process. As the size and scale of the environmental crisis is more widely grasped, we are seeing our own connection to this destruction. We have become a planetary presence that is not always benign.

The American museum of natural history: universe and earth evolution

This simultaneous bifocal recognition of our cosmological context and our environmental crisis is clearly demonstrated at the American Museum of Natural History in New York with two major permanent exhibits. One is the Rose Center that houses the Hall of the Universe and the Hall of the Earth. The other exhibit is the Hall of Biodiversity.

The Hall of the Universe is architecturally striking. It is housed in a monumental glass cube, in the center of which is a globe containing the planetarium. Suspended in space around the globe are the planets of our solar system. In a fascinating mingling of inner and outer worlds, our solar system is juxtaposed against the garden plaza and street scenes of New York visible through the soaring glass panels of the cube. After first passing through a simulation of the originating fireball, visitors move onto an elevated spiral pathway. The sweeping pathway ushers visitors into a descending walk through time that traces the 12 billion-year-old cosmic journey from the great flaring forth in the fireball, through the formation of galaxies, and finally to the emergence of our solar system and planet. It ends with the evolution of life in the Cenozoic period of the last 65 million years and concludes with one human hair under a circle of glass, with the hairsbreadth representing all of human history. The dramatic effect is stunning as we are called to reimage the human in the midst of such unfathomable immensities.

The Hall of Earth reveals the remarkable processes of the birth of earth; the evolution of the supercontinent, Pangaea; the formation of the individual continents; and the eventual emergence of life. It demonstrates the intricacy of plate tectonics, which was not widely accepted even 50 years ago, and it displays geothermal life forms around deep-sea vents, which were only discovered a decade ago. This exhibit, then, illustrates how new our knowledge of the evolution of the earth is and how much has been discovered within the last century.

In contrast to the vast scope of evolutionary processes evident in the Hall of the Universe and the Hall of the Earth, the Hall of Biodiversity displays the extraordinary range of life forms that the planet has birthed. A panoply of animals, fish, birds, reptiles, and insects engages the visitor.

A plaque in the exhibit observes that we are now living in the midst of a sixth extinction period due to the current massive loss of species. It notes that while the five earlier periods of extinction were caused by a variety of factors, including meteor collisions and climate change, humans are, in large part, the cause of this present extinction spasm.

With this realization, not only does our role as a species come into question, but our viability as a species remains in doubt. Along with those who recognized the enormity of the explosion of the atomic bombs in Japan, we are the first generations of humans to actually imagine our own destruction as a species.

The exhibition notes, however, that we can stem this tide of loss of species and habitat. The visitor walks through an arresting series of pictures and statistics that record the current destruction on one side and that highlight restoration processes on the other. The contrasting displays suggest that the choice is ours: to become a healing or a deleterious presence on the planet.

These powerful exhibits on cosmic evolution and on species extinction illustrate how science is helping us to enter into a macrophase understanding of the universe and of ourselves as a species among other species on a finite planet. The fact that the Rose Center is presenting the evolution of the universe and the earth as an unfolding story in which humans participate is striking in itself. Indeed, the introductory video to the Hall of the Universe observes that we are "citizens of the universe," born out of stardust and the evolution of galaxies, and that we are now responsible for its continuity. In addition, the fact that the Hall of Biodiversity suggests that humans can assist in stemming the current extinction event is a bold step for an "objective" and "unbiased" science-based museum.

Scientists are no longer standing completely apart from what they are studying. They are assisting us in witnessing the ineffable beauty and complexity of life and its emergence over billions of years. They are pointing toward a more integrative understanding of the role of the human in the midst of an extinction cycle. Some of this shift in the museum's perspective arose in the late 1990s when the curators were searching for an ornithologist. Of the final six candidates, four of them had had their birds go extinct while they were studying them. This was alarming to the museum curators, who realized they could not simply stand by and witness extinction with disinterested objectivity.

It can be said, then, that this new macrophase dimension of science involves three intersecting phases: (i) understanding the story of the universe with the best scientific methods, (ii) integrating the story as a whole (cosmic, earth, human), and (iii) reflecting on the story with a sense of our responsibility for its continuity.

Environmental ethicists and scholars of the world's religions are also being called to contribute to this large-scale macrophase understanding of the universe story. The challenge for religion and ethics is both to re-vision our role as citizens of the universe and to reinvent our niche as members of the earth community. This requires reexamining such cosmological questions as where we have come from and where we are going. In other words, it necessitates rethinking our role as humans within the larger context of universe evolution as well as in the closer context of natural processes of life on earth. What is humankind in relation to 13.7 billion years of universe history? What is our place in the framework of 4.6 billion years of earth history? How can we foster the stability and integrity of life processes? These are critical questions underlying the new consciousness of the universe story. This is not simply a dynamic narrative of evolution; it is a transformative cosmological story that engages human energy for a future that is sustaining and sustainable.

Cosmological stories

Since the earliest expressions of human culture, humans have struggled to understand and define our place in the universe. We have developed cosmologies, which are stories that describe where we have come from and where we are going. The religious and cultural traditions we have honored for millennia all bear witness to our deep desire to find meaning in what we see and feel around us.

Over the last two centuries, however, the scientific paradigm has taken root and, in many cases, has become the dominant worldview. Through the scientific method, science tends to objectivize what it describes. In recent years, scientific and religious cosmologies have therefore coexisted uneasily. Some scientists and philosophers have come to the conclusion that the universe, while appearing to follow certain natural laws, is largely a random and accidental accretion of objects, with little meaning and certainly no larger purpose. Scientific facts are separate from human values. One of the aims of the Journey of the Universe perspective is to counteract this view with a presentation of a dynamic and creative universe. Relying on the best of modern science, we discover how we are part of this ongoing journey and now are shaping its future form. This can be an important context for ecological, economic, and social transformation on behalf of our emerging planetary community.

The goal: providing an integrating story

The goal of the Journey of the Universe is to tell the story of cosmic and earth evolution, drawing on the latest scientific knowledge in a way that makes it both relevant and moving. What emerges is an intensely poetic story that evokes emotions of awe and excitement, fear and joy, belonging and responsibility.

This universe story is a dramatic one. Throughout billions of years of evolution, triumph and disaster have been only a hairsbreadth apart. Violence and creativity are pervasive. The ability of matter to organize and reorganize itself is remarkable — from the formation of the first atoms to the emergence of life. We are coming to realize that the energy released

> *Throughout billions of years of evolution, triumph and disaster have been only a hairsbreadth apart.*

at the very beginning has finally, in the human, become capable of reflecting on and exploring its own journey of change. Simple hydrogen has become a vibrant living planet, with beings that now are able to investigate how this has happened and to imagine a life-sustaining future.

Waking up to our fundamental relationship with the cosmos will be a means of reengagement with life. The Journey of the Universe enables us to connect more deeply with the universe and the earth of which we are a part. In doing this, we will appreciate the need for a sustainable human presence on the planet.

Thus the integrated story of the origin and development of the universe, of earth, and of humans could become an inspiring vision for our time.[12] This is because this story is giving us a sense of common evolutionary heritage and shared genetic lineage. This new understanding of the kinship we share with each other and with all life could establish the foundations for rediscovering our past and sustaining the future.

We can be inspired by this scientific view of nested interdependence — from galaxies and stars to planets and ecosystems — so that we sense how personally we are woven into the fabric of life. We are part of this ongoing journey. From this perspective we can see that our current destructive habits toward the environment are unsustainable. In an evolutionary framework, the damage we are causing is immense — indeed, cataclysmic. We can thus recognize ecological, economic, and social change as not only necessary but inevitable. But this will require expanding our frame of reference and broadening our worldview. We are already in the process of doing this as we create the foundations for a sustainable future.

References

1. Crutzen, PJ (2002). The effects of industrial and agricultural practices on atmospheric chemistry and climate during the Anthropocene. *Journal of Environmental Science and Health, Part A*, 37, 423–424.
2. Christian, D (2005). *Maps of Time: An Introduction to Big History*. Berkeley: University of California Press.
3. Brown, CS (2007). *Big History: From the Big Bang to the Present*. New York: New Press.
4. Great Transition Initiative [online]. Available at www.gtinitiative.org [accessed on 8 August 2013].
5. Macy, J (2007). *The Great Turning*. Berkeley, CA: Center for Ecoliteracy.
6. Layard, R (2006). *Happiness: Lessons from a New Science*. New York: Penguin.
7. Journey of the Universe [online]. Available at www.journeyoftheuniverse. org [accessed on 8 August 2013].
8. Hawken, P (2008). *Blessed Unrest: How the Largest Social Movement in History Is Restoring Grace, Justice, and Beauty to the World*. New York: Penguin.

9. Wilson, EO (1999). *Consilience: The Unity of Knowledge*. New York: Vintage.

10. Chaisson, EJ (2002). *Cosmic Evolution: The Rise of Complexity in Nature*. Cambridge, MA: Harvard University Press.

11. Steffen, W, J Rockström and R Costanza (2011). How defining planetary boundaries can transform our approach to growth. *Solutions* [online] 2(3), 59–65. Available at www.thesolutionsjournal.com/node/935 [accessed on 8 August 2013].

12. Christian, D (2012). Big history for the era of climate change. *Solutions* 3(2), 71–74. Available at www.thesolutionsjournal.com/node/1066 [accessed on 8 August 2013].

28

It Is Time to Fight the Status Quo

Bill McKibben

My solution is: get outraged.

Having written the first book about global warming 23 long years ago, I have watched the issue unfold across decades, continents, and ideologies. I have come to earth summits and conferences of the parties from Rio to Kyoto to Copenhagen, and many places in between.

All along, two things have been clear.

One, the scientists who warned us about climate change were absolutely correct — their only mistake, common among scientists, was in being too conservative. So far, we have raised the temperature of the earth about 1°C, and two decades ago, it was hard to believe this would be enough to cause huge damage. But it was. We have clearly come out of the Holocene and into something else. About 40% of the summer sea ice in the Arctic is gone; the ocean is 30% more acid. There is nothing theoretical about any of this any more. Since warm air holds more water vapor than cold, the atmosphere is about 4% wetter than it used to be, which has loaded the dice for drought and flood. In my home country, 2011 smashed the record for multibillion-dollar weather disasters — and we were hit nowhere near as badly as some. Thailand's record flooding late in the year did damage equivalent to 18% of the country's gross domestic product (GDP). That is almost unbelievable. But it is not just scientists who have been warning us. Insurance companies — the people in our economy who we ask to analyze risk — have been bellowing in their quiet, actuarial way for years. Here is Munich Re, the world's largest insurer, in their 2010 annual report: "The reinsurer has built up the world's most comprehensive natural catastrophe database, which shows a marked increase in the number of weather-related events. For instance, globally, loss-related floods have more than tripled since 1980, and windstorm natural catastrophes more than doubled, with particularly heavy losses from Atlantic hurricanes. This rise cannot be explained without global warming."

Two, we have much of the technological know-how we need to make the leap past fossil fuel. Munich Re again: "Whilst climate change cannot be stopped, it can be kept within manageable proportions, thus avoiding the possibility that climate change tipping points will be reached."

What does this mean in practice? Go to China where, yes, they are emulating the West by putting up lots of coal-fired power plants. But they are also busy building, say, solar hot-water heaters: 60 million arrays, providing hot water for 250 million Chinese, almost a quarter of the country — compared with less than 1% in America. I could list here a long tally of solutions (wind, geothermal, conservation, bicycles, trains, hybrid cars, tidal power, local food) and I could list an equally long tally of policies that everyone knows would help bring them quickly to pass: most important, of course, putting a stiff price on carbon to reflect the damage it does to the environment. That price signal would put markets to work in a serious way. It would not guarantee that we could head off climate change, because we have waited a very long time to get started, but it is clearly our best chance.

So, if we have an emergency, and we have the tools to fight it, the only question is why we are not doing so. And the answer, I think, is clear: it is in the interest of some of the most powerful players on earth to prolong the status quo. Some of those players are countries, the ones with huge, fossil-fuel reserves: recent research has demonstrated that the nations with the most coal, gas, and oil are the most recalcitrant in international negotiations.[1] And some of those players are companies: the fossil fuel industry is the most profitable enterprise in history, and it has proven more than willing to use its financial clout to block political action in the capitals that count.

If we are going to impose a stiff-enough price on carbon to keep those reserves in the ground (which we simply must do — physics and chemistry do not allow us any other out), then we have to overcome the resistance of those companies and countries. We cannot outspend them, so we have to find different currencies in which to work: creativity, spirit, and passion. In other words, we have to build movements — not only creative, hopeful movements that can summon our love for the planet, but also angry, realistic movements willing to point out the ultimate rip-off under way, as a tiny number of people enrich themselves at the expense not only of the rest of us, but also at the expense of every generation yet to come, not to mention every other species.

> *We have to build movements — not only creative, hopeful movements that can summon our love for the planet, but also angry, realistic movements willing to point out the ultimate rip-off under way, as a tiny number of people enrich themselves at the expense not only of the rest of us, but also at the expense of every generation yet to come.*

As it happens, such movements are possible. We built one in the last year around the Keystone Pipeline, which would have run from the tar sands of Canada down to the Gulf of Mexico. The pipeline was a certifiably bad idea — burning the world's tar sands alone would raise the planet's temperature almost a half degree. (Burning all the coal will add, wait for it, 15°.) And so people came together in huge numbers — we had the largest civil disobedience action in America in 30 years with 1253 people arrested. We ringed the White House with people standing shoulder-to-shoulder, five deep. We inundated the Senate with 800,000 messages in 24 h, the most concentrated burst of environmental activity in many years. And it kind of worked — though the battle rages on, the president at least decided to deny the permit for the pipeline.

Our campaign preceded, and then was dwarfed by, the wonderful Occupy movement, which raised specific issues, like the Keystone Pipeline, but mostly concentrated on larger questions of fairness. It showed a great depth of concern about inequality and corporate power, the very set of arrangements that have produced climate change. And it offered a number of solutions — getting money out of politics, above all — that would really help.

But talking endlessly about these solutions at international conferences is not going to produce them. They go against the power of the status quo, and hence they will be enacted only if we build movements strong enough to force them. We need politicians more afraid of voter outrage than they are of corporate retribution. And so — at 350.org, and many other places — we will go on trying to build that movement. We will focus on pipelines and coal mines, and on subsidies to the fossil fuel industry. We will demand fee-and-dividend systems that tax fossil fuel and give the proceeds to citizens. We will write and march and, when necessary, we will go to jail. And we need those who spend too much of their time at international conclaves to join us, when you can. We will never get the solutions we need — the solutions everyone has known about for two decades — unless we build the movement first.

Reference

1. Clark, D (2012). Revealed: how fossil fuel reserves match UN climate negotiating positions. *The Guardian*. Available at www.guardian.co.uk/environment/blog/2012/feb/16/fossil-fuel-reserves-un-climate-negotiating?newsfeed=true [accessed on February 2012].

29

Can We Avoid the Perfect Storm?

David W. Orr

It is quite possible that by the year 2100 human life will have become extinct or will be confined to a few residential areas that have escaped the devastating effects of nuclear holocaust or global warming.

Brian Barry[1]

Evolution equipped us to deal with threats from dependably loathsome enemies and fearsome creatures, but not with the opaque and cumulative long-term consequences of our own technological and demographic success. As cartoonist Walt Kelly once put it, "We've met the enemy, and he is us."

Deforestation, agriculture, and the combustion of fossil fuels have committed the world to a substantial and possibly rapid warming that will last for hundreds or thousands of years. Rising temperatures, whether gradual or sudden, will progressively destabilize the global climate system, causing massive droughts, more frequent storms, rising sea level, loss of many species, and shifting ecologies, but in ways that are difficult to predict with precision in a nonlinear system. These changes will likely result in scarcities of food, energy, and resources, undermining political, social, and economic stability and amplifying the effects of terrorism and conflicts between and within nations, failed states, and regions.

Action to head off the worst of what could occur is difficult because of the complexity of nonlinear systems, with large delays between cause and effect, and because of the political and economic power of fossil fuel industries to prevent corrective action that would jeopardize their profitability. Political leadership has been absent in large part because no government is presently organized to deal with the permanent emergency of climate destabilization. The effects of procrastination will fall with increasing weight on coming generations, making our role as the primary cause of worsening climate destabilization the largest moral lapse in history.

> *The effects of procrastination will fall with increasing weight on coming generations, making our role as the primary cause of worsening climate destabilization the largest moral lapse in history.*

Climate destabilization is not just an issue of technology and policy, but a symptom of deeper problems rooted in our paradigms, philosophies, and popular delusions. In particular, a great deal of the conventional economic wisdom — including "neoliberalism," the "Washington consensus," and the prevailing faith in infinite economic growth — has been proved wrong in many ways and tragically so for the poorest.

The "perfect storm" ahead, in short, is caused by the convergence of steadily worsening climate change; spreading ecological disorder (e.g., deforestation, soil loss, water shortages, species loss, ocean acidification); population growth; unfair distribution of costs, risks, and benefits of economic growth; national and ethnic tensions; and political incapacity.

Nonetheless, we might still head off the worst of a future that Cambridge University scientist Martin Rees[2] describes as possibly "our final hour." We have good reason to believe that this will be the closest of close calls, but we must hope that humankind will emerge someday from what biologist E. O. Wilson calls "the bottleneck" chastened but improved.

From the other side of that bottleneck, the components of a transition strategy, presently hotly disputed, will appear as merely obvious and necessary. The journey to a more resilient and durable future for humanity will require, first, a strategy to overcome the political gridlock that variously afflicts all developed countries and to build an informed, energetic constituency to launch the essential steps during the transition. Early warnings about climate change began in the 1960s, but neither the international community nor any developed country has yet adopted policies adequate to the situation. In the years of lassitude and drift, we exhausted whatever margin of safety we might otherwise have had. In the United States, in particular, the federal decision-making capacity on energy and climate policy is presently broken, impairing its capacity to lead on these issues.

As a result, in the United States and elsewhere, grassroots organizations are mobilizing communities around transition strategies that address energy, food, and economic issues without assistance from central governments. Similarly, mayors, cities, regional organizations, and states are engaging with the public, colleges and universities, corporations, and faith communities in a broad effort to lower carbon emissions and build economic and social resilience. The National Sustainable Communities Coalition,[3] for example, proposes a strategy of "full-spectrum sustainability" that coordinates issues of food, energy, finance, education, economic development, building, and resource flows so that each part reinforces the others and hence the prosperity and resilience of the entire community. These efforts coincide with a growing recognition that security, in the full sense of the word, must be broadened to include access to food, clean water, energy, employment, health, shelter, safety, ecological health, and climate stability.

Grassroots organizing as well as urban and regional coalitions are necessary to mobilize the public and build the infrastructure for local resilience, but they will be insufficient without a larger strategy that eventually generates a constituency for policy changes and shared sacrifice at a scale appropriate to the global emergency. Efforts at local and regional levels must be linked with a larger strategic vision that harnesses the big economic drivers in the economy. Policy analyst Patrick Doherty[4] proposes, for example, to join local action with the emerging demand for housing in smart-growth regions that have good transit and easy access to urban amenities. The combination of bottom–up organizing with a larger grand strategy suggests the possibility for new political coalitions that cross worn-out national, political, ethnic, and class divisions and for new opportunities to create an engaged and ecologically competent citizenry networked across the planet.

To limit the possibility of runaway climate change, we must also rethink energy strategies, beginning with lucid judgments about what is necessary and what is not. Necessary energy consumption must be made as efficient as technology and design permit, while waste and ephemeral energy use must be phased out. At the same time, we must make a rapid transition from fossil fuels to renewable energy. Since Amory Lovins[5] first made the case in *Foreign Affairs* in 1976, the evidence has become incontrovertible that radically improved efficiency is the fastest, cheapest, and smartest way to reduce carbon emissions, while improving the economy and virtually everything else. A recent report by Deutsche Bank and the Rockefeller Foundation,[6] for example, showed that an investment of US$269 billion in energy efficiency in US building stock would save US$1.1 trillion over 10 years and create 3.3 million jobs. The findings are similar to those of dozens of reports over decades. Of all of the changes necessary to stabilize the climate and build resilient economies, energy efficiency is the least difficult because the technology is available now and is economically advantageous. Adoption, however, requires accurate information, clear price signals, and policies that make financing affordable and straightforward.

On the supply side, wind power, photovoltaics, and more exotic technologies are capturing the world market for energy services at double-digit rates. The transition reflects the unusual convergence of economically smart choices by energy users with moral considerations. But there is a great deal more that governments can do to incentivize both efficiency and deployment of renewable energy, including adoption of feed-in tariffs to encourage rapid diffusion of solar technology, development of simple financing mechanisms, establishment of uniform codes that make installations straightforward and predictable, guarantees for long-term tax credits, financing of research as well as start-up companies, and policy measures that level the playing field for energy, whether by placing a rising price on carbon or desubsidizing fossil fuels and nuclear power.

Since the failure to anticipate and respond to climate destabilization is the largest political failure in history, a further transition strategy must address the problems of governance and politics that led to the present predicament. Most governments rest on foundations dating from the early industrial age, in what was then perceived to be an "empty world." The world is now "full" and the health of the biosphere everywhere is in decline. Governments have grown, not as a part of well-thought-out plans, but mostly in response to wars and economic crises. They are organized as silos, fiefdoms, and separate bureaucracies that often work at cross-purposes. The time horizon for most governments typically extends no further than the next election. But the challenges ahead are those of permanently managing complex, nonlinear changes in which cause and effect are separated in both space and time. All of these problems are compounded by (i) a vitriolic campaign virtually everywhere against the idea of governance, funded by those with a lot to gain from less of it; (ii) the dominance of neoliberal ideas in the global economy that render the abstraction of the market sacrosanct; (iii) the narrow bandwidth of the media; and (iv) the corruption of government and politics by vast amounts of equally addictive oil and drug money.

The new and permanent challenge for governments everywhere will be to balance human demands for resources, energy, and waste cycling with the declining carrying capacity of ecosystems. The United States during the Nixon presidency made a start toward ecological governance with the passage of the National Environmental Policy Act (NEPA) (1970). NEPA called for a systems approach to environmental decisions, evaluation of alternatives to proposed actions, and consideration of the long term. In the intervening years, the vital signs of the earth have deteriorated faster than anyone in 1970 expected. And the prospect of declining climate stability lends urgency to the challenge of rethinking how we conduct the public business at all levels.

In the broadest terms, the challenge for governments, on one hand, is to develop the capacity to foresee and forestall adverse changes by (i) developing the capacity for systems planning; (ii) implementing full-cost accounting; and (iii) extending time horizons for decisions from years to decades and centuries. On the other hand, governments must build capacity to govern smarter by promoting synergies between public and private sectors that catalyze virtuous cycles of change.

Further, governments and our political discourse must transcend the old right-left dichotomy characteristic of industrial age politics. The challenge ahead will be to creatively join conservatism and liberalism in search of a livable future. Interestingly, the necessary changes would blend the thinking of Edmund Burke, the founder of modern conservatism, with that of Thomas Jefferson, associated with modern radicalism. In different ways, each argued for the protection of future generations from "intergenerational tyranny." The prospect of political change, however, is complicated and difficult, and there is no assurance that governments that are

> *The challenge ahead will be to creatively join conservatism and liberalism in search of a livable future.*

effective in the face of rapid climate destabilization will also be democratic.[7] It is easier and perhaps more plausible to imagine a future of hyper-efficient, solar-powered, sustainable, and authoritarian societies than reformed and effective democracies.

What we do know is that governments will be under increasing climate-change-driven stresses that will jeopardize food supplies, water, key infrastructure, and probably population shifts from vulnerable coastlines and desiccated and storm-devastated interiors. In such circumstances, public order will be difficult to maintain without the perception of shared sacrifice, common vision, and leadership.

Finally, we live amid the ruins of failed systems — communism, socialism, and capitalism — and urgently need a new vision of the human prospect and potentials grounded in science, philosophy, and inclusive spirituality, not wishful thinking, greed, fear, and illusion. This new vision must begin with the hard fact that climate destabilization and its collateral effects will cause great suffering and trauma and exact an increasing psychological toll on all of us.[8] Old and familiar places and entire ecologies will be mutilated, some beyond recognition, undermining our sense of place and safety. Climate refugees (the United Nations estimates up to 250 million or more by 2050) will be the first to suffer the traumas of displacement and perhaps violence. But the fact is that we are all refugees from the only paradise humans have ever known — the 12,000-year interlude that geologists call the Holocene. We now live in a less benign and far less certain age called the Anthropocene. In this new age, the duress of scarcity, heat, and alternating dryness and deluge may bring out both the best and worst of human behavior. In either case, it will certainly dissolve the false optimism inherent in the "modern project."

Such prospects make it all the more urgent to develop plausible alternative visions grounded in emerging realities, but with hope on a further horizon. The scientific evidence suggests that we are entering a "long emergency" for which there will be no quick fixes or painless solutions. Any worthy vision must hold out solid hope of the millennial kind. It must include rights for future generations.[9] It must create a more inclusive framework for justice, fairness, decency, sustainability, and human rights (e.g., the Earth Charter).[10] It must preserve a stock of irreplaceable knowledge[11] while protecting and extending the hard-won gains of civilization, but over time spans and conditions that we can barely fathom.

References

1. Barry, B (2005). *Why Social Justice Matters.* Cambridge: Polity Press.
2. Rees, M (2003). *Our Final Hour.* New York: Basic Books.
3. Becker, W, P Doherty, M Mykleby and DW Orr. *The National Sustainable Communities Coalition* (in process).
4. Doherty, P and C Leinberger (2010). The next real estate boom. *Washington Monthly*, 42, 22–25.
5. Lovins, A (1976). Energy strategy: The road not taken? *Foreign Affairs*, 55, 65–75.
6. Rockefeller Foundation and Deutsche Bank Climate Change Advisors (2012). *United States Building Energy Efficiency Retrofits.* New York: Rockefeller Foundation.
7. Burnell, P (2009). *Climate Change and Democratization.* Berlin: Heinrich Böll Stiftung.
8. Coyle, K and L van Susteren (2012). *The Psychological Effects of Global Warming on the United States.* Washington, DC: National Wildlife Federation.
9. Gardiner, SM (2011). *A Perfect Moral Storm: The Ethical Tragedy of Climate Change.* New York: Oxford University Press.
10. The Earth Charter Initiative [online]. Available at www.Earthcharterinaction.org [accessed on 8 August 2013].
11. Lovelock, J (1998). A book for all seasons. *Science* 280, 832–833.

30

Sustainable Shrinkage: Envisioning a Smaller, Stronger Economy

Ernest Callenbach

Growth is the ideology of the cancer cell.

Edward Abbey

In 1987, when the United Nations' Brundtland Report, *Our Common Future*, appeared to worldwide fanfare, its slogan of "sustainable development" reassured environmentalists who focused on the term "sustainable," while pleasing business interests who understood "development" to mean continued material growth. It seemed we could have it all. But many thoughtful observers then and since have pointed out that "sustainable development" is an oxymoron. On a finite planet, we cannot have both sustainability and continued material growth. More than two decades after the Brundtland Report, it is past time to abandon this linguistic sleight of hand and rally around a new, shocking but this time realistic slogan: sustainable shrinkage! Within this new perspective, we can get on with saving species, restoring wastelands, improving efficiency, putting our life-support systems on sustainable bases — in short, finding solutions.

But we will do so with a new urgency and clarity, conscious that if we are to survive on our little planet in some reasonably civilized way, human activity (and its impacts) must shrink. If we do not shrink it, Gaia will shrink it for us, catastrophically.

What to shrink?

Population must shrink

Nobody knows exactly how many people eating what kinds of food the earth can support in acceptable comfort, but we know there are too many of us already. We are steadily decreasing the fertility of the globe's limited arable soils, increasing our dependence on fertilizers produced with fossil fuel, and rapidly pumping dry the essential aquifers on which millions depend. If climate change thins the Himalayan glaciers as it is thinning lower-elevation ones, several billion people will be unfed. They will not go peacefully. While it is shameful that world food supplies are distributed so unfairly, greater equality of access is both highly improbable under capitalism and moot in the long run: humans, like any other species, tend to use up whatever food is available.

Consumption must shrink

Sheer numbers matter in food consumption. Sheer wealth matters in food and everything else. Rich people and rich countries (North America, Europe, Japan) buy more, mine more, burn more, dispose of more. Ecological impacts of manufacturing, shipping, distribution, use, and disposal are directly proportional to the money spent, with only rare exceptions — solar panels and wind machines, for instance. Unless we shrink overall consumption, we have no chance of cutting global-heating emissions, oceanic biology impoverishment, habitat loss, extermination rates — or avoiding feedback phenomena (methane release, for instance) that threaten runaway planetary warming. The only means yet known to reduce consumption is economic recession/depression; we badly need to find others.

How to shrink?

Supply the right incentives

The best candidate so far for reducing consumption is a substantial carbon tax, the only workable way to motivate ourselves and our corporations to stop trashing our planetary home. Idealism or even pious hopes for long-term survival do not significantly motivate either ordinary people or corporate/political leaders. A carbon tax would force us all to get smarter about using energy (where cap-and-trade systems only make us smarter about tweaking the rules). Businesses would be intensely and permanently motivated to reduce their energy use. We would drive less and travel less. We would waste less of everything: food, wood, steel, glass. We would spend more time at home, with family and friends and neighbors. We would wear sweaters instead of turning up the heat and replace air conditioners with swamp coolers. We would find amusements less expensive than shopping and more rewarding of the incredible responsiveness, ingenuity, flexibility, endurance, and spontaneity of our species. We would no longer have a problem deciding where to store unused stuff. We might even get outside and enjoy hiking in nature, without the distraction of cell phones.

Switch from consumption to maintenance

For the past several decades, most Americans' real income has been stagnant. This has been mitigated by the influx of women into the workforce and by super-cheap, mainly Chinese imports; many people have been able to live a reasonably comfortable life by buying a lot of stuff at Walmart. But as our chronic unemployment continues and real incomes dwindle, this will not be so easy. We will actually have to face frequent choices between making things last and doing without. Doing without sometimes seems painful, especially to children and others who do not understand budgets, but it can also usefully simplify life.

Build to last

On the whole, however, we will try to make things last. Modern appliances are not designed to be repaired but rather to be thrown away and replaced.

But sometimes repairs can be improvised — there is a vigorous subcategory of Internet information about fixing almost anything (go to RepairClinic.com, for example). Laws such as the European "take-back" regulations can force manufacturers to redesign their products for recycling and repairability both. Patching of clothes, which was fashionable among hippies in the 1960s and 1970s, will come back, and indeed some people will relearn how to sew simple garments. We are already keeping our cars longer and buying used rather than new.

Control shrinkage instead of letting it control us

Smart shrinkage does not mean collapse. To get a rough idea of what is required, think back to about 1965, when our impacts on the planet were roughly half what they are now. It took more than five decades to contrive the auto-dependent, truck-dependent, space- and energy-hogging way of life we now enjoy, and though we need to shrink it faster than we have been, the pace need not be unduly shocking. For example, average new-house area is now 2000 square feet, compared to 2200 a decade ago. When gas prices hit US$4 a gallon, we cut down a bit on driving, but people were not committing suicide because of the price hike; quite a few just sold their sport utility vehicle (SUVs) and bought fuel-efficient cars. Walmart made its giant worldwide fleet of diesels more efficient. Utility magnates had second thoughts about nuclear power and started investing in solar. Imagine gas creeping up toward US$10 a gallon and you can construct your own idea of what sustainable shrinkage would actually mean — challenging, but not the end of the world as we know it. We can adjust if we have to. The real planet-scouring trouble will only come if we *do not* adjust.

Decline need not mean fall

The good news is that shrinkage may also mean transformation. When old institutions falter, they make room for new and more responsive and efficient ones. We stand near the end of an unprecedented period of heavy industrial and population expansion, and we confront an utterly new and yet age-old challenge: living better on less, figuring out how to live on a limited planet in an enduringly comfortable way.

Nobody, outside of a few visionaries, has bothered to think much about what a stable-state society might look like. However, in England especially, a movement called New Economics is now afoot, which tries to incorporate real-world environmental factors into economics.

And even in the United States, a few socially and psychologically astute economists have realized that the abstract formulas of traditional economics do not in fact match how people or economies actually behave, which is of course not straightforwardly rational. We have to devise a new economics sophisticated and flexible enough to equip us to think about a stable-state world.

The coming transformation

Material growth in the industrial era has been astonishing, with many good results as well as bad. But what if material growth as we have known it is no longer possible, and the rosy growth projections are wrong? Let us look at a few particulars.

What if world oil supplies, no matter where we drill, become inexorably more expensive? What if extraction from tar sands consumes so much energy, not to mention water, that if all the costs are accounted for it is only marginally economical, not to mention environmentally unacceptable? What if profit making in most industries (obviously in airlines and trucking, but really almost all) becomes much more difficult, and taxpayer subsidies get harder to finagle? What if procurement of certain essential minerals becomes critically difficult and expensive? What if nuclear power, with its pipe dreams of a renaissance, is in fact a doomed 20th century technology barely surviving on public-money life support? What if our vaunted agribusiness system, which puts between four and ten calories of fossil energy into every calorie of food, cannot sustain seven billion humans?

And, most ominous of all on the economic side, what if the stupendous stimulus outlays of governments cannot return us to business as usual, or indeed anything like it? What if the real incomes of American and other advanced-country working people continue to decline toward third-world levels, while the Wall Street bankers get ever richer? Can we imagine such a society remaining politically stable? How do we avoid despair, which is certainly not a constructive stance? And how do we avoid false hope, a witless nostalgia for the return to things as they were (and, in the United States, a possible gateway to a homegrown fascism)?

In the face of such grim circumstances, let us try to see what gradual sustainable shrinkage means and what our chances are of achieving it. It took us 60-odd postwar years to build a petroleum-dependent, suburbanized world. Can we retool and rebuild in a sustainable way?

Privileging density and conservation

Some of the requirements for sustainability are familiar, but that does not make them easy. Our fossil-fuel energy systems must be replaced by renewable sources. Our sprawling autodependent urban agglomerations must be rebuilt into compact ecocities that offer access by proximity to the necessities of life (including jobs) and to each other. Consider cities like San Francisco: They cover their rooftops with solar cells. They create green jobs for workers displaced from dying industries. They offer a compelling alternative to American-style autodependent suburban sprawl, making life easier for pedestrians and bicyclists and harder for cars. Or look at countries like Sweden that limit nuclear power and favor centralized town heating — keeping people warm collectively. Consider that computerization and miniaturization do more with less material and less energy, enabling a new kind of global shared brain. And intelligent engineering can vastly reduce the energy requirements of both our domestic and industrial machinery. Squeezing "negawatts" (Amory Lovins's term for watts that we do not have to generate, if we conserve instead) out of our system is cheaper than any way of producing megawatts. Conservation is always the first choice, and conservation is something that, being social animals, we mainly copy from each other. In an era of shrinkage, this will seem more and more obvious.

Rediscovering our social roots

We will find, as unemployed and underemployed and health-bankrupt Americans already know, that we have to share housing, both with family and others. It is not easy to live near or with other people, but that is our history as a species. We are groupy and interdependent even in the best of times. So we will learn to live together better. We will share space, friends, amusements, vehicles, tools — we may even learn again to sing and dance and play games together. Humans are a sociable species, playful, sexy. Spending more time together rather than interacting with expensive electronic toys will mean going back to our human nature. Consider that communicating via Facebook and e-mail only uses about 7% of our species' communication bandwidth, the verbal; the rest — expressions, gestures, postures, and probably even pheromones — lies dormant. Face-to-face contact will make us psychologically healthier and physically better off too, because people in supportive groups live longer and less anxious lives.

Encouraging population stability

And, though demographers continue to prognosticate further growth in world population, at some point (even without plagues or other disasters) this trend will reverse. What would it be like if — through better access to general health care, including contraception and abortion, and a growing realization that fewer children would mean happier lives for both kids and parents — world population began gently to decline? (Not just rise more slowly, which is the extent of most hopes heretofore.) In places like the United States, Western Europe, and Japan (in the absence of massive in-migration), there would be plenty of decent, modest-priced apartments for rent. Some office buildings abandoned by failing corporations would be converted into dwelling space. There would be a surplus of electricity and gas, so utility rates would fall. Because of fewer people, the water supply in most regions would be ample. Instead of a globe overloaded with grow-ing population and increasingly hungry consumers, our planet might be capable of supporting the people it has.

Restoring nature

How would shrinkage affect our immediate natural environment? We would not need to pave over more land — indeed we could rip up unneeded roads and maybe even tear down a few dams and restore salmon runs. We could put a lot of people to work restoring natural areas, which developers would no longer covet. A few minutes' walk outside town, there would be wild places that humans would enter as guests, not masters.

Redefining a healthy economy

Because "growth" is the ignition fuel for speculation, the stock market would dwindle in importance. Economists would proclaim the economy to be in ruins, but people would be better off: even if we continued our present scandalous division into rich and poor, nobody need be hungry or unhoused. Because there would be fewer people, we would not have to invest in more power plants and roads and cars and schools and shopping centers and courts and police and prisons and psychiatrists. We could cut back on petroleum-intensive farming and pesticides and herbicides.

Our food production would become more local, more healthful, and less energy-consumptive. Our manufacturing would follow nature's example in recycling waste, turning outputs into inputs, achieving the efficiencies of zero emissions. Our fisheries would learn how to sustain yields instead of maximizing them in the short run until collapse. Since trees sequester a lot of carbon, we would defend them against land development and deforestation.

These are big changes, and some of them will require capital, which will be harder to get. But some will thrive in conditions of declining capital, which will make them newly attractive. Saving money is the same as making money (sometimes better) and it is almost always less destructive ecologically. Some of the necessary changes will bring joy and happiness. Some will demand harder and smarter work — which may be good for our health. A lot of the changes, it is crucial to note, will involve the creation of many new jobs: the renewable-energy industry (solar and wind, mainly) already provides more jobs in the United States (about 88,000) than coal mining (about 81,000); intensive agriculture has higher outputs per acre than commercial fossil-fuel-driven farming, but it requires more labor. This is *good*.

While some changes will require massive technological innovations, many will spring up and spread by ordinary cussed human determination, like the gardening that is taking over areas of Detroit and Flint, Michigan, that General Motors has abandoned. Some innovations are within the power of present-day corporations, financed by our existing financial institutions: rooftop solar if we adopt German feed-in tariffs, plug-in cars, more efficient appliances. Some changes will happen faster if helped along by governments: incandescent lightbulbs are now illegal to import into the European Union, which is consequently far ahead of the United States in adopting compact fluorescents.

A stable or shrinking economy will still be tumultuous, full of opportunities for entrepreneurs and jobs for all kinds of people. The standard work week may shrink too, as in France and more recently in Germany — a kind of job sharing. Some industries will contract drastically, as airlines and construction are doing now; but others will grow, like medical services. The huge energy throughputs of the Internet can be reduced, and participant sports (not spectator sports) can grow. Battery building and other types of energy storage will thrive, while internal combustion engine manufacture will decline. Wind turbines will become a big business (they already are), while coal- and nuclear-plant construction will collapse. There will even be a new construction-and-destruction industry of retrofitting car-dependent suburbs into compact, dense towns with lively centers and good transport connections, taking the place of the sprawl-construction industry. Airplane builders will convert themselves into train and streetcar and bus manufacturers. Bicycles, already bigger in unit sales than cars, will further expand, along with low-energy devices like scooters and light motorbikes. In fascinating, titanic struggles, power companies and oil companies will joust over propulsion energy for vehicles. Centralized power generators will be mortally threatened by distributed-energy solar and wind entrepreneurs.

None of this, any more than life in the past, is going to be easy. For people interested in the combats inherent in business life, it will be an exciting and challenging time. We will slowly shift toward "distributed" everything: electric power, ethanol production from agricultural wastes, construction supplies, food. Shrinkage will bring localization, even perhaps political devolution: Vermont and Texas may secede, while Blue States may try to recapture some of the national taxes that are transferred to Red States.

We cannot entirely give up on Washington, DC. Some innovations, like a smart grid or high-speed trains, demand government initiative. Some changes, like green taxes to motivate lower-carbon energy use, will test to the utmost whether our social institutions are capable of fundamental changes. We are social animals, and now we must see whether we can be, as Aristotle put it, political animals as well.

Part of that is envisioning a lively and inventive and wholesome future of sustainable shrinkage. Because this future will have to respond to real-world constraints, it will look something like my Ecotopia, though every bioregion and cultural region will invent its own adaptations. The coming world will host new ideas about everything from microbiology to cosmology, with biology the central science. Our descendants will enjoy new ways of living and working together. They will probably wonder, if they bother to look back, how we ever lived in such extravagant and wasteful ways. But they will share hopes we can only dimly envision. We who are alive now are all runners, on their behalf, in the marathon of hope for the earth. When necessary, we will carry on against grim odds. But we must never give up that hope.

31

How to Apply Resilience Thinking: In Australia and Beyond?

Brian Walker

Resilience, in the context of earth's ecosystems, is defined as the capacity to absorb a shock, reorganize, and continue to function as before. This basic ability is often taken for granted by the global economy, and yet evidence is mounting that crucial ecosystems are in decline. Without a rethinking of how we use the earth's resources and the development of an approach based on resilience, many of those declines may be irreversible.

Australia's recent experience in confronting declines in its agricultural productivity suggests how this approach can work. In the 18th century, European settlement of Australia followed a familiar pattern: the rapid conversion of natural ecosystems to agriculture. The people prospered, populations expanded, and, as the saying goes, Australia grew rich on the sheep's back. Over the past few decades, however, worrying signs appeared: rangelands were changing from grassy to shrubby states that supported fewer livestock; agricultural soils showed evidence of salinity due to rising water tables following tree clearing, and even wider evidence of increasing acidity due to fertilizers; conflicts over use of limited water arose; and conservationists warned of rapidly declining biodiversity.

The tone of the debate about how to use the country's resources began to change, but it was not an easy debate to win. Those who had much to lose from changes in resource policy objected and things got heated politically. During the last decade of the 20th century, the State of New South Wales (NSW), which had the biggest share of agricultural production in the country and most of the Murray–Darling Basin (the breadbasket of Australia), took the initiative. The NSW government's first step was to address the problem of conflicting policies under different departments. They created a high-level Natural Resources Commission with a cross-government mandate. Next came the creation of Catchment Action Plans for the 13 water catchments into which the state was divided. Two pilot resilience-based schemes were prepared during 2008–2010 by members of the Catchment Management Authorities, a mixture of farmers and technical staff. Driving the whole approach was the idea of building resilience in the catchment areas.

Some local stakeholders were initially skeptical but, in the words of a Catchment Board Chairman and farmer, "This resilience approach is the way to go; it cuts through the dross we've had to deal with and gets to what matters." The pilot schemes have now been completed, and the NSW government is deciding on whether to adopt the measures statewide. In the meantime, the other catchment areas in NSW and other states are adopting the approach. The future is always uncertain, but the future of NSW's natural resources looks more promising than it did a decade ago.

> *"This resilience approach is the way to go; it cuts through the dross we've had to deal with and gets to what matters."*

The NSW story demonstrates a creative approach to the global challenge facing ecosystem managers. With a few local exceptions, the ecosystems of the world, natural and agro-ecosystems, are in decline. Rivers, lakes, groundwater reserves, the atmosphere, ocean fisheries, agricultural soils, tropical (and many temperate) forests are all fully or overused. They are either declining in area and abundance or declining in their diversity, productivity, and capacity to maintain themselves. The globalized economy has extended resource use and harvesting to a multinational scale, fueled by the ideology of boundless consumption that

> **With a few local exceptions, the ecosystems of the world, natural and agro-ecosystems, are in decline.**

treats the ecosystem as a contested open-access resource instead of a global commons. Our misuse of ecosystems is due in part to not recognizing the crucial feedback effects between social behavior and ecosystem function and a failure to understand the cross-scale feedbacks.

As a consequence, many systems have already shifted into degraded states from which they cannot recover, like the change from a viable agricultural landscape to a salinized one, or from an abundant fish stock to one that is too depleted to recover. We are running many others too close to the margin. The identification of likely planetary boundaries[1] for self-regulation of many of the biophysical processes involved has placed special attention on the limits to resource use. Serious declines in human well-being are, however, not restricted to crossing these planetary boundaries. At all scales, from local to regional to global, exceeding the self-regulatory capacity of our ecosystems has ramifying consequences for human well-being. Climatic change; rising sea levels; decreases of fresh water, fish stocks, and forests; and scarcity of farmland could variously trigger large-scale human migrations, social breakdown and revolutions, and conflicts (including nuclear conflicts).

Awareness of these dangers has led to increasing interest in the ideas of resilience, and its application to the policy and management of social-ecological systems. The NSW story is one example but the idea is spreading to agencies and government departments in other countries, notably in Europe, and to high-level policy advocacy, as shown by the United Nation's recent report, *Resilient People, Resilient Planet: A Future Worth Choosing*. What these approaches share is a recognition of three interrelated aspects. The first is a recognition of critical levels, or thresholds, in both social and ecological systems that trigger shifts in the system dynamics to a different (usually less desirable) structure and function. The pilot schemes in NSW identified sets of likely critical thresholds that needed priority attention and that would guide future investment of resources. An important point is that these threshold levels are not fixed and can change as the system is changed by what we do to it.

The second aspect of resilience has to do with the adaptive capacity of the system, its ability to change and self-organize, or to manage resilience, so as to avoid crossing a threshold. Some of this capacity has to do with the ecological system itself but much of the loss in adaptability is due to human agency, and the adaptive capacity of the system is thus dependent on political leadership and organization, particularly in the interaction between local and regional or national governments. In the NSW example, the pilot schemes identified interactions with higher scales of government as a limiting factor to building resilience. Rules about how state and federal funding could or could not be used constrained options on managing resilience at local levels.

The third aspect of a resilience approach, and the one I wish to concentrate on here, comes under the general title of transformability, or the capacity to transform into a different kind of system. When a social-ecological system has undergone a regime shift into an undesirable, alternate state from which recovery is not possible, or when such a shift is looming and clearly inevitable, the only option is to transform it into a different kind of system. Much of the world today faces the necessity of transformational change, at all scales. Until 2012, some irrigation farming areas in NSW had not had a water entitlement for several years and, despite occasional relief during high rainfall years, there is not enough water to ensure irrigated farming. It is necessary to transform these areas to some other kind of land use. There are three requirements to effecting this kind of transformation:

1. Get beyond the state of denial. Nobody likes fundamental change and individuals, communities, and societies will resist it as long as they can, often to a point where their options for a relatively graceful transformation are severely reduced.
2. Identify options for change, which may be present already or which may need to be explored and created. Because it is both dangerous and very difficult to experiment with a whole system, options for change are best developed through safe experiments at fine scales, creating what the transition approach to sustainability calls "safe arenas" for experimenting.[2]
3. Building capacity to change, which usually requires government help at the regional or national level. Ironically, government often promotes

damaging business-as-usual practices by handing out subsidies and "special circumstances" (e.g., drought) packages to local authorities, which are essentially help not to change. Instead, government should encourage bottom–up experimentation.

The three components of transformability are difficult enough to orchestrate in a naturally fluctuating environment. The world today is not like that. The speed and magnitude of directional change, environmentally and socially, are now such that what is needed is continual transformational change in human-dominated systems. As climate change ecologist Stafford Smith and others have forcefully argued, adapting to a particular "new" climate is illogical when continuous adaptation is necessary.[3]

What is needed, therefore, is an approach to learning how to change in a continuous way. Adopting this approach will not be easy. The first step is to move beyond the state of denial and, to achieve that, it is necessary to frame the problem — the uncertainties and the possible solutions — in a way that is acceptable and meaningful to people. The second step requires changes to be initiated at fine scales, with successful changes feeding back to the higher scales. Such an approach envisions the world as a multiscale, interconnected system evolving through constant experimentation toward a self-organizing, highly adaptable system that also satisfies human needs.

Whether or not this is possible will require a longer-term view of resilience at the global scale — just as time is running out to form such a consensus.

Acknowledgments

I thank Paul Ryan for his comments on the NSW example and Nick Abel for valuable suggested changes.

References

1. Rockström, J *et al.* (2009). Planetary boundaries: Exploring the safe operating space for humanity. *Nature*, 461, 472–475.
2. Loorbach, D and J Rotmans (2010). The practice of transition management: Examples and lessons from four distinct cases. *Futures* [online]. doi:10.1016/j.futures.2009.11.009.
3. Stafford Smith, M, L Horrocks, A Harvey and C Hamilton (2011). Rethinking adaptation for a 4°C world. *Philosophical Transactions of the Royal Society*, A16, 196–369.

32

Endangered Elements: Conserving the Building Blocks of Life

Penny D. Sackett

The earth is finite and so are the chemical elements of which it is composed. Those elements, represented by the symbols that fill the boxes of the periodic table, fuel all human consumption. Yet we are mining and redistributing these fundamental elements at such a rapid rate that many are already in short supply or likely to become so in the next few decades. To maintain supply lines to the dinner table and to industry, we must completely reframe our understanding of mining, consumption, human environments, and waste, recognizing that the accessible elemental resources of our future are largely stored aboveground in the familiar objects of our daily lives.

The situation is so critical that in a recent report of the Royal Society of Chemistry, a color-coded periodic table indicated the degree to which the basic building blocks of human consumption are now "endangered elements."[1] Chemical elements are being shifted out of their natural reserves in deposits in the earth's crust and into human consumables at a remarkable rate. As far back as 20 years ago, a study conducted at Kyoto University based on data from that time concluded that 80% of the world's mercury (element number $Z = 80$) reserves; 75% of its silver ($Z = 47$), tin ($Z = 50$), and lead ($Z = 82$); 70% of gold ($Z = 79$) and zinc ($Z = 30$); and 50% of copper ($Z = 29$) and manganese ($Z = 25$) had already been processed through human products.[2]

Some of the elements under serious threat are familiar. Silver, for example, which is used as a catalyst for a wide variety of chemical reactions in manufacturing, and zinc, used to protect iron and steel against corrosion.

Other, less well-appreciated elements that form the basis of modern life are also being consumed unsustainably, including tellurium ($Z = 52$) and hafnium ($Z = 72$), both of which are used in electrical devices and special metallic alloys. Indium ($Z = 49$), a common ingredient of solar cells and computer displays is on the endangered list, as is neodymium ($Z = 60$), an important building block of magnets used in many industries (e.g., for wind turbines, car batteries, and computer hard-disk drives) as well as in ceramics and glasses.

The rapid disposal of mobile phones, laptop computers, and batteries are placing large stores of some of the rarest elements directly into the waste bin, including gold, silver, and indium. It is important to realize, however, that mining urban dumps will not provide a full solution to the endangered element dilemma. This is because most "aboveground" metals are contained in products that are *actively in use* by humans rather than those used for processing, manufacturing, or discarded as waste. As an example, nearly half the world's past and current zinc reserves appear to be aboveground and in use. So changing the pattern of human consumption of elements will also need to play a role in maintaining their availability.

Unfortunately, accurate estimates of the exact amount of the elements currently in human use around the world are hindered by large gaps in our understanding. Reasonably robust global estimates do exist for the amount of in-use aluminum, lead, copper, zinc, and iron.[3] Of these, lead, copper, and zinc are on the endangered list. Comparison with underground global ore reserves[4] indicates that, as a fraction of all past and current such reserves, 45% of lead, between 33 and 43% of copper, and at least 45% of zinc was already aboveground and in use by 2005.

Japan's National Institute of Material Science (NIMS) has conducted what may be the most detailed national inventory of elements in the "urban mines" of consumer products. In 2008, it estimated that discarded high-tech devices and other products *in Japan alone* contain a remarkable fraction of the *world's* reserves of some elements. Japanese urban areas are estimated to contain 16% of the world's gold, 22% of its silver, 15% of its indium, 19% of its antimony ($Z = 51$), nearly 11% of its tin, and more than 10% of its tantalum ($Z = 73$).[5]

In order to ease the increasing risk of demand outstripping supply for some of these substances, it may be possible in some cases to substitute other elements in manufacturing processes,[1] though this simply pushes the problem from one spot in the periodic table of elements to another. In other cases, however, only a particular element of nature will do, as in the case of phosphorus.

Phosphorus ($Z = 15$) is required for living cells and is a major and essential component of agricultural fertilizers, yet some researchers predict that global phosphorus production may reach its peak as early as 2030.[6] According to the Royal Society, rock phosphate reserves are likely to be exhausted in North America, northern and southern Africa, Russia, and southeast Asia before the end of this century.[7] The price of the phosphate rock and two common types of phosphate fertilizer produced from it have exhibited a sharp peak in the last decade as well as an overall increase.[8] Phosphate prices and shortages are even more important given the growing and often malnourished global population. The 2009 World Food Summit estimated that a 70% increase in food production would be required by 2050.[9]

The relative scarcity of some elemental reserves relative to the expected demand in the next few decades is exacerbated by their uneven distribution across the earth's surface. More than 75% of the known reserves of phosphate rock are in the hands of a single country (Morocco).[10] The US Government Accounting Office estimates that 97% of the "rare earth" oxide reserves are in China.[11] China has decreased export quotas and increased export tariffs, causing shocks to industry and spurring efforts by other nations to develop alternate sources of rare earth metals.[12] The reserves of many other elements are also concentrated in only a few nations.

In assessing the implications of these data, it should be remembered that the term "reserves" is generally taken to mean the identified geological source of an element or mineral that, at the specified time of the determination, could be extracted and produced *economically*.[10] It does not imply that the facilities to do so are actually present or operational. If a new deposit is discovered and/or economic conditions change, the amount of an element "in reserve" could increase.

In fact, even though the demand for minerals increased exponentially over the last century, new technology and mining in new locations usually enabled global supply to meet demand.[13] In stable periods between short-term spikes, real prices have changed little for most elements. Indeed, despite increased consumption, the reserves of most elements have remained relatively constant over the decade 1997–2007.[13] The question is whether the doubling in real price since 2002 is just another short-term spike or instead represents a new trend due to the exhaustion of easy-to-access, high-grade ore mines and rapidly increasing new demand from large developing nations.

There is reason to suspect the latter. Newer geological reserves tend to have lower ore concentration and to be found in more hostile, difficult-to-access regions farther from consumers — and the consumption of elemental resources is increasing much faster than the global population.[13] Between 1950 and 2000, the world's population slightly more than doubled, while the production of precious metals grew fivefold. Between 1947 and 2000, per capita zinc consumption in the United States rose from 6.3 to 210 kg. For comparison, the average citizen of Cape Town, South Africa, used about 18 kg of zinc in 2002.[3] In the future, if citizens in developing countries use metals to the same extent and in the same way as those in developed countries currently do now, even more metals would be stored "in use" in human products — between three and nine times more.[3]

The time has come for a new concept of mining to meet this burgeoning demand. For many elements, the future may lie not in single-take, geological mining but in continuous "re-mining" aboveground in the generally urban locations of our consumer products and trash dumps. We must recognize and utilize these potential "mines" that we have already created at locations aboveground, rather than placing faith in undiscovered, remote, and increasingly economically unviable resources deep beneath the earth's surface.

> *The time has come for a new concept of mining.*

However, there is a long way to travel to reach sustainable, closed-cycle use of elements. For true sustainability, all goods should be made of re-mined elements, that is, with 100% recycled content. In fact, only lead, ruthenium ($Z = 44$), and niobium ($Z = 41$) are found in products in re-mined fractions larger than 50%, though 16 other elements have re-mined fractions between 25 and 50%.[14]

The good news is that some industries, governments, scientists, and local communities have already begun serious programs to speed sustainable use of the natural resources catalogued in the periodic table of elements.

The chemical industry is in a key position. Chemical companies are in the business of sourcing elements and more complex chemicals in order to recombine them into innovative products that meet a wide variety of industrial needs in, for example, agriculture, construction, medicine, manufacturing, and personal-care products (such as cosmetics, shampoo, etc.). In its just-released long-term business strategy, BASF, the world's largest diversified producer of chemicals, has indicated that it intends to use sustainability as a strategic driver for the company, in particular re-mining the rare earth elements from its own activities.[15] BASF's goal is to be a leader in chemical solutions for a sustainable world in the next decade; doing so will require stable and secure supplies of basic chemical elements.

The 3M company instituted a waste-reduction program in 1975 and has documented its progress.[16] Between 1990 and 2010, 3M reduced the tonnage of waste it produced (defined primarily as unused raw materials) per sales dollar by 66%. The company's strategy, which it calls "Pollution Prevention Pays," is financially motivated, as the slogan indicates. By reformulating its products, redesigning equipment, modifying processes, and reusing and recycling waste, 3M estimates that it has prevented more than three billion pounds of pollutants and saved nearly US$1.4 billion, based on the combined results of the *first year* of each of its individual programs.[17]

According to a recent study, public–private partnerships appear to be the most common policy tool used by nations to maintain the supply of element and mineral resources.[13] The partnerships are used to pool resources and expertise, negotiate external contracts and acquisitions, and build national capacity. Strategic partnerships with other nations and recycling are also important for many countries. Further, efforts to increase renewable energy will reduce risk, as mineral extraction is energy-intensive and mineral prices roughly track those of crude oil. Research and development is also important, including an emphasis on efficient practices and achieving similar material characteristics with different elemental compositions.

Japan, for example, has instituted an Element Strategy Initiative based on these four pillars: (i) *substitution* (of an endangered element for a more readily available one), (ii) *regulation* (to avoid shortages and chemical hazards), (iii) *reduction* (e.g., by increasing process efficiencies in manufacturing), and (iv) *recovery* (including recycling and urban mining).[12] The initiative's goals are to reduce the risk of shortages and increase the stock of usable ore in a nation that is otherwise poor in geological mineral resources.

Material scientists are tackling elemental *substitution* on many fronts. In one example, they have discovered that when common nitrogen is added appropriately to a form of carbon known as graphene, a catalyst results that could substitute for the platinum ($Z = 78$) catalyst currently used in clean fuel-cell vehicles.[12] Within five years, chemists may be able to develop a replacement for the endangered rare earth neodymium, widely used in magnets.[1]

Cost-effective urban mining will require a suite of new technologies as well as product redesign to allow easier separation of elements. One possibility would make use of microorganisms engineered to have increased abilities to adsorb particular metals through proteins in their cytoplasm or cell surface.[18] If mixed in solution with waste, the metals can then be "harvested" by separating the microbes and then processing them to remove the trace metal. In principle, the microbial cells can then be reused to repeat the process with another batch of waste.

Citizens can contribute in a very personal way to re-mining in their local communities. Urine is phosphorus rich and a natural consequence of human food production. Two Swedish cities now require the use of toilets that separate urine from solids as a step toward realizing the Swedish government's goal of re-mining 60% of the phosphorus contained in sewage by 2015.[6] Doing so will obtain a source of phosphorus native to Sweden, augmenting imported phosphate rock.

Mining phosphorus from wastewater and agricultural runoff will reduce the environmental damage caused by algal blooms in downstream ecosystems. As the algae die and sink, they are decomposed by oxygen-consuming bacteria, which rob deeper animal life of oxygen. In extreme cases, fishing dead zones are created. Great scope for improvement exists, as currently only about one-quarter of agricultural phosphorus is recycled back into fields,[19] with much of the rest running off, to the detriment of the environment.

Most conservation solutions can produce additional benefits beyond sustainable use of elements. Price volatility and geopolitical tensions can be reduced through a more even distribution of elements. Urban re-mining would reduce both the environmental damage caused by geological mining and the amount of landfill space required for discarded goods. A cost-effective substitute for endangered elements currently used in the batteries of clean vehicles would reduce the greenhouse gas emissions associated with transportation.

Effective strategies to achieve elemental sustainability and concomitant benefits will require a systems approach that examines all facets of the consumer cycle as well as market and nonmarket approaches to properly account for the true, full value of linked element-energy-environment resource use.[20]

First steps can be taken now by

- taking better stock of the rich veins of chemical elements tied up in our consumer goods and discarded into waste streams;
- reducing unnecessary consumption;
- increasing the efficiency with which we use the most endangered elements;
- substituting into consumer goods elements that are more readily available and more easily re-mined;
- improving the efficiency of reextraction of the elements from urban mines;
- designing and engineering for a closed life cycle of elements — extraction, production, consumption, and reextraction for further reuse; and
- developing new relationships between suppliers (re-miners), producers, manufacturers, and consumers to effectively transport materials from those who see it as waste to those who see it as a resource.

But perhaps most importantly, achieving sustainable use of the elements will require re-visioning our interaction with rural and urban environments, our concept of mining, and our attitudes toward waste. Consumption will need to be seen as a continuous cycle: a cycle with no off-ramps for trash, junk, or waste. What we now call our possessions, our homes, our cities, our soil, our organic waste, and urban scrap heaps are not (permanent) *ends*, but very literally

> *Achieving sustainable use of the elements will require re-visioning our interaction with rural and urban environments, our concept of mining, and our attitudes toward waste.*

the *means* to the next cycle of human consumption — the banks that hold our globally shared reserves of precious chemical elements.

References

1. Royal Society of Chemistry (2011). *A Sustainable Global Society*. Chemical Sciences and Society Summit White Paper. Cambridge, UK: RSC.
2. Halada, K (2008). Concept and technology for utilizing "urban mines". *Nims Now International*, 6(5), 3–5.
3. UN Environment Programme (2010). *Metal Stocks in Society: Scientific Synthesis* [online]. New York: UNEP. Available at www.unep.org/metalstocks [accessed on 8 August 2013].
4. U.S. Geological Survey (2005). Commodity Publications [online]. Available at http://minerals.usgs.gov/minerals/pubs/commodity [accessed on 8 August 2013].
5. NIMS (2008). Japan's Urban Mines Are Comparable to the World's Leading Resource Nations [online]. Available at www.nims.go.jp/eng/news/press/2008/01/p200801110.html [accessed on 8 August 2013].
6. Cordell, D, J-O Drangert and S White (2009). The story of phosphorus: Global food security and food for thought. *Global Environmental Change*, 19(2), 292–305.
7. Royal Society (2009). *Reaping the Benefits: Science and the Intensification of Global Agriculture*. London: Royal Society.
8. World Bank Commodity Prices [online]. Available at http://databank.world bank.org/ddp/home.do?Step=12&id=4&CNO=1175 [accessed on 8 August 2013].

9. Declaration of the World Summit on Food Security, Rome, 16–18 November 2009 [online]. Available at ftp://ftp.fao.org/docrep/fao/Meeting/018/k6050e. pdf [accessed on 8 August 2013].

10. U.S. Geological Survey (2011). Mineral Commodity Summaries [online]. Available at http://minerals.usgs.gov/minerals/pubs/commodity/phosphate_ rock/mcs-2011-phosp.pdf [accessed on 8 August 2013].

11. U.S. Government Accountability Office (2010). *Rare Earth Materials in the Defense Supply Chain.* GAO-10-617R [online]. Washington, DC: GAO. Available at www.gao.gov/new.items/d10617r.pdf [accessed on 8 August 2013].

12. Nakamura, E and K Sato (2011). Managing the scarcity of chemical elements. *Nature Materials*, 10, 158–161.

13. Hague Centre for Strategic Studies (2010). *Scarcity of Minerals: A Strategic Security Issue* [online]. The Hague: HCSS. Available at www.hcss.nl/reports/ scarcity-of-minerals/14 [accessed on 8 August 2013].

14. UN Environment Programme (2010). *Recycling Rates of Metals: A Status Report.* New York: UNEP.

15. BASF (2011). *BASF Strategy: We Create Chemistry* [online]. Ludurigeshafen, Germany: BASF. Available at www.slideshare.net/basf/basf-we-create-chemistry-strategy [accessed on 8 August 2013].

16. 3M (2012). *Managing Waste: Thinking beyond Recycling* [online]. Available at http://solutions.3m.com/wps/portal/3M/en_US/3M-Sustainability/Global/ Environment/ManagingWaste/#Waste%20redefined [accessed on 8 August 2013].

17. 3M (2011). *2011 Sustainability Report* [online]. St. Louis, 3M. Available at http://multimedia.3m.com/mws/mediawebserver?mwsId=SSSSSu7zK1fslx tUO8_ZP8mvev7qe17zHvTSevTSeSSSSSS--&fn=GRI%20Report.pdf [accessed on 8 August 2013].

18. Kuroda, K and M Ueda (2010). Engineering of microorganisms towards recovery of rare metal ions. *Applied Microbiology and Biotechnology*, 87, 53–60.

19. Childers, D *et al.* (2011). Sustainability challenges of phosphorus and food: solutions for closing the human phosphorus cycle. *Bioscience*, 61, 117–124.

20. PMSEIC Working Group (2010). *Challenges at Energy-Water-Carbon Intersections* [online]. Canberra, Australia: PMSEIC. Available at www. chiefscientist.gov.au/wp-content/uploads/EnergyWaterCarbon_web_ FAISBN.pdf [accessed on 8 August 2013].

33

Well-Being, Sufficiency, and Work-Time Reduction

Anders Hayden

Since the Industrial Revolution, two main motivations have driven the movement for work-time reduction. Free time away from the job improves individual well-being, while reducing work hours can cut unemployment by better distributing the available work. These historical motivations for work-time reduction have been joined by a new rationale: the need to reduce the impact of human societies on the environment.

The urgency of reducing humanity's impacts on the earth is well documented. Estimates of our ecological footprint suggest that we need 1.5 planets to sustain current consumption practices, while studies of humanity's "safe operating space" have concluded that we have already crossed some critical planetary boundaries, including safe levels of carbon dioxide in the atmosphere.

Two dominant responses to this threat have emerged. One has been to carry on with business as usual, pursuing endless economic expansion while downplaying or denying the severity of environmental problems. But in some countries, business as usual has given way to a second paradigm: the idea of green growth through eco-efficiency and low-impact technologies. While laudable, evidence to date suggests that such efforts do not go far enough, as steady production and consumption growth frequently outpaces eco-efficiency improvements, resulting in continued increases in environmental impacts. Sustainable outcomes also require ideas of sufficiency, which see a need to limit the relentless expansion of output. Work-time reduction would be one way to do this that could also improve well-being.

Noticeable differences already exist among wealthy nations in terms of average hours worked per employee, which, in combination with hourly labor productivity and the percentage of the population that is employed, determine a nation's level of production. Since the 1970s, a gap has emerged between long-hours nations, such as the United States, and several shorter-hours nations in Europe, including the Netherlands, France, Germany, and the Scandinavian countries. This gap in work hours had become, by the mid-1990s, the main factor behind the United States' greater output per capita than Europe.[1]

In effect, in recent decades, American society opted almost exclusively for higher output, while Europeans chose to use at least part of their increase in hourly productivity for greater leisure. They have done so through a range of measures, including standard workweeks of less than 40 h (e.g., France, Netherlands, Denmark); paid vacations of five or six weeks per year (several countries); generous parental leaves (e.g., Scandinavia); educational and sabbatical leave options (e.g., Denmark, Belgium); and rights for employees to choose shorter work hours while keeping the same hourly pay and prorated benefits (e.g., Netherlands).

While advocates of work-time reduction have highlighted the potential ecological benefits for many years, empirical evidence has emerged recently to support these claims. A study by two American economists found a significant association between work hours and energy consumption.[2] Their economic model showed that if European nations adopted American work hours, they would consume some 25% more energy (putting their Kyoto Protocol targets out of reach); meanwhile the United States would consume roughly 20% less energy if it moved to

> *If European nations adopted American work hours, they would consume some 25% more energy, putting their Kyoto Protocol targets out of reach.*

Europe's work/leisure balance (putting it within close striking distance of its original Kyoto target).

In comparing member countries in the Organisation for Economic Co-operation and Development (OECD) with some non-OECD nations, John Shandra and I found statistical support for the idea that longer work hours are associated with larger ecological footprints.[3] The main factor is the contribution of longer work hours to higher gross domestic product, which, in turn, is associated with larger environmental impacts. We also found some evidence of a time-scarcity effect, in which long work hours led to a more environmentally damaging mix of consumption and lifestyle practices, although more research is needed on this specific issue.

Two Swedish researchers looked at the household level and concluded that a 1% decrease in work time reduces household energy use and greenhouse gas emissions by 0.8% on average — mainly by lowering incomes and consumption.[4] Looking ahead, they compared two scenarios for Sweden: (i) keeping the standard workweek at 40 h and using all future labor productivity gains to increase incomes and consumption; or (ii) using half the productivity improvement to reduce the workweek to 30 h by 2040. They concluded that the second scenario would result in significantly slower growth of energy demand, making it easier to meet the country's climate targets.

Work-time reduction is also an important element of an ecologically sound response to problems of unemployment. Some selected forms of expansion — such as green job creation through investments in a low-carbon energy system, energy efficiency retrofits of homes and offices, and growth in other ecologically sound sectors — are clearly still needed in order to make the transition to a sustainable economy. In addition, work-time reduction would be a way to equitably distribute available work rather than simply trying to revive conventional, ecologically damaging forms of growth. In Germany, *kurzarbeit* policies encourage shorter hours in place of blanket layoffs. Workers can shift, for example, to a four-day week and the government tops up their pay on the fifth day. The OECD credits these policies with preventing nearly half a million people from losing their jobs and helping keep German unemployment from rising significantly despite a deep economic contraction in 2008–2009.

One of the best outcomes of less work is the possibility for a better life. Fewer hours worked can open up time for a range of freely chosen and self-directed activities outside of the work-and-spend cycle: more time for friends and family, community involvement, political participation, learning, self-improvement, personal projects, and so on. For many people facing high levels of time pressure and stress, the opportunity to do

> *One of the best outcomes of less work is the possibility for a better life.*

less and relax more could bring significant physical- and mental-health benefits. When France introduced a 35-h workweek, despite the considerable political controversy and some loss of income growth, the vast majority of employees who gained shorter hours said their overall quality of life improved.[5] Meanwhile, studies from Germany show that individuals who work fewer hours have higher levels of life satisfaction; similar evidence at the country level shows that European nations with shorter work hours also have higher levels of life satisfaction.[6]

Work-time reduction as a key part of an ecological strategy has recently gained institutional recognition. The UK Sustainable Development Commission identified "sharing the work and improving the work-life balance" as one of 12 steps to a sustainable economy.[7] Meanwhile, the UN Environment Programme, in a report on green jobs, acknowledged that "channeling productivity gains toward more leisure time instead of higher wages that can translate into ever-rising consumption … increasingly makes sense from an ecological perspective."[8]

We should harbor no illusions that such a transition will be easy to achieve — history since the Industrial Revolution has shown that overcoming employer resistance has typically required significant political mobilization. The weakening of the labor movement in many countries and competitive pressures of globalization have created new obstacles to further reducing work hours in ways that simultaneously improve quality of life and preserve adequate incomes for employees — indeed, there are pressures to increase work hours. But as it becomes increasingly clear that humanity is surpassing critical ecological thresholds, we may find a new openness in the years ahead to an alternative vision of progress that is not premised on endless economic growth.

References

1. Prescott, EC (2004). Why do Americans work so much more than Europeans? *Federal Reserve Bank of Minneapolis Quarterly Review*, 28(1), 2–13.
2. Rosnick, D and M Weisbrot (2006). *Are Shorter Hours Good for the Environment? A Comparison of U.S. and European Energy Consumption.* Washington, DC: Center for Economic and Policy Research.
3. Hayden, A and J Shandra (2009). Hours of work and the ecological footprint of nations: an exploratory analysis. *Local Environment*, 14(6), 575–600.
4. Nässén, J and J Larsson (2010). *Would Shorter Work Time Reduce Greenhouse Gas Emissions? An Analysis of Time Use and Consumption in Swedish Households*. Working Paper [online]. Available at http://jorgenlarsson.nu/wp-content/uploads/Would-shorter-work-hours-reduce-greenhouse-gas-emissions-100326.pdf [accessed on 8 August 2013].
5. Méda, D (2001). Travailler moins pour vivre mieux? In *35 heures: Le temps du bilan*, B Brunhes *et al.* (eds.), Paris: Desclée de Brouwer.
6. Alesina, A, E Glaeser and B Sacerdote (2005). *Work and Leisure in the US and Europe: Why So Different?* NBER Working Paper 11278. Cambridge, MA: National Bureau of Economic Research.
7. Jackson, T (2009). *Prosperity Without Growth? The Transition to a Sustainable Economy*. London: Sustainable Development Commission.
8. UN Environment Programme (UNEP) (2008). *Green Jobs: Towards Decent Work in a Sustainable, Low-Carbon World*. Nairobi: UNEP.

34

Millennium Consumption Goals (MCGs) at Rio+20: A Practical Step Toward Global Sustainability

Mohan Munasinghe

Unsustainable patterns of consumption and production have led to multiple problems threatening our future — like poverty, resource scarcities, hunger, disease, and environmental harm. Focusing on correcting key drivers such as consumption and production leads to integrated solutions that can solve many problems simultaneously, where piecemeal solutions have failed before.[1] The consumption-driven global economy already uses natural resources equivalent to almost 1.5 earths, with the world's richest 1.4 billion consuming almost 85% of global output — over 60-fold the consumption of the poorest 1.4 billion.[2] The consumption by the rich is not only ecologically unsustainable, but also crowds out the prospects of the poor and exacerbates inequalities that increase the risk of conflict and global unrest.

To address this challenge, Millennium Consumption Goals (MCGs) have been proposed as one key building block of a comprehensive framework for sustainable development that might emerge from the Rio+20 Earth Summit.[3-6] The MCGs have three major objectives:

- *Environmental*: to reduce humanity's global ecological footprint to less than one planet earth.

- *Social*: to meet the basic consumption needs of the poor and make the distribution of consumption more equitable, within this global-resource-use envelope.
- *Economic*: to promote prosperity within a sustainable economy that is economically efficient, but respects critical environmental and social sustainability constraints.

Specific target areas where MCGs would apply are summarized in Box 1.

Generally, the national ecological footprint is correlated with per capita income.[7] For example, the 2007 national footprint calculations show that high-income countries used resources over sixfold their nationally available biocapacity (sustainable level of resource use), middle-income countries around twofold, and low-income countries 1.2-fold. At the high end, Qatar and the United Arab Emirates (UAE) are over 10, while the United States, Belgium, and Denmark are all over 8. Many countries essentially impose their footprint globally, and suck up natural resources from abroad. This phenomenon highlights imbalances in trade, where the consumption by the rich depends upon exploiting production conditions in poor countries where natural resources and labor are underpriced. This cycle further depletes the dwindling domestic resources of poor countries.

While the MCGs are a novel concept, they have roots in the original Agenda 21 of 1992,[8] which stressed the need for "changing unsustainable consumption and production." Sustainable consumption and production were also highlighted at the 2002 World Summit on Sustainable Development in Johannesburg. The MCG concept is directly based on a comprehensive and integrated transdisciplinary framework called *Sustainomics*, which was also presented at the 1992 Rio Earth Summit.[2,9] Sustainomics sets out a step-by-step methodology to make development more sustainable, which empowers people to take immediate action by eliminating existing unsustainable activities. It is based on a balanced consideration of economic, social, and environmental concerns. Sustainomics seeks to transcend traditional boundaries of space, time, unsustainable values, and narrow stakeholder interests. It uses transdisciplinary thinking as well as both conventional and new analytic tools.

A comprehensive path to sustainable development was laid out with great enthusiasm and hope in Agenda 21 at the 1992 Rio Earth Summit.[8]

Box 1. Specific Target Areas for Millennium Consumption Goals

MCGs seek to achieve sustainable development by making consumption and production more sustainable in environmental, social, and economic terms.[13] The first MCG addresses poor people's chronic underconsumption:

- meet everyone's basic consumption needs (food, water, energy, shelter, health, education, etc.).

Next, several key resource-related MCGs tackle unsustainable consumption by the rich:

- greenhouse gas emissions reduction;
- energy use (conservation, fossil fuels, renewable energy, transport, buildings, urban planning, etc.);
- water use (conservation, quality, reuse, etc.);
- land and biomass use (urban habitats, rural land, buildings, forests, protected areas, agro-ecological balance, biodiversity, etc.);
- ores, metals, and industrial minerals;
- construction materials and minerals; and
- pollution and waste (air and water effluents, solid waste, toxic waste and chemicals, etc.).

Other MCGs would aim to increase human and ecological well-being by bringing about less material-intensive lifestyles and improving livelihoods. Focus areas include:

- food and agriculture (e.g., reducing food losses and waste, increasing agricultural yields, reducing land degradation, and deforestation, etc.);
- health and obesity (e.g., diet, smoking, exercise, etc.);
- transportation, housing, and habitats (e.g., reduced energy use, better space planning, more sustainable cities, etc.); and
- livelihoods, recreation, and leisure (e.g., through reduced working hours and better working conditions).

Finally, the MCGs could target:

- economic-financial systems (progressive taxation, banking reform, measures of well-being, etc.); and
- military expenditures.

After a period of inaction, the original goals of Agenda 21 (considered to be too ambitious and expensive by donor nations) were replaced by the more modest Millennium Development Goals (MDGs), launched in 2000 to improve the well-being of billions of poor people.[10] Even here, the results have been mixed,[11] and the current economic crisis along with emerging problems like energy, food, and water shortages as well as climate change make it unlikely that many MDG targets will be met.

The MCGs will complement the Millennium Development Goals and serve as one essential brick that will support any or all of the much larger schemes to be discussed at Rio+20, including Agenda 21, the Green Economy, the Sustainable Development Goals, and the Gross National Happiness initiative (promoted by Bhutan).[6] The MCGs would aim to curb consumption by the affluent evenhandedly in all countries, thereby freeing up resources to meet the basic needs of the poor. Instead of viewing the affluent as a problem, the novel approach of the MCGs would persuade them to contribute to the solution without having to reduce their quality of life. This will require both top–down and bottom–up processes to set global targets and then allocate consumption equitably among countries, sectors, cities, communities, and firms.

The problems of setting and implementing mandatory national targets are illustrated by studying the issue of greenhouse gas (GHG) emissions, which are the cause of global warming. The most widely known example of a global consumption target is the 1997 Kyoto Protocol where the developed (Annex 1) countries agreed to reduce their collective greenhouse gas emissions by 5.2% during 2008–2012, relative to their 1990 emissions baseline. However, there was no enforcement mechanism. Ultimately, the United States refused to ratify their target of 7%, and even signatories like the European Union countries (8%) and Japan (6%) have not met their goals. Recent international meetings on climate change have failed to revive Kyoto or develop any binding targets. Instead, most countries appear to be more comfortable with pledges to meet voluntary targets, which are inadequate to address growing global warming. Meanwhile, discussions to determine how the emissions mitigation burden should be shared among nations drags on, based on past and existing emission levels, resource endowment and availability, economic capability, equity, and other country-specific criteria. At the last international negotiations in

Durban (COP17 in December 2011), countries could only agree that a global agreement might be implemented by 2020, which, according to scientific evidence, is too late to avoid "dangerous levels of climate change."[12]

But we need not wait for governments to take action. While top–down, international negotiations on a lasting agreement for sustainable development will continue through the Rio+20 summit, the Millennium Consumption Goals Initiative (MCGI) has already launched a bottom–up effort, which has attracted worldwide support from a broad coalition of stakeholders.[5,13] The MCGI emphasizes voluntary actions by many pioneering individuals, communities, organizations, firms, cities, regions, and nations, who are willing to set up their own specific voluntary MCGs, monitor and implement them, and report progress.

In particular, MCGs can provide a readily implementable framework for the middle tier of decision makers (e.g., mayors of cities, leaders of community organizations, and CEOs of companies), permitting them to act more decisively and quickly. Authorities at national and international levels would have to take enabling actions to create a locally driven and country-specific approach. Specific activities to implement the MCGs would include interventions in key areas of the economy, and could range in scale from the household to the company or community. It is possible to achieve many MCGs by implementing existing policy tools (including cost-reflective prices, accurate product labeling and information, public education, environmental laws, the polluter-pays principle, etc.) and by adopting best practice methods and processes, especially among producers (firms). More public education (especially for the young) is essential to ensure the widest possible support for the measures.

Energizing communities that include high-consumption households and businesses can often change behavior more quickly than central government policies and long-term investments. Already, many large cities in Europe and elsewhere have declared voluntary targets to reduce consumption of resources like energy and water and production of carbon emissions, usually by 20% or more within the next 5 to 10 years.[14] Progressive business leaders have also pledged to overcome barriers faced by consumers, such as lack of information and a sense of powerlessness, as well as to address the availability and affordability of sustainable products. Major reductions in resource use per unit of output are possible.[15] Thus, several giant multinational companies and other firms have declared energy, water use, and carbon emissions reduction goals on their websites over time periods from 2020 to 2050.[16,17] This is a welcome contrast to the continuing reluctance of world leaders to decisively address pressing sustainable development issues. In summary, voluntary MCGs could be pursued by the willing, at whatever level they choose, and could focus on the goals they prefer.

Focusing on the rich worldwide has a big potential payoff. Since the affluent account for over 80% of consumption and pollution, even modest shifts in their consumption can effectively reduce the environmental burden and free up resources to raise poorer peoples' living standards. They are better educated, better organized, and more effective. Research indicates that there is a great deal of overconsumption and waste here, so initial cuts can be made with little pain and even an

> *Since the affluent account for over 80% of consumption and pollution, even modest shifts in their consumption can effectively reduce the environmental burden and free up resources to raise poorer peoples' living standards.*

increase in well-being. For example, at the individual level, healthier diets and lifestyles will not only save resources but will also improve quality of life.[18] Furthermore, there is significant scope for savings in food, given that food waste within homes is around 30% in Western Europe and closer to 50% in North America.[19]

Often, win–win outcomes (i.e., saving both resources and money) have not been pursued because waste and overuse are encouraged both globally and locally by distorted policies (like subsidized prices for energy, water, and agriculture) as well as market failures (like externalities, where hidden pollution costs are imposed on innocent parties and not incurred by the polluters). Ensuring that markets set resource prices that reflect their true economic values and getting polluters to actually pay for the damages caused by their actions are among the first measures that will help eliminate unsustainable consumption. Government laws and regulations are crucial, but sustainability-conscious businesses and civil society need to cooperate, rather than exploit loopholes.

Changing such mindsets will be a challenge. The Washington Consensus that dominated government thinking in the 1990s and led to the current economic collapse still persists. But many ordinary citizens, businesses, and mid-level policymakers are already ahead of national political leaders in terms of willingness to address an array of sustainable development issues. While understanding that pricing and other market-based policies generally lead to more efficient allocation of scarce resources devoted to consumption and production, they also realize that unrestrained market forces will not ensure sustainability unless there are constraints based on environmental and social criteria. That is why we urgently need the MCGs, which place the emphasis directly on sustainable consumption and production, to ensure a sustainable future for our children and grandchildren.

References

1. Munasinghe, M (2011). Addressing sustainable development and climate change together using sustainomics. *Wiley Interdisciplinary Reviews: Climate Change*, 2(1), 7–18.
2. Munasinghe, M (2009). *Sustainable Development in Practice: Sustainomics Framework and Applications*. London: Cambridge University Press.
3. Euro STEP [online]. Available at www.eurostep.org/wcm/eurostep-weekly/1308-rich-countries-called-upon-to-take-responsibility-for-global-environmental-damage.html [accessed on 8 August 2013].
4. Munasinghe, M (2011, January 31). Millennium consumption goals (MCG): How the rich can make the planet more sustainable. *The Island* [online]. Available at www.island.lk [accessed on 8 August 2013].
5. Millennium Consumption Goals [online]. Available at www.millenniumconsumptiongoals.org [accessed on 8 August 2013].
6. Rio+20. Compilation document [online]. Available at www.uncsd2012.org/rio20/compdocument.html [accessed on 8 August 2013].
7. Global Footprint Network [online]. Available at www.footprintnetwork.org/en/index.php/GFN [accessed on 8 August 2013].
8. UN Department of Economic and Social Affairs. Division for Sustainable Development [online]. Available at www.un.org/esa/dsd/agenda21 [accessed on 8 August 2013].

9. Munasinghe, M [online]. Available at www.mohanmunasinghe.com/ sustainomics.cfm [accessed on 8 August 2013].

10. UNDP. Eight goals for 2015 [online]. Available at www.beta.undp.org/undp/ en/home/mdgoverview.html [accessed on 8 August 2013].

11. United Nations. Millennium Development Goals Report [online] (2010). Available at www.un.org/millenniumgoals/pdf/MDG%20Report%202010%20 En%20r15%20-low%20res%2020100615%20-.pdf [accessed on 8 August 2013].

12. Gogo, J (2012). Zimbabwe: COP17 post-mortem. *allAfrica.com* [online]. Available at http://allafrica.com/stories/201204020099.html [accessed on 8 August 2013].

13. Rio+20. Millennium Consumption Goals Initiative (MCGI) [online]. Available at www.uncsd2012.org/rio20/index.php?page=view&type=510&n r=312&menu=20 [accessed on 8 August 2013].

14. Climate Alliance [online]. Available at www.climatealliance.org [accessed on 8 August 2013].

15. UNEP. Decoupling Natural Resource Use and Environmental Impacts from Economic Growth [online]. Available at www.unep.org/resourcepanel/ decoupling/files/pdf/decoupling_report_english.pdf [accessed on 8 August 2013].

16. Novozymes. Water [online]. Available at www.novozymes.com/en/sustainability/ sustainability-priorities/water/Pages/default.aspx [accessed on 8 August 2013].

17. Tesco. Corporate Responsibility Report 2011 [online]. Available at www.tesco-plc.com/media/60113/tesco_cr_report_2011_final.pdf [accessed on 8 August 2013].

18. UNEP (2011). *Visions for Change: Recommendations for Effective Policies on Sustainable Lifestyles*. New York: UNEP. Available at www.unep.fr/shared/ publications/pdf/DTIx1321xPA-VisionsForChange%20report.pdf [accessed on 8 August 2013].

19. Human Rights Council. Report submitted by the Special Rapporteur on the right to food, Olivier de Schutter (UN General Assembly, 26 December 2011). Available at www.ohchr.org/Documents/HRBodies/HRCouncil/RegularSession/ Session19/A-HRC-19-59_en.pdf [accessed on 8 August 2013].

35

Happiness and Psychological Well-Being: Building Human Capital to Benefit Individuals and Society

George W. Burns

Happy people are healthy people. Happy people live longer and enjoy a greater quality of life. They function at a higher level, utilizing their personal strengths, skills, and abilities to contribute to their own well-being as well as that of others and society. They are more likely to be compassionate and, therefore, to contribute to the moral fiber of society in diversely beneficial ways. They are less prone to experience depression and, if they do, tend to manage it better and more quickly. They are less likely to experience anxiety, stress, or anger. As a result, happy people engage in fewer acts of violence or antisocial behaviors. They enjoy stronger and more-lasting relationships, thus facilitating society's social capital. In all, they contribute to society in economic, social, moral, spiritual, and psychological terms.

Compared to unhappy or depressed people, the happier ones are less of a burden to health services, social welfare agencies, or police and justice systems and so are less of a burden to the economy.[1] In other words, building greater levels of individual

> *Building greater levels of individual happiness not only benefits a particular person but also leads to the healthy, happy functioning of society as a whole.*

happiness not only benefits a particular person but also leads to the healthy, happy functioning of society as a whole.

Given this, in conjunction with the worldwide escalation in rates of depression, is there any better reason for communities, states, and nations to be addressing the question: How can we create an environment that will best facilitate the happiness of our citizens? But to address that question, we perhaps need to ask some preceding ones: What are the factors that contribute to an individual's — and, in turn, to society's — happiness? How can society create a conducive context for the development of happiness?

Fortunately, in the last decade or so, burgeoning research in the field of positive psychology has taught us much about the state of happiness. Most research prior to this, at least in the Western world, had focused on psychological abnormalities, dysfunction, and idiosyncrasies — despite happiness being the next most important life goal for most people once our physical needs for food, shelter, and health have been met. So what have we learned from this research?

Relationships

First, as a contributor to happiness, research shows that relationships top the scale. Researchers in one study asked: What contributes to the top 10% of happy people being happy? What are the keys to happiness for these "very happy" people? The answer was clear: the single-most important variable was that "very happy" people had good social relationships with other people.[2] Other research supports this, claiming that "relationships are an important, and perhaps the most important, source of life satisfaction and emotional well-being."[3]

Spirituality

Second on the list of what most contributes to happiness is a sense of spirituality. In fact, a sense of spirituality strongly correlates to a life well-lived. This relationship between happiness and taking a "big picture" view of life is born out in research across gender, age, religion, and nationality.[4]

Spiritual strivings are clearly linked with higher levels of subjective well-being, particularly in regard to greater positive effect and higher satisfaction with both life and marriage. Drawing from such data, my colleague Helen Street and I wrote in our book, *Standing without Shoes*, that "numerous researchers have found that those of us with strong spiritual beliefs are happier and better protected against depression than those who have no particular sense of spirituality. Similarly it seems that people cope better with major adversity in their life and major physical illness if they have a sense of established spirituality."[5]

Strengths

In another area, researchers have found that when we use our strengths, skills, resources, and abilities, we feel in touch with our "true selves" and do the things that are right for us to do — we experience a sense of energy and function at optimal levels. The acknowledgment and use of one's strengths are a significant predictor of both psychological and subjective well-being, which in turn contributes to the optimal functioning of society.[6] One study of positive psychotherapy conducted in a clinically depressed population found that identifying one's signature strengths and finding ways to use them led to clinically significant and sustained decreases in depression.[7]

While the pursuit of happiness is both personal and subjective, and ultimately an individual responsibility, if the state wants its citizens to be functioning well and contributing to the well-being of society, then it needs to create a conducive atmosphere in which individuals can pursue happiness, which leads to the next question: How can communities, societies, and governments create such an atmosphere?

Some suggestions

In regard to relationships, spirituality, and the identification and use of strengths, the path to developing happiness first needs to incorporate policies and practices that (i) respect, value, and encourage positive, healthy, and mutually respectful relationships; (ii) promote a strong sense of family values and ties; (iii) allow the freedom for citizens to develop healthy, happy relationships; and (iv) encourage the maintenance of those relationships.

Second, concerning spirituality, it befits governing bodies to create an environment in which individuals are (i) free to follow their individual spiritual paths; (ii) free to hold those beliefs without fear of retribution; and (iii) allowed to engage freely in spiritual practices, assuming that those beliefs are beneficial to both individuals and society.

Third, a healthy, well-functioning society — along with a healthy, well-functioning individual — is one in which citizens' contributions are based on their personal strengths. To receive the benefits of this, society needs to provide opportunities for citizens to (i) discover their strengths; (ii) develop and train those strengths; and (iii) apply such strengths effectively.

Happy people contribute much to society — to both the social fabric of society and its effective functioning — and they are less of a drain on its resources. It is therefore in the interests of countries and communities to examine the research on what facilitates happiness and to provide a context in which these factors can develop. Not only will individual citizens be healthy, happier, and more productive, but so will the community and the world as a whole.

References

1. Burns, GW (ed.) (2010). *Happiness, Healing, Enhancement: Your Casebook Collection for Using Positive Psychotherapy.* Hoboken, NJ: John Wiley & Sons.
2. Diener, E and M Seligman (2002). Very happy people. *Psychological Science*, 13, 81–84.
3. Reis, HT and SL Gable (2003). Toward a positive psychology of relationships. In *Flourishing: Positive Psychology and the Life Well-Lived*, CLM Keyes and J Haidt (eds.), Washington, DC: American Psychological Association, pp. 129–159.
4. Meyers, D (2000). The funds, friends, and faith of happy people. *American Psychologist*, 55, 56–57.
5. Burns, GW and H Street (2003). *Standing without Shoes: Creating Happiness, Relieving Depression, Enhancing Life.* Sydney: Prentice Hall.

6. Linley, PA and GW Burns (2010). Strengthspotting: finding and developing client resources in the management of intense anger. In *Happiness, Healing, Enhancement: Your Casebook Collection for Using Positive Psychotherapy*, GW Burns (ed.), Hoboken, NJ: John Wiley & Sons, pp. 3–14.

7. Seligman, MEP, T Rashid and AC Parks (2007). Positive psychotherapy. *American Psychologist*, 61, 774–788.

36

Time for a Bold Vision: A New, Green Economy

Van Jones

Editor's Note:

This chapter has been excerpted from the author's recent book Rebuild the Dream (Nation Books, 2012) and edited for Solutions.

Many politicians want us to lower our expectations about the economy. I say it is time to raise them. We should go beyond the shriveled thinking imposed on us by today's mania for austerity. Even the Contract for the American Dream — 10 steps for fixing the economy, selected from over 25,000 ideas submitted online by both experts and everyday Americans — should be seen as just a springboard — and not a ceiling — for what Americans might dare to dream and do together.

The time has come to propose solutions at the scale of the problems we face. Here I offer my own thoughts on one way we might do this. We must revive the economy, but in a way that respects people and the planet. After all, the last version of America's economy — the version that collapsed in 2008 — was built up on three fundamental fallacies:

1. First of all, *the failed economy was based on consumption rather than production.*
2. Second, *the failed economy was based on credit rather than on smart savings and thrift,* which our grandparents believed in.
3. Third, *the failed economy was based on ecological destruction rather than on ecological restoration.*

All three of these fallacies contributed to the mess we are in today. To heal our finances and fix the flaws in our last economic model, we must bring our monetary world into alignment with a deeper wisdom.

Three principles of the next American economy

The next American economy must be the reverse of the economy that let us down:

1. It must be driven by local production rather than by global consumption.
2. It must be based on thrift and conservation rather than on credit and waste.
3. It must be grounded in ecological restoration rather than in environmental destruction.

If we honor all of these principles together — local production, thrift, conservation, and ecological restoration — the next US economy will be more productive, more stable, and more sustainable. That is the very definition of a green economy.

And just as we have no choice but to change course economically, we have no choice but to change course ecologically. Since I wrote my last book, *The Green Collar Economy,*[1] things have mostly gotten worse — in many cases, much worse. Our children face a future without sufficient resources to live on, given our levels of consumption, waste, and pollution — especially greenhouse gas pollution.

Catastrophic climate change, driven by human activity, is still the biggest threat to human societies, not to mention innumerable other species. The Intergovernmental Panel on Climate Change (IPCC) in late 2011 released its most recent assessment of the unmistakable cause–effect relationship between CO_2 emissions and extreme weather. As I write these words, our planet has reached 390.31 ppm atmospheric carbon in the atmosphere. That figure is well above the 350 mark that experts agree is safe.

CO_2-driven climate change is a serious threat. It is killing our oceans. In June 2011, the International Programme on the State of the Ocean (IPSO) warned that we are on the brink of the greatest extinction of marine species ever seen, unprecedented in known history. A lot of the CO_2 gets sucked into the oceans, and as a result, the seas are acidifying 10 times faster than 55 million years ago, when a previous mass extinction of marine species occurred.

Mass extinction affects the land as well, and not just because of climate change. According to the World Resources Institute (WRI), for every hour that passes, four species (animals and plants) go extinct, and more than 4500 acres of trees are lost. The International Union for Conservation of Nature's (IUCN) most recent Red List of threatened species[2] shows that 21% of all known mammals, 30% of amphibians, 12% of birds, 28% of reptiles, 37% of freshwater fishes, 70% of plants, and 35% of invertebrates are under threat of extinction.

The new economics foundation (nef), based in London, calculates how much of the earth's resources and ecosystem services humans use each year (we use natural resources to do everything from building cities and roads to providing food, creating products, and absorbing CO_2) and then compares that to how much the earth can make, or replenish, in that year. The nef calculates that we used 1.3 to 1.5 planet's worth of resources in 2011. In other words, humans used at least 130% of the resources that the earth can generate in a year. For the rest of the year, we accumulated debt by

Even with modest United Nations projections for population growth, consumption, and climate change, by 2030, humanity will need the capacity of two planets. Last time I checked, we had only one.

depleting our natural capital and letting waste accumulate. The nef estimates that even with modest United Nations projections for population growth, consumption, and climate change, by 2030, humanity will need the capacity of two planets. Last time I checked, we had only one.

Today we find only about one barrel's worth of oil for every four barrels the planet consumes. Back in 1993, the Worldwatch Institute warned us that:

> At some point, the economic costs of deteriorating forests, dying lakes, damaged crops, respiratory illnesses, increasing temperatures, rising sea levels, and other destructive effects of fossil fuel use become unacceptably high. Basic economics argues for a switch to solar energy. Rather than wondering if we can afford to respond to these threats, policymakers should consider the costs of not responding.[3]

The message is clear: we need to move on from burning carbon-based fuel. There is a reason we call them fossil fuels: because they are dead. They are made of material that has been without life for eons. In the case of petroleum, it is material that has been dead for 60 million years; in the case of coal, for 300 million years. Right now, the United States powers itself by burning dead stuff it pulls out of the ground. Any shaman will tell you that a society that powers itself with death should not then be surprised to find death everywhere — in its children's lungs in the form of asthma, in its oceans in the form of oil spills, and coming from the skies in the form of climate change. It is time to evolve. It is time to power civilization with living energy from the sun, the wind, our crops, our labor, and our own creativity.

Alternative to suicide: green and clean economy

Fortunately, there is an alternative to this suicidal gray economy that is killing jobs and the planet. A cleaner, greener economy has the potential to increase the work, wealth, and health of ordinary Americans in a way that respects the earth. The cornerstone of the new economy must be clean technologies and manufacturing, especially in the energy sector.

For too long we have acted as if we had to choose between strong economic performance and strong environmental performance. We have been torn between our children's need for a robust economy today and our grandchildren's need for a healthy planet tomorrow. We have been trapped in the "jobs versus environment" dilemma.

The time has come to create "jobs *for* the environment." We seem to forget that everything that is good for the environment is a job. Solar panels do not put themselves up. Wind turbines do not manufacture themselves. Houses do not retrofit themselves and put in their own new boilers and furnaces and better-fitting windows and doors. Advanced biofuel crops do not plant themselves. Community gardens do not tend themselves. Farmers' markets do not run themselves. Every single thing that is good for the environment is actually a job, a contract, or an entrepreneurial opportunity.

We have our own "Saudi Arabia" of clean, renewable energy in America. In the plains states, off our coasts, and in the Great Lakes area, we have abundant wind energy. With American-made wind turbines and wind farms, we could tap those wind resources and create jobs doing it. We also have abundant solar resources — not just in the Sunbelt and in our deserts, but on rooftops across America. With American-made solar panels and solar farms, we could tap the energy of the sun to create electricity. Then we could build a national smart grid — an Internet for energy — to connect our clean-energy power centers to our population centers. That would create jobs and let us begin to run America increasingly on safe, homegrown energy.

When we do this, we will not be starting from scratch. According to the Brookings Institution, the United States already has 2.4 million green jobs. A national commitment to building a green economy can create many millions more.

The new, improved "red scare" is green ... but just as bogus

Some on the Far Right reject this agenda, saying, "But we don't want the government getting involved in our energy system." That is similar to saying, "Get your government hands off my Medicare!" Just as Medicare is already a government program, the public sector is already

deeply involved with the energy system — through regulation, subsidies, and taxation — in every country in the world. What needs to
change is this: the world's governments need to stop partnering with the
problem makers in our energy sector — the big carbon polluters — and
do a better job of partnering with the problem solvers — the pioneers of
renewable energy.

Funding the transition to America's next economy

The transition to a cleaner, greener economy will be neither cheap nor
easy. One way to handle the expense is to make sure that greenhouse gas
polluters pay some of the tab for the transition. In this scenario, the United
States just needs to follow a simple principle: nobody in America should
be allowed to pollute for free. Nobody. Not a strolling citizen who might
be tempted to litter; not a small-business person who might want to ille-
gally dump her trash; and not the biggest polluters on earth, who belch
megatons of greenhouse gases into our atmosphere and do not pay a cent
for the privilege.

Carbon tax or carbon trading

Society can put a price on carbon pollution in one of two ways: through
a tax on carbon or with a cap-and-trade system. With the tax approach,
the government would determine the extra price to place on carbon.
It then would let the market sort out the amount of carbon that industry
ultimately produces. With emissions trading, the government would
determine the allowable amount of carbon pollution. It then would let
the market figure out the price. These two ideas are basically flip sides
of the same solution, with the government playing the opposite role in
each. The money generated could go toward supporting the transition.

   This is not pie in the sky; in the first and only mandatory carbon emissions trading scheme in America, it is already working brilliantly. A new
report, *The Economic Impacts of the Regional Greenhouse Gas Initiative
on Ten Northeast and Mid-Atlantic States*, quantifies the economic benefits from the implementation of a 10-state Regional Greenhouse Gas
Initiative (RGGI).[4]

To quote the report, key findings include the following:

- The regional economy gains more than US$1.6 billion in economic value added (reflecting the difference between total revenues in the overall economy, less the cost to produce goods and services).
- Customers save nearly US$1.1 billion on electricity bills, and an additional US$174 million on natural gas and heating oil bills, for a total of US$1.3 billion in savings over the next decade through installation of energy efficiency measures using funding from RGGI auction proceeds to date.
- 16,000 jobs are created region wide.
- Reduced demand for fossil fuels keeps more than US$765 million in the local economy.
- Power plant owners experience US$1.6 billion in lower revenue over time, although, overall, they had higher revenues than costs as a result of RGGI during the 2009–2011 period.

Massachusetts benefited most, creating 3800 jobs and nearly US$500 million in economic activity between 2008 and 2011, because it used the bulk of its money to help fund its aggressive energy-efficiency agenda. A similar program at a national scale would enable hundreds of thousands of Americans to go to work, would create or grow hundreds of private firms, and would put the United States in a position to compete with China (which is now eating our lunch using our technology).

Other policies to jump-start the green economy

If Republicans and Blue Dog Democrats continue to oppose cap and trade, there are other ways to stimulate green growth. The federal government could simply mandate that our utilities buy more clean energy; this policy — called a Renewable Energy Standard — would create an instant market for entrepreneurial purveyors of advanced batteries, smart-grid technologies, and clean energy. Alternatively, the Environmental Protection Agency (EPA) could directly regulate carbon polluters under the Clean Air Act, as the Supreme Court says is lawful; Democrats would have to maintain a filibuster to keep the Clean Air Act from immediately being amended. If the EPA were to exercise this authority, clean-energy entrepreneurs would have a guaranteed market.

There is no rational reason that any of these solutions could not be implemented on a bipartisan basis. As it is, too many of our clean and green industries are teetering on the brink. The Chinese government is pumping money into its solar companies to flood the world market with cheap solar panels; once it achieves a monopoly, it will jack the prices back up. Meanwhile, the US government will not even commit to maintain the modest subsides it has made available to domestic clean-energy producers. At a time when we need jobs, our government is throwing away the industries of tomorrow.

It is important to remember that the green sector of America's economy — often associated with expensive ecoproducts such as home solar systems, organic food, and hybrid cars — is no longer just for affluent people who are willing to spend more money. It is also for middle-class, working-class, and low-income people who want to earn more money and save more money.

With the right policies, we can help rebuild the middle class; fight pollution *and* poverty; beat global warming *and* the global recession; and create an inclusive, green economy.

Final thoughts

We must reject the idea that people who love America and who respect the free market are just supposed to sit back and give the country over to the global corporations. We cannot accept the idea that the American people can do nothing but suffer until eventually an international company decides that

> *We must support the idea that there is something very American about Americans working together with America's government to solve America's problems.*

it wants to create a job somewhere — and then hope that "somewhere" is in America. We need Uncle Sam to do more than just cross his fingers and wait for the global market to magically fix everything for us. We must support the idea that there is something very American about Americans working together with America's government to solve America's problems.

People who actually love the country — and who understand something about economics besides a slogan — need to speak out. Having a blind religious faith in markets has nothing to do with the kind of economic thinking and investment strategy that built America's middle class. That is the kind of thinking that is actually destroying the middle class in the United States and killing the American Dream.

References

1. Jones, V (2008). *The Green Collar Economy: How One Solution Can Fix Our Two Biggest Problems*. New York: HarperOne.
2. IUCN (2008). The IUCN Red list [online]. Available at www.iucn.org/about/work/programmes/species/our_work/the_iucn_red_list [accessed on 8 August 2013].
3. Brown, LR *et al.* (1993). *State of the World 1993*. Gland, Switzerland: Worldwatch Institute.
4. Hibbard, PJ, SF Tierney, AM Okie and PG Darling (2011). The *Economic Impacts of the Regional Greenhouse Gas Initiative on Ten Northeast and Mid-Atlantic States*. Boston: Analysis Group.

37

A World That Works for All

L. Hunter Lovins

The global economy rests on a knife's edge. The financial crash of 2008 caused US$50 trillion and 80 million jobs to evaporate.[1] And the wreck is not over. This chapter describes the major challenges facing the economy and proposes solutions.

The challenges

The International Labor Organization sets forth the following grim statistics[2]:

- Studies of 69 of 118 countries with available data show an increase in the percentage of people reporting worsening living standards in 2010 compared to 2006.
- People in half of 99 countries surveyed say they have little confidence in their national governments.
- In 2010, more than 50% of people in developed countries lacked decent jobs (in Greece, Italy, Portugal, Slovenia, and Spain, it is more than 70%).·
- The share of profit in gross domestic product (GDP) increased in 83% of countries studied between 2000 and 2009, but productive investment stagnated globally during the same period.

- Growth in corporate profits increased dividend payouts (from 29% of profits in 2000 to 36% in 2009) and financial investment (from 81.2% of GDP in 1995 to 132.2% in 2007). Bankers regained their bonuses, but workers face falling wages.
- Food price volatility doubled from 2006 through 2010 compared to the prior five years. Financial investors benefit from this; food producers do not. Remember, it was a food riot that touched off the Arab Spring in Tunisia.

Nobel Laureate economist Joseph Stiglitz observed, "Unless we have a better understanding of the causes of the crisis, we can't implement an effective recovery strategy. And, so far, we have neither." His diagnosis: ideological driven release of the financial sector from the regulations that had prevented collapse since the 1930s, bubble-fueled consumption, and growing inequality. His prescription: promote energy conservation, reduce inequality, reform the global financial system to drive productive investment instead of a buildup of cash, and strong government expenditures to aid restructuring.[3]

Despite warnings that the economy faces continuing peril,[4] governments are doing none of this. Fixated on austerity (read: ensuring profits for bankers, rather than investing in real prosperity in communities), governments threaten their citizens' quality of life not only in the euro-zone countries facing difficulties — Portugal, Ireland, Italy, Greece and Spain — but across the globe. Despite the Millennium Development Goals, developing nations struggle to lift from poverty the half the world's population that lives on less than US$2 a day. But the situation is worsening: millions of drought-driven refugees in the Horn of Africa join people threatened by too much or too little glacial meltwater and monsoon floods from the Himalayas to Colombia.[5] It is clear that climate change will hit the most vulnerable hardest.[6,7] Yet, these poorest three billion emit only 7% of global emissions. The richest 7% (about half a billion people) spew out 50%.[8] The primary crises the globe faces are created by an economy geared to overconsumption in the North.

The global dependence on fossil fuels that drives the climate crisis, in turn, endangers the economy. Six months before the financial collapse, oil prices rose to US$150 a barrel. When gasoline in the United States exceeded US$5 a gallon (far below prices in Europe), American workers chose to drive to work instead of paying their mortgages; the housing market collapsed and the September 2008 financial collapse ensued.[9]

Between 2005 and 2010, Exxon, Chevron, Shell, and BP reduced their US workforces by 11,200 workers[10] but pocketed US$4 billion a year in tax subsidies. Globally, subsidies to the fossil-fuel industry top US$550 billion every year,[11,12] at least 12 times any subsidies given to energy efficiency and renewable energy.[13] In 2011, Exxon made US$5 million in profit every hour, or more than US$41 billion, but paid lower taxes than the average American.[10] In 2012, as oil prices hit US$120 a barrel, oil companies made an additional US$5 billion from American workers.[14] Prices could reach as high as US$250 a barrel if Iran blockades the Strait of Hormuz.[15]

In 2010, the third edition of *Global Biodiversity Outlook*,[16] building on the 2005 Millennium Ecosystem Assessment,[17] warned that climate change and other assaults are tipping three of the earth's major ecosystems into collapse: By the end of this century, if we proceed with business as usual, there will be no living coral reefs on the planet. The Amazon now releases more carbon than it soaks up. The acidifying oceans risk ending life as we know it.[16]

These "drivers of change" mean that something is going to give.

> *Something is going to give.*

The solutions

Solutions to these challenges will come from a combination of international leadership, good policy at the national level, action by states and provinces, a suite of market-based measures, and a growing commitment by individuals to create the future we want.

International leadership is represented by Bhutan's courageous commitment to measure its national accounts with the metric of gross national happiness.[18,19] Asking what we want more of rather than counting only gross national product — the flow of money and stuff through the economy — grew from the work of Herman Daly in the 1970s on the Index of Sustainable Economic Welfare. In 1995, Clifford Cobb, Ted Halstead, and Jonathan Rowe proposed the Genuine Progress Indicator

(GPI), taking Daly and Cobb's work further to value volunteer work, cost of crime and family breakdown, the cost of underemployment, ozone depletion, and the loss of old growth forests. They calculated the GPI from 1950 comparing it to the GDP, finding that we are not even breaking even. This same finding by the Chinese green GDP project resulted in its being consigned to an academic exercise, but it now appears to be re-emerging.[20]

More recently, the recognition that GDP is a wholly insufficient metric became the basis of the French Commission on the Measurement of Economic Performance and Social Progress,[21] the Chinese Green GDP,[22] the United Kingdom's Happy Planet Index,[23,24] the GPI, and an array of "circular economy" applications. Introduced in the 1970s by Walter Stahel,[25] the concept of the circular economy became the basis of Chinese development policy in 2008.[26,27] A new report describes how it would net the European manufacturing sector US$630 billion by 2025.[28] These initiatives, as well as the 40th anniversary update to *Limits to Growth*[29] and the new report *Beyond GDP*,[30] challenge the myth that growth is necessary for prosperity.[31,32]

National policies like Germany's feed-in tariff (FiT) have unleashed that country's renewable energy industry, underpinning German prosperity. In their first four years, FiTs created 300,000 new jobs and cut the unit cost of solar panels enough to reach grid parity (costing the same as grid electricity) by 2013.[33] The program added only two to three euros per month to electricity bills, roughly US$50 per customer annually, for a total of €8.6 billion. Deutsche Bank found that far from costing the economy, the savings outstripped the total cost of payments made by households. Had customers bought electricity from conventional coal generation, they would have paid an additional €9.4 billion.[34] If the United States implemented a similar program, it would create 2.5 million jobs.[35]

The green economy is emerging best, however, at the local level, as people realize that they must build their own plan for resilience in the face of an unaccountable global economy.[36] The failure of global leadership to agree to climate protection at Copenhagen, Cancún, and Durban has spurred cities to implement sustainable practices. Denmark's Samso Island is 100% renewably powered.[37] The German town Wildpoldsried is as well, producing 321% more energy than it uses and selling the excess for US$5.7 million each year.[38] Over half of Germany's renewables are owned not by utilities but by farmers and citizens.[39] San Francisco is on track to be 100% renewable by 2020, Scotland by 2020, Germany by 2050. This is good news, as already half of the world's people live in cities, and three-quarters will by 2050. Projections warn that in the next decade or so, China will seek to move into cities yet unbuilt more people than there are in the United States. Just the copper wire this would require is more than current world copper production.[40] In the business as usual scenario, by 2030 China will want more oil than the world now produces.[41]

Tools like Natural Capitalism Solutions' LASER (Local Action for Sustainable Economic Development)[42] have helped communities from Kazakhstan, to South Africa, to New Zealand, to Newburg, New York, implement renewable energy and a whole array of measures to build stronger locally based economies. Cities are developing locally appropriate sustainability indicators to enable them to judge whether they are gaining or losing, and they are adjusting policies to deliver greater well-being.[43]

Agricultural approaches like Allan Savory's holistic management (which takes carbon from the air and returns it to the soil while increasing grazing output) and organic farming (which the UN Food and Agriculture Organization now admits will do a better job of feeding the world's people) are coming to be recognized as superior to industrial agriculture.[44]

At the same time, companies are implementing more sustainable practices. When Walmart asked its global supply chain of 60,000–90,000 companies to measure its carbon footprint and report it to the Carbon Disclosure Project,[45] the attention drove sustainability into even very small companies. More than 27 studies from the likes of the wild-eyed environmentalists at Goldman Sachs[46] show that the companies that are the leaders in environmental, social, and good governance policies have a 25% higher stock value and the fastest-growing stock value; they also deliver superior financials and are better investment risks. Companies like Puma, Novo Nordisk, Baxter, and many others are counting the costs and risks of unsustainability in their financial reports. They have found that behaving more responsibly enhances core business value.

This Natural Capitalist[47] approach is taking hold in companies in three ways. First, companies are eliminating waste and implementing more efficient use of resources. This drives profitability and buys time to solve climate change, resource constraints, and other challenges.[48] Second, companies are redesigning how we make and deliver everything using sustainable approaches such as biomimicry,[49] and leading companies are also profitably implementing cradle-to-cradle design.[25,28,50] The third principle — that we manage all institutions to be restorative of human and natural capital, the forms of capital that underpin all life and thus the economy — is being embedded in innovative business schools. It is becoming the management philosophy of a whole new generation of business people.[51–53]

The world has reached, in the words of Canadian activist and author Naomi Klein, "a no kidding moment."[54] The Arab Spring and the global phenomenon of Occupy Wall Street are challenging dictatorial regimes and the dominant economic paradigm, delegitimizing many aspects of the old order.[55] The new economic model of co-op capitalism[56] arising in these movements values community, networks, and collaboration over competition and acquisition. From occupiers who are helping foreclosed homeowners reclaim their houses, to Spain's *indignados*, to the embattled activists in Syria, to farmers in Japan challenging the nuclear industry, to the villagers in Wukan voting out corrupt officials, the global conversation has entered a new phase. People are realizing that the powerful interests that ruled the last century will not solve their problems. They are retaking control over their own lives.

For this global populist movement to make a difference, it will have to do more than protest. As it installs new governments, it must craft policies to relieve debt and encourage productive investment. Globally we need to enable countries like Greece and the whole of the developing world to escape the crushing debt that stifles efforts to build prosperity. Locally, it would be far better to pay people who are at risk of defaulting on their mortgages, enabling them to pay the banks and stay in their homes, than to bail out the banks, which are only hoarding their newfound cash.

The world needs to recognize that there is a difference between debt-fueled consumption and borrowing to invest in productive assets for the future. Economic policies and obsolete subsidies that reinforce inequality and constrain the transition to a green economy must be swept away.[57]

> *Economic policies and obsolete subsidies that reinforce inequality and constrain the transition to a green economy must be swept away.*

At present, we tax what we want: income and employment. And we subsidize what we do not: pollution and depletion of resources. This must be reversed. As Al Gore and David Blood wrote in their *Manifesto for Sustainable Capitalism*,[58] corporations must migrate away from short-term fixation on quarterly profits and share price.

Al Gore talked about it, Unilever CEO Paul Polman is doing it. He refused to issue quarterly reports just to fuel Wall Street's appetite for volatility. The company's share price fell 8%. His answer: good, that's not the sort of investor I want. His plan: double sales and halve the environmental impact of Unilever's products over the next 10 years, improve the nutritional quality of its food products, and link half a million smallholder farmers and small-scale distributors in developing countries to its supply chain. Polman states, "The Occupy Wall Street movement sends out a very clear signal. If you look out ive or 10 years … consumers will not give us a sense of legitimacy if they believe the system is unfair or unjust. Companies that miss the standards of acceptable behaviour to consumers will be selected out."[59] This is the sort of leadership to which all companies should aspire.

It is important, however, to recognize what markets are good at and for, and what government is better at. Market mechanisms are extremely powerful. Approaches like cap and trade work, drive environmental protection, *and* enhance profitability. But in the end, markets only allocate scarce resources efficiently in the short term. Adam Smith, the father of markets, was very clear that this is all they were ever intended to do. They were never created to protect grandchildren. This is the job of a free people coming together in a democracy and asking, as Rio+20 is now doing, what is the future we want?[60] This is why humans created governments and it is what we should insist that they attend to.

Smith carefully distinguished between economic activity that enables nations to afford military forces to protect their boundaries and the broader suite of activities that bring happiness to individuals. A moral philosopher, Smith rejected the notion that greed was good, stating in *The Theory of Moral Sentiments* (the book he was writing when he died), "that to feel much for others, and little for ourselves, that to restrain our selfish, and to indulge our benevolent affections constitutes the perfection of human nature; and can alone produce among mankind that harmony of sentiments and passions in which consists their whole grace and propriety." Smith continued: "The chief part of happiness arises from the consciousness of being beloved."[61]

Which returns the conversation to the concept of gross national happiness. On 18 March 1968, Robert Kennedy put it elegantly:

> Too much and for too long, we seemed to have surrendered personal excellence and community values in the mere accumulation of material things. ... The gross national product counts air pollution and cigarette advertising, and ambulances to clear our highways of carnage. It counts special locks for our doors and the jails for the people who break them. It counts the destruction of the redwood and the loss of our natural wonder in chaotic sprawl. ... Yet the gross national product does not allow for the health of our children, the quality of their education or the joy of their play. It does not include the beauty of our poetry or the strength of our marriages, the intelligence of our public debate or the integrity of our public officials. It measures neither our wit nor our courage, neither our wisdom nor our learning, neither our compassion nor our devotion to our country, it measures everything in short, except that which makes life worthwhile.[62]

It is time for the world to reject the life-destroying economics of GDP and commit to achieving ever greater gross national happiness.

References

1. Lee-Brago, P (2011). ILO: recession, massive job loss threaten global economy. *Philippine Star* [online]. Available at www.philstar.com/Article.aspx?articleId=743718&publicationSubCategoryId= [accessed on 8 August 2013].
2. Third World Network (2011). ILO says world heading for a new and deeper jobs recession, warns of more social unrest [online]. Available at www.twnside.org.sg/title2/resurgence/2011/254/econ2.htm [accessed on 8 August 2013].
3. Stiglitz, J (2011). To cure the economy. *Project Syndicate* [online]. Available at www.project-syndicate.org/commentary/stiglitz143/English [accessed on 8 August 2013].

4. Roubini, N (2011). Is capitalism doomed? *Al Jazeera* [online]. Available at http://english.aljazeera.net/indepth/opinion/2011/08/201181610494541 1574.html [accessed on 8 August 2013].

5. Spotts, PN (2006). Little time to avoid big thaw, scientists warn. *Christian Science Monitor* [online]. Available at www.csmonitor.com/2006/0324/ p01s03-sten.html [accessed on 8 August 2013].

6. Oxfam International (2009). 54% increase in number of people affected by climate disasters by 2015 could overwhelm emergency responses [online]. Available at www.oxfam.org/en/pressroom/pressrelease/200-04–21/increase-number-people-affected-climate-disasters [accessed on 8 August 2013].

7. Millions of African climate refugees desperate for food, water (2011). *AlterNet* [online]. Available at www.alternet.org/food/151578/millions_of_african_ climate_refugees_desperate_for_food, water [accessed on 8 August 2013].

8. Angus, I and S Butler (2011). *Too Many People*. Chicago: Haymarket Books.

9. Location, location, location efficiency: Can smart growth help beat the mortgage crisis? (2010). *Natural Resources Defense Council* [online]. Available at www.nrdc.org/media/2010/100127.asp [accessed on 8 August 2013].

10. Leber, R (2012). ExxonMobil made $41.1 billion in 2011, but pays estimated 17.6 percent tax rate. *ThinkProgress* [online]. Available at http:// thinkprogress.org/green/2012/01/31/415242/exxonmobil-made-411-billion-in-2011-but-pays-estimated-176-percent-tax-rate [accessed on 8 August 2013].

11. Energy subsidies: getting the prices right (2010). *International Energy Agency* [online]. Available at www.iea.org/files/energy_subsidies.pdf [accessed on 8 August 2013].

12. Harvey, F (2011). We're headed for irreversible climate change in five years, IEA warns. *Guardian* [online]. Available at www.guardian.co.uk/environment/ 2011/nov/09/fossil-fuel-infrastructure-climate-change?newsfeed=true [accessed on 8 August 2013].

13. Morales, A (2010). Fossil fuel subsidies are 12 times support for renewables, study shows. *Bloomberg* [online]. Available at www.bloomberg.com/news/ 2010-07-29/fossil-fuel-subsidies-are-12-times-support-for-renewables-study-shows.html [accessed on 8 August 2013].

14. Johnson, B (2012). Gas spike takes $5 billion from the 99 percent and gives it to big oil. *ThinkProgress* [online]. Available at http://thinkprogress.org/

green/2012/02/29/434623/gas-spike-takes-5-billion-from-the-99-percent-and-gives-it-to-big-oil [accessed on 8 August 2013].

15. Vanderbruck, T (2012). Iran, oil and Strait of Hormuz. *Oil-Price.net* [online]. Available at http://oil-price.net/en/articles/iran-oil-strait-or-hormuz.php [accessed on 8 August 2013].

16. Convention on Biological Diversity (2010). *Global Biodiversity Outlook 3* [online]. Available at www.cbd.int/gbo3 [accessed on 8 August 2013].

17. Millennium Ecosystem Assessment [online]. Available at www.maweb.org [accessed on 8 August 2013].

18. Wellbeing & Happiness: Defining a new economic paradigm [online]. Available at http://www.2apr.gov.bt [accessed on 8 August 2013].

19. Marks, N (2010). The happy planet index. TED [online]. Available at www.ted.com/talks/nic_marks_the_happy_planet_index.html [accessed on 8 August 2013].

20. Lelyveld, M (2012). China's "Green GDP" resurfaces. *Radio Free Asia* [online]. Available at www.rfa.org/english/energy_watch/greengdp-0213 2012120520.html [accessed on 8 August 2013].

21. Stiglitz, J, A Sen and J-P Fitoussi (2009). Report by the Commission on the Measurement of Economic Performance and Social Progress [online]. Available at www.stiglitz-sen-fitoussi.fr/documents/rapport_anglais.pdf [accessed on 8 August 2013].

22. Watts, J (2011). China's green economist stirring a shift away from GDP. *The Guardian*. Available at www.guardian.co.uk/environment/2011/sep/16/china-green-economist-gdp [accessed on 8 August 2013].

23. Happy Planet Index [online]. Available at www.happyplanetindex.org [accessed on 8 August 2013].

24. New Economics Foundation [online]. Available at www.neweconomics.org [accessed on 8 August 2013].

25. Product Life Institute [online]. Available at www.product-life.org [accessed on 8 August 2013].

26. Chinese leaders join lawmakers, political advisors in panel discussions. *Chinese Consulate in New York* [online] (2012). Available at http://newyork.china-consulate.org/eng/xw/t912428.htm [accessed on 8 August 2013].

27. Green GDP to be expanded nationally (2007). *China Daily* [online]. Available at www.chinadaily.com.cn/china/2007-01/18/content_786230.htm [accessed on 8 August 2013].

28. Ellen MacArthur Foundation (2012). *Towards the Circular Economy* [online]. Available at www.ellenmacarthurfoundation.org/about/circular-economy/towards-the-circular-economy [accessed on 8 August 2013].

29. Club of Rome and Smithsonian Institution (2012). Perspectives on *Limits to Growth*: challenges to building a sustainable planet [online]. Available at http://si.edu/Content/consortia/limits-to-growth.pdf [accessed on 8 August 2013].

30. Daly, L and S Posner (2012). *Beyond GDP* [online]. Available at www.demos.org/publication/beyond-gdp-new-measures-new-economy [accessed on 8 August 2013].

31. Beyond GDP initiative [online]. Available at www.beyond-gdp.eu [accessed on 8 August 2013].

32. AtKisson, A and J Edahiro (2012). *Life Beyond Growth* [online]. Available at http://lifebeyondgrowth.wordpress.com [accessed on 8 August 2013].

33. Roney, JM (2010). Solar cell production climbs to another record in 2009. *Renewable Energy World* [online]. Available at www.renewableenergyworld.com/rea/news/article/2010/09/solar-cell-production-climbs-to-another-record-in-2009 [accessed on 8 August 2013].

34. Paying for renewable energy: TLC at the right price — achieving scale through efficient policy design (2009). *Deutsche Bank* [online]. Available at www.dbcca.com/dbcca/EN/investment-research/investment_research_2144.jsp [accessed on 8 August 2013].

35. Bill Clinton interview (2011). *The Daily Show* [online]. Available at www.thedailyshow.com/watch/tue-november-8-2011/bill-clinton-pt--2 [accessed on 8 August 2013].

36. Transition Network [online]. Available at www.transitionnetwork.org [accessed on 8 August 2013].

37. Burund, M (2008). Living a green dream on Danish island. *PlanetArk* [online]. Available at www.planetark.org/dailynewsstory.cfm/newsid/49847/story.htm [accessed on 8 August 2013].

38. Allen, C (2011). German village achieves energy independence … and then some. *BioCycle* [online]. Available at www.jgpress.com/archives/_free/002409.html [accessed on 8 August 2013].

39. Wind-Works [online]. Available at www.wind-works.org/coopwind/CitizenPowerConferencetobeheldinHistoricChamber.html [accessed on 8 August 2013].

40. Hilderson, P (2012). *Global Sustainability Perspective*. Chicago and Rome Jones Lang LaSalle.

41. Brown, L (2006). China forcing world to rethink its economic future. *EcoEarth.Info* [online]. Available at www.ecoearth.info/shared/reader/ welcome.aspx?linkid=56248 [accessed on 8 August 2013].

42. LASER [online]. Available at www.global-laser.org [accessed on 8 August 2013].

43. Sustainable Measures [online]. Available at www.sustainablemeasures.com [accessed on 8 August 2013].

44. Scialabba, NE (2007). *Organic Agriculture and Food Security* [online]. Chicago and Rome UN Food and Agriculture Organization. Available at ftp:// ftp.fao.org/paia/organicag/ofs/OFS-2007-5.pdf [accessed on 8 August 2013].

45. Press release (2007). Walmart announces partnership with Carbon Disclosure Project to measure energy used to create products. Available at http:// walmartstores.com/pressroom/news/6739.aspx [accessed on 8 August 2013].

46. Sachs, G (2007). *GS Sustain* [online]. Available at www.natcapsolutions.org/ Presidio/Articles/Climate/GoldmanSachsReport_v2007.pdf [accessed on 8 August 2013].

47. Natural Capitalism Solutions [online]. Available at www.natcapsolutions.org [accessed on 8 August 2013].

48. World Business Council for Sustainable Development (WBCSD) [online]. Available at www.wbcsd.org/home.aspx [accessed on 8 August 2013].

49. Biomimicry Institute [online]. Available at http://biomimicryinstitute.org [accessed on 8 August 2013].

50. Interface [online]. Available at www.interfaceglobal.com [accessed on 8 August 2013].

51. Bainbridge Graduate Institute [online]. Available at www.bgi.edu [accessed on 8 August 2013].

52. Association for the Advancement of Sustainability in Higher Education [online]. Available at www.aashe.org/resources/sustainability-business management-programs [accessed on 8 August 2013].

53. Education Revolution [online]. Available at www.educationrevolution.org [accessed on 8 August 2013].

54. Occupy everywhere: Michael Moore, Naomi Klein on next steps for the movement against corporate power (2011). *Democracy Now!* [online]. Available at www.democracynow.org/2011/11/25/occupy_everywhere_michael_moore_ naomi_klein [accessed on 8 August 2013].

55. Stiglitz, J (2011). The global 99 percent. *Slate* [online]. Available at www. slate.com/articles/business/project_syndicate/2011/11/occupy_wall_street_ and_the_global_trend_against_inequality_.html [accessed on 8 August 2013].

56. Hertz, N (2011). *Co-op Capitalism: A New Economic Model from the Carnage of the Old* [online]. Manchester: Co-operatives UK. Available at www.uk.coop/coopcapitalism [accessed on 8 August 2013].

57. New Economics Foundation. A New Economic Model [online]. Available at www.neweconomics.org/projects/new-economic-model [accessed on 8 August 2013].

58. Gore, A and D Blood. *A Manifesto for Sustainable Capitalism* [online]. Available at www.generationim.com/media/pdf-wsj-manifesto-sustainable-capitalism-14-12-11.pdf [accessed on 8 August 2013].

59. Confine, J and P Polman (2012). The power is in the hands of the consumers. *The Guardian* [online]. Available at www.guardian.co.uk/sustainable-business/unilever-ceo-paul-polman-interview [accessed on 8 August 2013].

60. The Future We Want [online]. Available at http://futurewewant.org [accessed on 8 August 2013].

61. Smith, A (2000). *Theory of Moral Sentiments*. New York: Prometheus Books.

62. Kennedy, R (1968). Remarks at the University of Kansas [online]. Available at www.jfklibrary.org/Historical+Resources/Archives/Reference+Desk/ Speeches/RFK/RFKSpeech68Mar18UKansas.htm [accessed on 8 August 2013].

38

Fighting Poverty by Healing the Environment

Christine Loh

Ecological restoration — the rehabilitation of degraded landscapes — is a bright spark in the effort to achieve sustainable development. If given a chance, damaged ecosystems can recover rapidly. Research shows that forest ecosystems recovered in 42 years on average, while ocean bottoms recovered in less than 10 years. Ecosystems affected by either invasive species, mining, oil spills, or trawling recovered in as little as 5 years.[1] The following case studies from China and Rwanda demonstrate the potential of ecological restoration for environmental health, local poverty alleviation, and sustainable development.

Ecological restoration in practice: China and Rwanda

The Loess Plateau in northwest China is home to more than 50 million people. Centuries of uncontrolled grazing, deforestation, and subsistence farming caused widespread erosion and environmental degradation, and plunged the region into poverty. Moreover, the erosion of the plateau led to silting of the Yellow River. (The Yellow River basin is home to one in nine (over 130 million) Chinese people, and most depend, directly or indirectly, on the river for their livelihood.[2]) A study conducted by China's Ministry of Water Resources with the assistance of the World Bank in the early 1990s found that restoring ecological function on the plateau would

293

be less expensive than continuously dredging the river. It also found that on much of the land, the ecological functions, such as soil retention, were worth more than the profits from continuing to exploit what was already a much-degraded region.

This study led to the creation of the US$240 million, 10-year Loess Plateau Watershed Rehabilitation Project in 1995,[2] which set 35,000 km² of land aside for restoration and sustainable agriculture. The project created many thousands of jobs for the poor local inhabitants in terracing and building small dams and sediment traps to slow runoff. It also encouraged the regeneration of grasslands as well as the planting of trees and shrubs on previously cultivated slopes to reduce erosion.

The outcome provided many useful lessons. Sediment flow into the Yellow River was reduced by more than 53 million tons just during the life of the project. A network of small dams stores water for use by towns and farmers when rainfall is low, and reduces the risk of flooding. Replanting and bans on grazing increased the perennial vegetation cover from 17% to 34%. Local food supply increased. More than 2.5 million people were lifted out of poverty. Farmer incomes rose from about US$70 per year per person to about US$200.[3] In addition, the project produced substantial benefits downstream as a result of reduced sedimentation, and globally through carbon sequestration.[2]

The Loess Plateau's restoration helped to inspire the government of Rwanda to adopt its own restoration policy in February 2011. Rwanda is one of the world's poorest and most densely populated countries, where 85% of the population practices subsistence farming on degraded lands. Poor forest management and land-use conflict led to a rapid loss of the country's forest cover in the 1990s. Its new Forest Landscape Restoration Initiative aims to reverse degradation of soil, water, land, and forest resources by 2035, and to use ecosystem restoration as a way to create jobs.[4]

The momentum in Rwanda has manifested in ambitious plans to enlarge forest coverage, restore biodiversity, reduce the risk of flooding and drought, ensure food security, and reduce dependence on petroleum by developing alternative renewable energy sources. In an innovative partnership with the Smith School of Enterprise and Environment, with support from the Climate Development Knowledge Network (CDKN),

Rwanda's Cabinet approved the Rwanda national strategy for climate change and low carbon growth in December 2010.

As seeing is believing, soil scientist and filmmaker, John D. Liu, has recorded the progress of the Loess Plateau transformation over 15 years, and is currently documenting the Rwandan initiative.[5]

Restoration opportunities

According to the International Union for the Conservation of Nature (IUCN), there are approximately 1.5 billion hectares of land worldwide with potential for forest landscape restoration. Asia and Africa hold the greatest promise: each have about 500 million hectares available for restoration without impacting current agricultural activities.[4] Restoration also

> *There are approximately 1.5 billion hectares of land worldwide with potential for forest landscape restoration.*

offers opportunities for the most polluting industries to mitigate their ecological footprint.

Take the energy sector. With rising global population and urbanization, energy demand will inevitably increase. The International Energy Agency (IEA) estimates the world will need to invest US$38 trillion in energy-supply infrastructure to meet the projected demand to 2035.[6] However, the IEA acknowledges the window for limiting the global average temperature increase to 2°C is closing fast (Box 1).[6]

Ecological restoration can provide a way forward. Companies in the energy sector already have to restore the environment where they have caused damage by extracting resources, but they could do more: they could look to offset their carbon emissions through large-scale ecological restoration.

It is already accepted that stopping deforestation and forest degradation is vital to tackling climate change, as those activities contribute 15–17% of all greenhouse gases. It only takes a small stretch of the imagination to see ecological restoration in the same light. If the principle is accepted, then the next step is to find ways to fit projects like the Loess Plateau and Rwanda's effort into an overall mitigation framework, especially for the energy and mineral mining sectors.

Box 1. Urban Restoration

The concepts behind ecological restoration can also be applied to urban jungles. The need is great: already one-half of the world's population lives in cities and, by 2030, city-dwellers will make up 60% of the global population.[7] While cities cover only about 1% of the land on earth, they have an outsized ecological footprint.

Many of the urban areas that will exist in 2030 have not yet been built, and some of what exists today will be replaced. As we remake our cities (and build new ones), there are many sustainable development opportunities that should not be missed. For example, we must lower urban heat-island effect (the byproduct of our massive use of concrete and asphalt to create dark-colored rooftops and pavements) and reduce water use, since many cities have to import water from their surrounding regions, which carries a high cost both to consumers and the ecosystems that supply the water.

Projects in Los Angeles are transforming neighborhoods into sustainable ecosystems that function like natural forests, where residents plant and care for trees and incorporate forest-mimicking technologies into their urban landscape. In these neighborhoods, trees shade walkways, streets, buildings, and recreation areas to reduce energy and water use. Native and drought-tolerant plants and grasses reduce the need for irrigation. Permeable paving replaces hard asphalt surfaces and allows rainwater to soak into the ground, thus reducing flooding and runoff into waterways. Swales — human-made trenches planted with native vegetation — slow the flow of rainwater, and raised berms create sunken gardens that trap rainwater and let it seep into the ground. Rain barrels or cisterns store rainwater for use in dry seasons.[8]

The Elmer Avenue Neighborhood Retrofit Project is a good example. This small neighborhood in Los Angeles' San Fernando Valley used to suffer from flooding during the rainy season. Retrofitting the storm drains took the street off the city's water grid. Now, all the rainwater that falls on Elmer Avenue and some adjacent streets is captured in a large underground infiltration gallery and allowed to soak into the ground. This system mimics a natural watershed, directing water into underground aquifers, thereby increasing local water supply.[8]

Large-scale projects, like the examples above, require the right government policies and possibly international funding, as well as deep societal collaboration. The Loess Plateau Watershed Rehabilitation Project, for example, involved many layers of bureaucracy for design and implementation, and Rwanda's Forest Landscape Restoration Initiative is a collaboration between the Rwandan government, IUCN, the Secretariat of the UN Forum on Forests, and many others. But the payoffs for these efforts can be substantial: For example, the IUCN estimates that restoring 150 million hectares of lost forests and degraded lands worldwide — the goal set forth by the Bonn Challenge Ministerial Roundtable in September 2011 — would be worth US$85 billion per year to national and global economies. We can hope that, with examples like the Loess Plateau and Rwanda to guide us, other nations will see that being good to the environment can be good for people as well.

References

1. Jones, HP and OJ Schmitz (2009). Rapid recovery of damaged ecosystems. *PLoS ONE*, 4(5), e5653. doi:10.1371/journal.pone.0005653.
2. Available at http://web.worldbank.org/WBSITE/EXTERNAL/EXTOED/EXT WBASSHEANUTPOP/0,,contentMDK:21601420~menuPK:6080533~pageP K:64829573~piPK:64829550~theSitePK:4422776~isCURL:Y,00.html World Bank (2007). Project Performance Assessment Report.
3. World Bank (2007). Restmoring China's Loess Plateau [online]. Available at www.worldbank.org/en/news/2007/03/15/restoring-chinas-loess-plateau [accessed on 8 August 2013].
4. IUCN (2011). Rwanda: Restoring nature for future prosperity [online]. Available at www.iucn.org/?6875/Rwanda--restoring-nature-for-future-prosperity [accessed on 8 August 2013].
5. Environmental Education Media Project. John D. Liu [online]. Available at www.eempc.org/john-d-liu [accessed on 8 August 2013].
6. IEA World Energy Outlook 2011. Executive summary [online]. Available at www.worldenergyoutlook.org/docs/weo2011/executive_summary.pdf [accessed on 8 August 2013].

7. UN Habitat 2010–2011. State of the World's Cities Report: Bridging the Urban Divide [online]. Available at www.unhabitat.org/content.asp?cid=8051&catid=7&typeid=46 [accessed on 8 August 2013].

8. TreePeople [online]. Available at www.treepeople.org/sun-valley-watershed. [accessed on 8 August 2013].

39

Re-Engineering the Planet: Three Steps to a Sustainable Free-Market Economy

Eckart Wintzen

Editor's Note:

This chapter, written by the environmental entrepreneur Eckart Wintzen (1939–2008) on 19 April 2000, has been edited for Solutions. The green venture capital company Ex'tent, founded by Wintzen, researches and promotes the ideas described in this chapter through the Ex'tax Project (www. ex-tax.com).

A cynic is a man who knows the price of everything and the value of nothing.

Oscar Wilde

Simply put, there are currently two pressing problems in the developed and in the developing worlds: unemployment and the depletion of the planet's resources. In my opinion, Western fiscal systems are the fundamental cause of both.

Our culture has devised systems of taxation in which the vast majority of government income from business (80%) is personnel related, while raw materials are rarely taxed, if at all.

In other words, the more people you employ, the more tax you pay. Companies therefore have a strong tendency to optimize their operations by reducing personnel to a minimum, even if this means using more energy and raw materials. The reason that our systems have been organized in this way is that, in the past, our rate of consumption has been marginal compared to our stockpile of natural resources. But as our population and technological sophistication have increased, our consumption patterns have skyrocketed. We are only just now beginning to glimpse the consequences of our profligacy.

Since the fiscal system is the source of these problems, the obvious solution is to change the fiscal system. I therefore propose reversing the current tax structure by levying a tax on raw materials while at the same time reducing labor-related taxes. In other words, the more raw materials you use, the more tax you pay. Under this system, companies will be encouraged to optimize their operations by manufacturing fewer or more durable products (thereby consuming fewer raw materials) and enhancing their software or service orientation (thereby requiring more personnel). Increased employment will be a direct side effect of this approach, and the end result will be a truly service-oriented economy in which businesses distinguish themselves by the degree of net value added to their products or services.

The planet's natural resources are our collective inheritance, and we should be striving to live off of the planet's interest, not recklessly squandering its capital. We must therefore learn to effectively manage the environment just as we would any other business. But as no business can be successfully run without precise

> *The planet's natural resources are our collective inheritance, and we should be striving to live off of the planet's interest, not recklessly squandering its capital.*

accounting practices, environmental resources cannot be sustained without accurate ecological bookkeeping. If consistently and broadly applied, ecological bookkeeping combined with proper taxation can, within a few decades, generate the new market mechanisms necessary for sustainable growth, a growth that ensures freedom of entrepreneurship without depleting the planet's resources.

Ecological bookkeeping

To effect this change, I propose a three-step plan. The first step is to make ecological bookkeeping mandatory for all companies in the developed world within, say, five years. The ecological bookkeeping I propose is based on the concept of *extracted value*, or the burden a product places on the ecosystem throughout its life cycle. This burden is expressed in financial terms based on the theoretical costs of either devising a sustainable alternative or reversing the environmental damage caused by a product to a level at which the natural ecosystem is able to diminish the residual effects.

Though the concept of extracted value is relatively new, I can envision a time not so very far in the future when the extracted value (with and without recycling) of a product, whether it be a can of beans or an automobile, will be listed on the packaging, right next to the number of calories or the miles per gallon. For ecological bookkeeping to be successful, we must devise an accounting system that can accurately translate the extracted value of a product into cold, hard cash. This system of objectively determined extracted values will reveal just how often we rob Peter to pay Paul in our current efforts to solve the environmental crisis. It will also expose those who pay only lip service to the objectives of true environmental responsibility.

Extracted value tax

The second step involves the implementation of an extracted value tax of 5% to come into effect concomitantly with mandatory ecological bookkeeping. After an initial introductory period, the extracted value tax will be increased by a certain percentage every year until, say, in 30 years time, it reaches 100%. This type of full-cost pricing will then include the environmental costs (extracted value) in the total life cycle of all goods. The gradual introduction of the extracted value tax will give businesses in the industrial sectors sufficient time to prepare an adaptation strategy and adjust their practices. It will also create a situation in which the economic interests of business coincide with those of the planet. But, most important, it will dramatically change the habits of both business and consumers.

Repairing the damage

The third step in this process is the simplest and also perhaps the most important: use a growing part of the revenue generated by the extracted value tax to repair the damage done to the environment. In this way, a fully sustainable economy is a feasible proposition.

Assigning values

In the effort to establish concrete extracted values, policymakers will be presented with a philosophical "Sophie's Choice": decide which irreplaceable natural resources are most valuable. What is the extracted value of the white rhinoceros species, for example, when compared to 100,000 barrels of oil? It is therefore imperative that these extracted values be determined on the basis of scientific fact. It is also important to note that the theoretical costs of cleaning up damage or replacing resources can only be based on current scientific and technological capabilities. As these capabilities change, so will the theoretical costs of repair and replacement.

On objections to change

In the scenario I have just described, corporations will be forced to develop new paradigms for doing business and consumers will be forced to develop new patterns of consumption. The ideas I have outlined here will undoubtedly be met with considerable resistance. Some will wonder how our society can be expected to undergo such fundamental change. In response, I would remind them that the changes I am proposing will be implemented over a period of a few decades. If we look back on all the technological and lifestyle changes that have taken place over the last 30 years, do these proposals still seem so drastic?

Change is inevitable, and the key to business success lies precisely in responding effectively to change. It is therefore only good business sense to anticipate change and let it work in our favor.

Earth Inc.'s shareholders

Ideally, we would have some kind of cosmic accountant, an omniscient bookkeeper who was there at the Big Bang and thus present at the moment of the opening balance, someone capable of tallying up our planetary credits and debits. *In lieu* thereof, however, we will have to rely on good science and our own judgment.

Sustainable development is possible, but only if we begin managing the environment according to sound business principles. The goal of every company is to ensure its continuation and economic growth for the benefit of its employees and its shareholders. Is it not time then for us all, as equal shareholders in Earth Inc., to guarantee the sustainability of our own future prosperity? We must do this neither out of pie-in-the-sky idealism nor vague messianic ambitions, but out of pure economic necessity, a source of inspiration that has been the mother of so many fruitful inventions in the past. We have to face the fact that the only real driving force in the world is business. Simple idealism is not going to get us anywhere.

Ecological bookkeeping is just a beginning. But as the ancient Chinese Taoist philosopher Lao Tzu once wrote: "A thousand-mile journey begins with one step." It only remains for us to take the next step on the road toward sustainable development together.

40

Raising Gross National Happiness through Agroforestry

Pahuna Sharma-Laden and Croix Thompson

In 2010, an earthquake devastated Haiti. The rebuilding work has been slow, with tens of thousands still living in emergency tents. It may not seem like a good time to talk about envisioning a sustainable future for the island, but that may be exactly what is needed to stave off the next disaster. Deforestation has been a major problem in Haiti, as with other Caribbean and Central American countries, where collectively 285,000 hectares of forest are lost each year. Haiti has been particularly hard hit, losing almost 10% of its remaining tree cover between 1990 and 2005. Tree cover cannot stave off an earthquake, but it is vital for increasing resilience in the face of floods and storms — both of which are expected to increase in this era of global warming.

Reforestation can lead the way to a more sustainable form of living. Agriculture is currently the leading driver of deforestation. Unsustainable agricultural practices such as "slash and burn" have been particularly detrimental to forests. Additionally, a growing population and its increasing need for fuelwood, timber, and other forest products have accelerated the rate of deforestation. Addressing the problem requires multiple approaches that encompass social, cultural, and economic dynamics.

Agroforestry is a land-use system that integrates agriculture, trees, people, and animals in the same space, resulting in improved soil quality, higher yields, and improved standards of living. Agroforestry has been practiced in varying forms for thousands of years, and as such it works well with the low-input land-management systems that are common in the developing world. In the practice of agroforestry called intercropping, nitrogen-fixing native and noninvasive tree species are selected and grown alongside agricultural crops.

This can dramatically benefit soil fertility: a study from Nepal on the impact of agroforestry on soil fertility and farm income showed that agroforestry intervention nearly doubled farm income per hectare from US$800 to US$1580.[1,2] Intercropping can also protect agricultural crops from unwanted exposure to the sun, providing a "shade system" that creates a microclimate, resulting in higher yields. Rows of shrubs and bushes are planted to create buffers and windbreaks, which prevent soil erosion and overgrazing by livestock. Agroforestry also emphasizes crop diversity, increasing resilience among small landholders. Trees provide fuel, fodder, and timber. Fruit trees specifically can provide valuable income: a study of 1000 farmers from 15 districts in Kenya found that tree fruits contributed 18% of crop revenue, while tea and coffee contributed an additional 29% of revenue.[2,3]

In a devastated country like Haiti, these benefits could help transform lives.

> *In a devastated country like Haiti, these benefits could help transform lives.*

Trees for the Future (TFTF), an agroforestry development organization, has led the way in planting more than 1.4 million agroforestry trees since 2011. Agroforestry species such as moringa (*Moringa* spp.) and jujube (*Ziziphus* spp.) have been intercropped with income-generating trees such as neem (*Azadirachta indica*). Plans in Haiti are to intercrop agroforestry trees with coffee and beans as well.

More than 3000 farmers in rural Haiti have adopted modern agroforestry techniques. Trees have been planted in four provinces about 6–8 h by road from Port au Prince, both north and south of the city. One particular site in Medor is so rural that the only way to get there is by foot, walking at least 12 miles from the closest city, Bethel. Each of the Haitian projects costs about US$15,000 per year. The key to success has been to use a participatory approach sensitive to cultural practices, especially traditional patterns of land tenure, land use, and vegetation use. For example, it is common practice in many parts of the developing world for a single tract of land to be divided between several farmers or a whole village. Local people therefore need to be the drivers of agricultural change because they are, in the end, responsible for the sustainability of such projects.

TFTF works directly with local communities to adapt agroforestry techniques to indigenous farming methods, building on local pools of knowledge. Projects in Haiti have used native trees that have a cultural value for the local people, such as the Hispaniolan pine (*Pinus occidentalis*). As a result, in some of our programs, there has been a resurgence of native trees. Our projects have even led to the regeneration of native species that we did not plant — in the case of Honduras, for example, flowering species used locally for medicinal purposes have reappeared.

Because of the damage done by Haiti's 2010 earthquake, it will take time for the country to realize all the benefits from agroforestry. But the agroforestry techniques already introduced are allowing farmers to overcome deforestation challenges in their communities. Teaching the farmers new techniques that build on local knowledge has enabled communities to take ownership of their projects and develop multigenerational reforestation plans while increasing harvest yields.

Worldwide, the scale of the challenge posed by deforestation is huge. The net loss of the world's forests is estimated at 7.3 million hectares per year.[4] Central America loses forests at a rate of 1.3% per year, Southeast Asia 1%, and sub-Saharan Africa around 30%. At these current rates of deforestation, it is estimated that the world's rainforests will disappear in the next 100 years. Yet, if farmers the world over commit to implementing agroforestry techniques, it will be possible to at least stabilize the deforestation rates.

A major benefit of agroforestry is that it does not require huge investments or aid. It is a practice that creates self-sufficiency, as evidenced in Haiti. This bottom–up approach is what we need in order to tackle the widespread problem of deforestation. Therefore, we recommend the following: Help farmers learn how to effectively replace conventional agricultural practices with agroforestry. This should be done by forming partnerships with local farmers and communities. Native species of cultural value should be used whenever possible, as should noninvasive, nitrogen-fixing, multipurpose agroforestry species. Farmers should be trained to use shrubs and bushes for fencing, which limits overgrazing by animals and subsequent topsoil erosion. Low-cost alternatives to fuelwood, such as solar cookers, should be developed. Farmers should be trained in developing useful, economically viable, and environmentally sound products that build self-reliance rather than dependency. Communities should be trained in backyard horticulture, nursery development, and rainwater harvesting, the latter of which builds resilience to droughts. In short, successful agroforestry programs build on communities' cultural values, norms, and traditions. Foreign ideas or technologies should be implemented with extreme caution, given that their sustainability depends on these communities.

Acknowledgments

We thank David Tye, Interim Executive Director of Trees for the Future, for his guidance and encouragement.

References

1. Neupane, RP and GB Thapa (2001). Impact of agroforestry intervention on soil fertility and farm income under the subsistence farming system of the Middle Hills, Nepal. *Agriculture, Ecosystems and Environment*, 84, 157–167.

2. Neufeldt, H *et al.* (2009). *Trees on Farms: Tackling the Triple Challenges of Mitigation, Adaptation and Food Security*. World Agroforestry Centre Policy Brief 077. Nairobi, Kenya: World Agroforestry Centre.

3. Place, F and J Wanjiku (2006). High value tree and crop enterprises in Kenya: How meso and micro factors affect adoption and revenues. Paper presented at the International Association of Agricultural Economists Conference, Gold Coast, Australia.

4. Forestry Department. Food and Agriculture Organization of the United Nations [online]. Available at www.fao.org/forestry/en [accessed on 8 August 2013].

41

Building Bridges between Science and Policy to Achieve Sustainability

Katherine Richardson and Ole Wæver

In 1987, the Brundtland Commission released a report that would define the next 25 years of progress toward a sustainable future. Breaking with earlier conventions that saw development exclusively in terms of economic growth, the report urged policymakers to include social and environmental impacts in their considerations. The Brundtland Report also introduced the concept of intergenerational equity, that is, no generation has the right to use the earth's resources in such a manner that it compromises the ability of future generations to meet their own needs. This means that development can only be sustainable if the consumption of natural resources is kept within the amount that the earth is able to replenish. A sustainable future may seem far away, but research advances over the past few decades have meant the vision outlined by Brundtland is closer than many think.

At the time of the Brundtland Report and the Earth Summit in Rio, the term *natural resources* typically referred to materials or substances that could be collected, mined, or harvested for human use. Since then, our perception of natural resources has expanded through a greater understanding of how the earth functions as a single interacting system, along with our role in influencing how that system functions. Thus, we now recognize specific processes or functions within the earth system as also being natural resources. Examples of such earth system resources include soil formation; pollination by insects; natural carbon sinks both on land and in the sea; the ozone layer, which reduces the amount of ultraviolet radiation reaching the earth's surface; and the capacity of the atmosphere to absorb greenhouse gas emissions. These earth system resources can also be overused.

This changed perception has helped inform a new global debate about how to equitably distribute these limited resources. A first step to sharing resources within a sustainable framework is to develop a globally accepted set of metrics to measure the consumption of these resources. Quantifying resource demand is more straightforward than quantifying supply, although there are as yet no universally accepted metrics for assessing resource demand. For some critical material resources (for example, oil, phosphorous, metals, etc.), considerable effort has been devoted to estimating the remaining global supply. Here, again, there is no general consensus as to the metrics to be used. However, for many of these resources, the discussion centers not on *if* they are exhaustible but, rather, *when* they will become so scarce that it will no longer be economically feasible to extract them. An important contribution to attaining sustainable development, then, becomes the establishment of mechanisms and incentives for the reuse of natural resources, where this is technically feasible.

Quantifying the global supply of earth system resources is much more difficult than quantifying the supply of material resources. For many of these resources, the limit of the resource available for human use or consumption is set by the willingness of society to accept the change in living conditions that overuse of a given earth system resource would imply. Science must guide society's decision makers in their determination of limits for the *total allowable take* (analogous to *total allowable catch* in society's management of fisheries) for critical resources. Two things are necessary for providing this guidance: (i) the development of scientific methodology to estimate the consequences of various scenarios for the societal use of resources, and (ii) mechanisms for collating and assessing the available scientific information and channeling it to policymakers.

Interesting new approaches are under development for estimating the consequences of various scenarios for earth system resource use. One such approach is the *planetary boundaries* concept,[1] which identifies nine critical resources and proposes, on the basis of existing scientific data, boundaries or limits for their use. The authors argue that such analyses can identify a "safe operating space for humanity." The planetary boundaries approach has only recently been introduced and it certainly needs refinement before it can be used in political decision making. Nevertheless, an indication that such an approach is of interest and potential value in the governance process can be found in the attention it has received among government officials and policymakers, most recently in the report of the United Nations General Secretary's High Level Group on Global Sustainability.

Thus far, global political leaders have established limits on human depletion of only two earth system resources: (i) the ozone layer and (ii) the natural concentrations of atmospheric greenhouse gases (i.e., an upper limit of 2°C for anthropogenic global warming). In the case of the former, Montreal Protocol regulations ensure compliance with the identified resource limits. With respect to use of the atmospheric greenhouse gas dump, negotiation is still under way in an attempt to achieve compliance with the accepted limit of the resource.

Setting a political limit on the size of the atmospheric greenhouse gas depot available for human greenhouse gas wastes would not have been possible without input from the UN Intergovernmental Panel on Climate Change (IPCC), which brings together the global scientific community to assess the available documentation for human influence on the global climate system and provides political leaders with guidelines concerning the consequences of setting different limits on the potential size of the resource available for human use.

In the same manner that the IPCC has provided the scientific basis upon which political decision making can be based, managing the human relationship with the earth system and its resources will require establishment of an internationally recognized and respected infrastructure. This infrastructure would convey a synthesis of the scientific understanding of the given resource's role in earth system function as well as human impact on the resource to decision makers. This infrastructure must form the bridge that carries scientific understanding of human impact on earth system function to political decision makers. Given the crucial role that this infrastructure will play in the transition to sustainable development, it is important to consider what characteristics might give it the greatest chance for success.

To be useful in the policy arena, the science being made available to policymakers can never be the pure academic product exchanged among researchers themselves. The scientific product presented to policymakers has to, by definition, be a negotiated conclusion presented in a politically manageable form that is shaped by the particular purpose and context. The appropriate framework for conveying scientific evidence to policymakers emerges through an interaction between political and academic actors. Although it is crucial that the knowledge *content* derives directly from current scientific understanding, the institutional *format* of the product will be decided primarily by politicians.

> *To be useful in the policy arena, the science being made available to policymakers can never be the pure academic product exchanged among researchers themselves.*

There is no international governance organ that *a priori* is assigned the task of establishing the infrastructure by which scientific evidence can be introduced to policymaking. There is some indication, however, that the UN could take an increasingly prominent role in establishing the infrastructure to convey a global scientific consensus regarding resource availability to international policymakers. However, the history of controversies surrounding the IPCC (unfair as these might be) creates a challenging basis from which to set up new similar structures. Politicians are now much more aware of both the political acrimony that can arise and the binding power that strong scientific input can place upon them than they were at the time of the IPCC's inception. Therefore, the possible effects of allowing the introduction of strong knowledge into the decision-making process will already be taken into account when setting up these structures. In other words, if politicians fear the policies that might ensue from certain knowledge, they may also fear the empowerment of relevant scientific knowledge.

Should each of the global resources for which humans must consider constraining their use have their own IPCC-like organization? Would the multiplying controversies and campaigns drown any chance of action? Or will having a number of different infrastructures generate a normalization of this procedure and institutionalize the format for providing a scientific basis for policymaking?

Before addressing these questions, two important points need to be made. First, a productive interface between science and politics will require an evolution in the societal understanding of science. Therefore, there needs to be a focus on science education and communication. Second, actual action on the difficult demands created by scientific understanding does not emerge automatically or easily. Complex political constellations, where interests, time horizons, and competences do not line up easily when it comes to resource management, mean that the overall banner of sustainability or a call to rational self-interest may not convey a strong enough sense of necessity.

Without generally resorting to fear mongering and panic politics, it can be productive in terms of generating a sense of necessity to draw on security theory to capture the conditions under which a threat becomes part of the national security debate. The way leading states frame their national identity and their values and visions has to converge with the supranational security agenda[2]; and a political process for sustainability and global stewardship could actually be designed to match political principles in play nationally. When, for example, the European Union has regularly played a leading role in environmental negotiations, it has been politically sustainable because it corresponded to a European longing for an international role and a rationale for European integration. Similar synergies might be envisioned for China and possibly Brazil, where policies for sustainability can be embedded politically in programs for national identity, domestic transformations, or foreign policy.

From this approach, the current drift toward recommending one general IPCC-like body for sustainability might be questioned. When we take into account that powerful actors will try to impose paralysis, one grand body might be dangerous—both because it is an all-eggs-in-one-basket approach and because the complexity and comprehensiveness of such an organ would make it unwieldy. The importance of fostering a general evolution in societal understanding of science also speaks for a "multitude-of-panels" approach. Rather than producing a predictable revolt against an alleged supranational philosopher-king, a creation of several such science–policy bridges could normalize the condition of doing politics based on a scientific approach. Of course, respecting different environmental boundaries may sometimes result in contradictory policy suggestions, which will produce mutual tensions and externalities. However, these tensions are real and must be politically—not scientifically—resolved. Having several panels and an emphasis on boundaries as a form of security policy helps to avoid the perception that science dictates *the* line to be followed and, thereby, empties politics of content. It remains a political task to choose among the different ways human society can evolve while still respecting the limits science has identified. This approach could tweak the connotations of sustainability from an ideal standard (beautiful but optional) to respect for environmental boundaries that cannot safely be crossed.

> *It remains a political task to choose among the different ways human society can evolve while still respecting the limits science has identified.*

Since the Earth Summit of 1992, an understanding has emerged of the functioning of the earth system and human influences within this system that provides a framework for managing natural resources sustainably. It helps us to identify the earth system resources that are essential for development of human societies and it helps us to predict the potential effects of human use of these resources on our own habitat. Armed with this knowledge, global policymakers can designate limits—the total allowable take—of these essential resources. However, the recognition that human activities constitute a controlling force in nature brings with it responsibilities. Now that we know that humans directly influence the earth system, we have a responsibility to actively manage that influence and to become stewards of the planetary processes that support human development. For a number of generations now, humans have been inadvertently impacting the earth system. With the knowledge gained over the last two decades, ignorance is only possible with a growing effort, and we must regard most current and future human impacts on the earth system as having been intentionally induced or, rather, as a form of geoengineering. Understanding the various processes that are important for earth system function also gives us the power to understand when we are actively manipulating these processes. Perhaps the greatest challenge facing society, in general, and political leaders, in particular, on the road to sustainable development is deciding who should have the right to alter or impact earth system functioning and for what reasons.

References

1. Rockström, J *et al.* (2009). A safe operating space for humanity. *Nature*, 461, 472–475.
2. Buzan, B and O Wæver (2009). Macrosecuritisation and security constellations: reconsidering scale in securitisation theory. *Review of International Studies*, 35, 253–276.

42

Bringing Mozart to the Masses: Venezuela's Music Revolution

Maria Páez Victor

As a sociologist, I often roamed the dirt tracks of the poor sections of my hometown Caracas, and it seemed to me that from the open windows, I would always hear someone singing or strumming the Venezuelan four-string guitar, *el cuatro*, or see some fellow unselfconsciously walking by whistling or singing. Later on, reading the memoirs of an English officer of Simón Bolívar's British Legion that fought for the Venezuelan Independence Revolution, I was struck by his observation that at the bivouacs after the day's march, as the men sat around the campfires, they created music. "Most of the natives are musicians and singers,"[1] he wrote.

Today, 200 years later, the officer's observation is solidly backed by the achievements of the extraordinary Venezuelan music program, *El Sistema*, which today has 300 centers, 310,000 students, and 500 orchestras in the country. Its hallmark is the excellence of its musicians, foremost of whom is Gustavo Dudamel, undoubtedly the world's most exciting classical music conductor.

El Sistema is a remarkable music and antipoverty program that was created in 1975 by Maestro José Antonio Abreu, who was determined to improve social justice through the balm of music. He started out with only

11 young musicians who shared his vision to give the poor and marginalized access to music education. Over 70% of the students in El Sistema come from poor families.[2]

A typical student in El Sistema comes from a *barrio*, a very poor neighborhood. He or she attends a *nucleus* after school, taught by an older student of El Sistema at no charge and on an instrument supplied for free. There are groups for preschoolers, school-age children, and teenagers. Participants learn how to play an instrument and how to perform in an orchestra. The child's family is important to the success of El Sistema and is considered part of the program. Children progress through the program to higher standards, including the National Simón Bolívar Orchestra, which plays all over the world. (Go to www.youtube.com to see a video of the orchestra's performance at London's Royal Albert Hall.)

In 1975 oil-rich Venezuela was a goose that laid golden eggs for the upper classes. From 1935 to 1998, this petroleum-rich country had a poverty level of 60%, with almost one-third of the population suffering from extreme poverty.[3] The majority of the people were thus excluded from the benefits of oil riches; that exclusion was economic, political, and also cultural. The arts were seen as the reserve of only the wealthy, with the poor excluded from museums, galleries, theaters, and music performances. Classical music was especially seen as the purview of the privileged.[4]

Maestro Abreu struggled for the necessary backing from successive governments, never obtaining from them the recognition and funds that his program deserved. It is a wonder, however, that even under those circumstances, his program and musicians survived.

That all changed with the election of President Hugo Chávez.

Today there is a happy convergence between the values of El Sistema and those of the Chávez government, including the antipoverty programs Chávez inspired.[5] In 13 years, they have reduced poverty to 27.8% and extreme poverty to 7.3%, an astounding achievement for any developing country.[6] El Sistema now receives 90% of its funding from the Venezuelan government. The opposition to President Chávez has bitterly attacked El Sistema because of this government support,[7,8] even though the positive results of the program are beyond question.

Maestro Abreu organized his program into a series of centers, or nuclei, in different localities. Music was not taught as a "training session" but as a way

of life. Young people were made to feel they had joined a sort of family that would support and encourage them to reach higher standards. Abreu believes in the young people and says, "Culture for the poor cannot be poor culture."[9]
Children learn to work as a team and to have self-discipline. Egotistic individualism is not encouraged, but creativity and personal development are.

> *Culture for the poor cannot be poor culture.*

The heart of the music program is acceptance and support: the child that wants to join is accepted unconditionally without any filtering or auditions. The instruments that are provided are not kept in the school, but entrusted to the child to take home and care for. One 10-year-old boy admitted that he had to have his cello right next to his bed in his humble bedroom because he could not sleep without it.[10]

El Sistema also includes choirs, and one choir in particular has stunned the musical world: it is composed of children who are deaf, blind, or otherwise disabled. They participate with their hands, wearing white gloves, as they signal the words of the songs. World-famous opera singer Placido Domingo was so moved watching this choir for the first time that tears rolled down his cheeks.[10]

Abreu believes that "the most holy of human rights is the right to art." His student, Gustavo Dudamel, former conductor of the Simón Bolívar Orchestra, now conducts the Los Angeles Philharmonic Orchestra. He is now disseminating the idea that music is a human right in the world of classical music, where he is a major player. Dudamel is also promoting El Sistema in Los Angeles.

In an orchestra, as in a family, fellow students are supporters, not rivals. The idea of music as an inherent human right constitutes a cultural revolution that may very well save the future of classical music itself.

> *The idea of music as an inherent human right constitutes a cultural revolution that may very well save the future of classical music.*

El Sistema has renewed music education by bringing in the talents and enthusiasm of those who had been excluded. It has brought a fresh wind to the musty halls where elites had wanted to keep classical music prisoner. And it all started in Venezuela, where revolution is a very good thing.

References

1. Vowell, RL (1831). *Campaigns and Cruises*. London: Longman & Co, p. 40.
2. Eichler, J (2010). The necessary cultural revolution. *Boston Globe*.
3. Social Indicators, National Institute of Statistics (INE). Reported in *Venezuelan News Agency* (5 November 2011). Available at www.avn.info.ve [accessed on 8 August 2013].
4. Reading: Fundamental axis of Venezuelan cultural policy [online] (14 September 2011). *Venezuela International*. Available at venezuelanalysis. com/analysis/6489 [accessed on 8 August 2013].
5. Fisher, N. Venezuela's cultural revolution (18 October 2010). *The New York Times*.
6. Social Indicators, National Institute of Statistics. Venezuela reduces poverty from 70% to 23%. (3 October 2010). *Aporrea.org* [online]. Available at www.aporrea.org/actualidad/n152754.html [accessed on 8 August 2013].
7. Wakin, DJ. Venerated high priest and humble servant of music education (1 March 2011). *New York Times*.
8. Review of the opposition views on Maestro Abreu in EncontrArte [online]. Available at encontrarte.aporrea.org/137/de-interes/a12423.htm [accessed on 8 August 2013].
9. Eichler, J. You're part of something bigger: Venezuela's El Sistema in the USA (22 July 2010). *Boston Globe* [online]. Available at Venezuelanalysis. com/analysis/5513 [accessed on 8 August 2013].
10. *To Play and To Fight (Tocar y Luchar)*. Directed by Alberto Arvelo. Los Angeles, CA: Cinevolve Studios, 2006.

43

Creating the Schools of the Future: Education for a Sustainable Society

Peter M. Senge

The prevailing system of management has destroyed our people. The destruction starts with toddlers. ... The fundamental task of leadership is transformation of this system ... [which is] the same system in education and business.

W. Edwards Deming, pioneer, total quality management

"How do you think about the future?" (President, School Superintendents of America) "We sort of think that you drank your juice, and then you drank ours." (11-year-old female student)

Intergenerational dialogue on systems thinking in education

I believe that the Industrial Age system of education that has spread around the world in the past 150 years will change dramatically in the coming decades. The assembly-line progression of grades (first, second, third, etc.) coordinated by a fixed curriculum and headed by teachers in charge of students' learning has grown increasingly out of touch with the realities of today: the global interconnectedness of economics, politics, and culture; the Internet, which puts more and more information at students' fingertips; and businesses that need people who can think for themselves and collaborate effectively in teams to solve complex problems. While mainstream school systems are obsessed with standardized test scores and intense individual competition, education innovators are focused on higher order skills like systems thinking and creativity in conjunction with basic skills in mathematics and language; personal maturation together with technical knowledge; and learning how to learn together in service of addressing problems that are real in students' lives.

These changes will continue to unfold not because such change is easy. Indeed, as most educators know only too well, few institutions are more immune to innovation than public education. These changes will happen because such fundamental change in the aims and process of education is not only possible but necessary if we are to create healthy societies in the shrinking, interdependent, and stressed world in which we now live.

> *Fundamental change in the aims and process of education is not only possible but necessary if we are to create healthy societies in the shrinking, interdependent, and stressed world in which we now live.*

Ironically, few activists engaged in building more sustainable societies focus on the leverage that could exist in fundamental innovation in primary and secondary education. Partly this reflects the perceived difficulty of such change, but more deeply it reveals a tragic blind spot. While many focus understandably on business — because business plays a huge role in shaping the current human footprint — the deep changes in values needed to shift the path of the human journey are unlikely to arise from business alone, or from the current business-government-civil society nexus of institutional power. Truly restorative practices and policies will take multiple generations to bring into the mainstream of our societies. The only institution with a time horizon commensurate with these changes is education, and especially primary and secondary education.

Mindful of this, for almost two decades, radical innovators in K-12 schools have been building the schools of the future, largely unnoticed by mainstream society, which is obsessed with saving a dying and hopelessly outdated education system. Their overarching aim is not education reform but recontextualizing the whole vision of education: schools and communities working together to shape a sustainable future. Though their particular strategies and tools differ, they all emphasize the following:

- *Systems thinking and learner-centered pedagogy*: tapping students' innate abilities to understand systems by shifting from teacher-centered instruction to designing learning environments that engage students in their own questions and aspirations.
- *Education for sustainability*: making the context for education our common task of building healthier communities based on social and biological well-being.
- *Authentic youth engagement and youth leadership*: engaging students as leaders in building healthier communities, within and beyond the school.
- *Building schools as learning communities*: involving everyone — adults and children — in a mutual learning process of individual and collective development.

Systems thinking and learner-centered education

Picture an eighth-grade science class with no teacher standing in front. Instead, the 30 or so students are glued to their computers, two to a machine, deeply engrossed in conversations with one another, designing the trail system for a new state park to be developed north of Tucson. Once the students lay out a proposed trail network, the simulation model calculates the environmental and economic consequences, prompting energetic debates over trade-offs between different options.

While you are standing in the back of the room, a couple of young boys come up and ask your advice. "We need your opinion," Joe says. "Jimmy [the boy's partner] has a trail system that he thinks is great because it makes a lot of money [routing hikers past the best views], but it also does a lot of environmental damage. Mine avoids the environmental-impact areas, but he thinks it is too close to the Indian burial grounds and will stir up protests."

You listen for a while as the two boys explain their different trails and show you some of the simulated consequences. There are no black-and-white answers, and it is clear that they understand this. This is about design and making choices. The bell rings and the boys say goodbye, agreeing to come back after school to see if they can work out a proposal to share with the rest of the class at the end of the week. (The students' proposals and analyses will be presented to the actual park planning commission at the end of the term.)

You leave that afternoon amazed by a science class that is so engaging for the students — it turns out that Joe and Jimmy had both been identified as "discipline problems" by former teachers — and wondering, what does it take to help more teachers become designers of learning spaces rather than "instructors" delivering content who then must "motivate" their students to learn what otherwise has little meaning to them?

Actually, I have been thinking about these questions for a long time — ever since I first visited that classroom in Tucson almost 20 years ago!

Today, the systems thinking, learner-centered approach has spread across grade levels and curricular domains from social studies and history to high school math and science.[1] Some of the most inspiring advances have been with young children — like the three six-year-old boys at a pioneering K-4 school in downtown Tucson who drew a systems diagram to understand why they were having fights on the playground.[2] "It all starts with mean words," says one of them in a video of their discussion. "Then we have hurt feelings, and then more mean words, and then we get fights." They then search for "the leverage … to break the reinforcing loop." One observes that "saying 'I'm sorry' kind of works. But the next time we start to get into a fight we are going to try these others," pointing to where else they could "intervene" in the loop.

Education for sustainability

Education for sustainability builds on systems thinking conceptual skills to establish a context of community responsibility and engagement, integrating ideas and approaches from many different content areas, including ecological literacy, place-based education, action learning, sustainable economics (the connections between economic, social, and natural systems), and visioning (the ability to envision and invent a rich, hopeful future).

Jaimie Cloud, a national leader in the field for some 15 years, identifies seven primary habits of mind, starting with "Understanding of Systems as the Context for Decision Making" and "Awareness of Driving Forces and Their Impacts," and including the following:

- *Intergenerational responsibility*: taking responsibility for the effect(s) of one's own actions on future generations.
- *Protecting and enhancing the commons*: reconciling the conflicts between individual rights and the responsibilities of citizenship to tend to common resources on which all depend.
- *Paradigm shifting*: recognizing mental models and paradigms as guiding constructs that shape action but that can change over time with new knowledge and applied insight.[3]

Education for sustainability is more than just a new curriculum. It is about how the content and process of education can be interwoven with *real-life contexts* to create opportunities for young people to take the lead in building sustainable communities and societies.

Youth engagement and youth leadership

Scott Beall of Brewster, New York, redesigned his 10th- and 11th-grade science classes as "Do Right Enterprises." For several years, Beall has taught students how to conduct energy audits and then has engaged local businesspeople as clients. Not only do the students learn how to apply science to practical analysis, but local businesses start to reduce their energy (and carbon) footprints. "We thought we were doing the students a favor by letting them come in and gather some data from our restaurant," said one local businessperson. "We had no idea how much waste they would find, and how much money we could save."

"There is no doubt that the kids in the Do Right course learn as much science content as [their] counterparts in more traditional science classes," says Beall. (Their New York Regents' science exam results tend to be as high or higher than those of students in more traditional classrooms.) But, continues Beall, "the big payoff is student motivation and a completely different understanding of what it means to *do science* rather than do schoolroom exercises."

Connecting systems thinking, education for sustainability, and authentic youth engagement creates a powerful base for leadership development. "I think we tend to greatly underestimate young people's capacities as leaders," says Les Omotani, former superintendent of the West Des Moines and Hewlett-Woodmere (Long Island) school districts. Starting many years ago, Omotani invited high school students to learn the leadership "disciplines of learning organizations" (e.g., systems thinking, personal mastery, building shared vision, working with mental models, and team learning)[4] and to serve as facilitators for community dialogues that the school hosted, part of a yearlong Youth Leadership Forum. "The young people learned that they could help adults have meaningful conversations about how to make the community, including the school, healthier," says Omotani.

Building schools as learning communities

All of this is feasible only when we are all willing to rethink basic assumptions about how schools work, from the classroom to the school as a whole, to the larger school system. For example, supporting teachers in shifting from the teacher-centered model to becoming designers of learner-centered classrooms requires implementing learning infrastructures that combine training, in-classroom coaching, and rich peer-learning networks. This means a deep commitment to engaging in a life-long developmental journey.[5] In short, the learning commitment will be no greater for the students than it is for the adults. Early on, pioneers like those in Tucson realized that this meant basic changes in school culture.

Of all professions, teaching is among the most individualistic. Whereas most people in business or architecture or law have an acute sense that their accomplishments result from team effort, teachers typically operate in a highly fragmented world of *their* courses, *their* skills, and *their* students. Educators often espouse the ideal of collaboration, but it takes time and commitment to go beyond platitudes to develop practical skills to deal with the inescapable conflicts of any collaborative work environment.

> *Educators often espouse the ideal of collaboration, but it takes time and commitment to go beyond platitudes.*

"Of all the changes I tried to lead as principal, helping teachers learn how to [work as a] team was probably the most difficult," says Mary Scheetz, the principal at that first middle school in Tucson, Orange Grove (and now assistant superintendent for curriculum and instruction in the Ritenour district in Saint Louis). "There is so much more potential for collaborative solutions than normally gets realized given the professional isolation common to most schools." Sheetz and Assistant Principal Tracy Benson (now coordinator of the Waters Foundation for Systems Thinking) made sure collaboration became part of teachers' daily lives by redesigning the school schedule so that each day all teachers had 45–60 min free to meet with one another.

"Collaboration only starts to make a difference when teachers have time to practice coordinating in real time," says Benson. "They need to know what Billy's teacher found out in his first period class or how a new systems idea intended to integrate across civics and science is actually playing out for the kids. This is what actually helps them feel like a team."

The real question

None of these ideas represent simple changes that will be achieved by a few bold school leaders. Rather, they will take leadership from innovative teachers, committed principals, and dedicated central administrators. They will take community leadership: parents, school board members, civic and business leaders. All must work together to help create new relationships and expectations. And it will take leadership from the very place that we look to least frequently — the students themselves. Make no mistake. The students are ready for the change.

A few years ago at a large community gathering in Saint Louis, part of the SoL Education Partnership national learning community, an audience of 250 people heard a series of student presentations on their sustainability projects. Few will forget Annalise, a 12-year-old who spoke about the wind turbine she and her classmates had gotten built at their middle school. The project started with class sessions where their science teacher talked about energy and the need to move more rapidly to renewable energy sources. She and four of her classmates — she gave each of their names — talked with the teacher about what they could do, and that is when the wind turbine idea was born. They then enlisted parents to help them sort out the different engineering and investment options. They presented their idea to the school principal and then to the mayor of the local town: "I was worried that our presentation did not go too well with the mayor — she really didn't say anything when we presented our ideas." But they were later called back for a second presentation to the mayor and members of the town council. Annalise closed her remarkable story, which took all of 3 min to share, with a photograph of the vertical wind turbine now standing in front of the school.

Having by now captured the undivided attention of the adult audience, Annalise set aside her notes and standing calmly, some 75 pounds of fierce determination, said, "We children are often hearing that 'you children are the future.' We don't agree with that. We don't have that much time. We need to make changes now. We kids are ready, are you?"

It is said in traditional Chinese culture that "the mark of every golden age is that the children are the most important members of a society and teaching the most revered profession." This is not an idealist statement. It is a profoundly pragmatic one. A simple way to express our strategic imperative today is to ask, how do we make the future *real*, as emotionally salient as the present? I believe this cannot be done by rational argument alone. The future becomes real when the voices of children and young people like Annalise are real. As the saying goes, we have not inherited our world from the past, we are borrowing it from the future. And our creditors want a voice in shaping that future.

Acknowledgments

This chapter was based on a piece in *Leader to Leader* (June 2012).

References

1. Systems Thinking in Schools. Waters Foundation and Creative Learning Exchange [online]. Available at www.watersfoundation.org and www.clexchange.org [accessed on 8 August 2013].
2. First-Grade Problem Solving. Waters Foundation [online]. Available at www.watersfoundation.org/webed/mod9/mod9-3-1.html [accessed on 8 August 2013].

3. Cloud Institute for Sustainability Education [online]. Available at www. cloudinstitute.org [accessed on 8 August 2013].

4. Senge, P (2006). *The Fifth Discipline: The Art & Practice of the Learning Organization*. New York: Currency Press.

5. Senge, P *et al.* (2012). *Schools That Learn: A Fifth Discipline Fieldbook for Educators, Parents, and Everyone. New York:* Crown Business.

44

A Values-Based Set of Solutions
for the Next Generation

Tim Kasser

Psychologists have collected data from thousands of people in dozens of nations around the world to understand what humans value and how they prioritize different aims in life. These studies consistently show that the human value system is composed of about a dozen basic types of values, including aims such as having caring relationships, having fun, pursuing spiritual understanding, and feeling safe. Thus far, the evidence suggests that people in every corner of the globe appear to care about and be motivated by each of these basic values, at least to some extent.

Not only do people have the same fundamental types of values, but these values are also organized in similar ways in people's minds.[1,2] Specifically, the evidence strongly suggests that the human value system is organized such that some values tend to be relatively consistent with each other, and thus easy to pursue simultaneously, whereas other values tend to be in relative conflict, and thus difficult to pursue at the same time. The extent of compatibility or conflict between values can be statistically represented in circumplex models (for an example, see Fig. 1). Values are placed near each other in the circumplex when the pursuit of one value facilitates success at another value; for example, most people experience the values of image and status as compatible, as buying an in-fashion

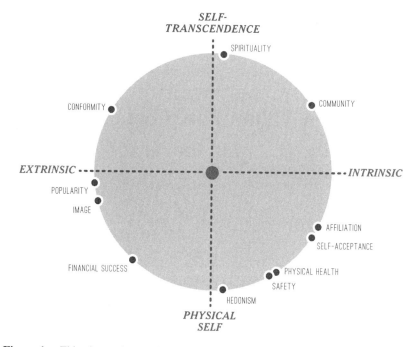

Figure 1: This circumplex model is based on circular stochastic modeling procedures applied to the goal-importance ratings of approximately 1800 college students in 15 cultures. Values adjacent to each other on the circumplex are experienced as relatively compatible, whereas values on opposite sides of the circumplex are experienced as in relative conflict. (*Credit*: Richard Morin/*Solutions*.)

Source: Grouzet et al., 2005.

handbag or automobile not only enhances one's image, but also conveys greater status. Values are placed on opposite sides of the circumplex when the pursuit of one value interferes with another; for example, most people find it relatively difficult to pursue spiritual goals while focused on hedonistic pleasures (it is difficult, for example, to party late on Saturday night and then pray early on Sunday morning).

Other studies offer additional support for the idea that the human value system is organized in this manner by showing that thinking about one set of values has predictable ripple effects on others.[3] Specifically, thinking about one value both *bleeds over* into compatible values and *suppresses* conflicting values. For example, if a person thinks about the importance of financial success, then image and popularity will usually rise in priority (as such pursuits are compatible with the desire for financial success), whereas giving back to the community will decline in importance (as that aim generally conflicts with the desire to make more money).

Because people's aims in life influence their attitudes and behaviors,[4] numerous studies show that prioritization of two particular sets of values affects outcomes relevant to many of the challenges humans currently face. The first set of values includes the *extrinsic* aims of financial success, image, and popularity. These values are called extrinsic because they are focused on rewards and other people's opinions, and usually are not satisfying in and of themselves. The second set of values involves the *intrinsic* aims of self-acceptance, affiliation, and community feeling. These values are called intrinsic because they tend to satisfy people's inherent psychological needs and thus are motivating in and of themselves.[5] Many studies show that the relative prioritization of intrinsic versus extrinsic values bears consistent associations with people's personal well-being, their relationships with other people, and their treatment of the environment.

For instance, dozens of studies have documented that the more people prioritize values such as money, image, and status, the lower their well-being and the greater their reported distress. As such extrinsic values rise in importance, people experience less happiness and life satisfaction, fewer pleasant emotions (like joy and contentment), and more unpleasant emotions (like anger and anxiety) in their day-to-day lives. They also tend to be more depressed and anxious, and are more likely to use substances like cigarettes and alcohol. Even physical problems like headaches, stomachaches, and backaches are associated with a strong focus on extrinsic values. In contrast, placing higher importance on intrinsic values (and successfully pursuing these values) is associated with being happier and healthier.[6]

Social behavior also relates to people's relative focus on extrinsic versus intrinsic values. People tend to be more empathic, cooperative, and caring when they prioritize intrinsic values, whereas a stronger emphasis on extrinsic concerns like money and image is associated with more manipulative and competitive behaviors. Unethical business and antisocial behaviors have also been shown to be more common among those who prioritize extrinsic values.[7] What is more, when they consider material belongings and image to be relatively important, people express more prejudicial attitudes toward other ethnicities and a stronger belief that downtrodden groups deserve what they have (or do not have).[8] Even brief reminders of extrinsic values can affect people's social behavior: one set of studies showed that subtly reminding people of money (by having them unscramble phrases with money-relevant words or view a computer screen-saver with a dollar sign on it) leads to less generous and helpful behaviors moments later.[9] This is a good example of the "suppression" effect, as the activation of the extrinsic value of financial success leads people to orient away from more intrinsic values such as generosity and caring for others.

Ecological behaviors and attitudes are also consistently associated with people's values. Studies have found that people who prioritize extrinsic values care less about the environment and other species, whereas intrinsic values promote more ecologically sustainable attitudes and behaviors.[10] And once again, even brief reminders of these values can affect ecological behaviors and attitudes. For instance, US college students led to think about times when their nation has acted to support freedom, to build family values, and to be generous to others (i.e., intrinsic values) later endorsed more sustainable ecological policies, such as support for public transportation and smaller homes.[11] And another study found that among people who tend to care a great deal about material possessions and social status, thinking for a few minutes about the intrinsic values of affiliation and being broadminded caused them to express stronger care for the environment and greater desire to help

> *Activating intrinsic values can cause a beneficial "bleed-over" in people's value systems, leading them to want to support the larger community of people, other species, and future generations.*

poor people in developing nations.[12] These results show that activating intrinsic values can cause a beneficial "bleed-over" in people's value systems, leading them to want to support the larger community of people, other species, and future generations.

These value dynamics are also relevant at the national level. Nations ranked as having citizens who especially endorse intrinsic over extrinsic values also have children with greater overall well-being, provide new parents with more generous leave after a baby is born, and emit less CO_2 per capita (even after controlling for national wealth).[13]

To summarize, the following three hopeful messages emerge from this body of empirical research:

- Intrinsic values are basic to the human value system, and thus can be encouraged and activated in all people.
- Intrinsic values can be an antidote to extrinsic values, as encouraging the former suppresses the latter.
- Intrinsic values hold promise not only for solving social and ecological problems, but also for helping people be happier and healthier.

Some possibilities for action

This values-based perspective suggests an empirically supported strategy for addressing humanity's greatest challenges: Discourage extrinsic values and encourage intrinsic values in people's lives and in society. Indeed, if one uses this perspective to look at seemingly disparate efforts to promote human well-being, social cohesion, or ecological sustainability, many such efforts, at base, critique the extrinsic values of status and possessions and instead promote intrinsic values such as self-acceptance and connection to others. Space limitations do not allow for a full exposition of this idea,[14] but consider the following six examples.

Voluntary simplicity

A not-insignificant minority of individuals in Western nations choose to drop out of the work-spend-work-some-more lifestyle and instead pursue the "inner riches" of personal growth, family, and volunteering. Examined through a values lens, such *voluntary simplifiers* have rejected extrinsic values in order to focus on intrinsic values. This suggestion is supported by empirical analyses showing that voluntary simplifiers prioritize intrinsic over extrinsic values more highly than do mainstream Americans. What is more, these differences in value prioritization explain, in large part, why voluntary simplifiers are both happier and living more sustainably than mainstream Americans.[15]

Mindfulness meditation

For at least the last couple thousand years, millions of humans have engaged in practices designed to enhance their awareness of their present state. Contemporary scientific studies document that cultivating this experience of mindfulness not only yields psychological and physical health benefits, but also helps people care less about material possessions and jockeying for social position and more about their own inner lives and their connection to the community. What is more, mindfulness also helps people live more sustainably and resist the endless pursuit of acquiring more material stuff.[15,16]

Time affluence

In many economically developed nations, work hours have been increasing over the last few decades. Consequently, people have less time to pursue their own interests, to be with their families, and to be involved in their communities. To counter these trends, the time-affluence movement has proposed polices to provide new parents with more generous paid leave, to extend paid vacations, and to decrease overall work hours.[17] Looked at through a values lens, each of these policies changes the focus from working and earning (i.e., extrinsic values) to family, opportunities for rejuvenation, and more equitable distribution of labor among citizens (i.e., intrinsic values).

Advertising

Citizens in contemporary consumer cultures are bombarded each day with thousands of commercial messages designed to stimulate their desire to consume. Viewed through a values lens, such messages activate and encourage the extrinsic portion of people's value systems. As such, efforts to remove advertising from public spaces (e.g., in subways, on highways, and in schools) and to ban advertising to children, who are particularly susceptible to such value messages, can be understood as attempts to discourage extrinsic values. This values-based approach would also be consistent with proposals to revoke government subsidies that allow businesses to deduct advertising expenditures from their tax returns and to instead tax such expenditures as a form of "value pollution."[18]

Alternative indicators of progress

Policymakers, business people, and the media typically use economic indicators, such as gross national product, consumer confidence, and stock market trends, to express the health and prosperity of a nation, despite the facts that these indicators were never designed for this purpose and that increases in these indicators have been associated with stagnation in citizens' well-being and with greater ecological degradation over time.[19] Many individuals and organizations have suggested developing alternative indicators, with proposals, including Lord Layard's happiness measures, the Kingdom of Bhutan's Gross National Happiness approach, the Happy Planet Index developed by the new economics foundation, and the recent recommendations of the Commission on the Measurement of Economic Development and Social Progress, created by French president Nicolas Sarkozy. While each alternative indicator has its own particular features, all of them de-privilege extrinsic values (by taking the focus off profit-making and economic growth at any cost) and incorporate data reflecting a nation's success on measures relevant to intrinsic values (e.g., equal distribution of wealth, environmental health, opportunities for free time, and mental health).

Challenging corporations

Publicly traded corporations are frequently blamed for social and ecological ills.[20] These organizations' mandate to maximize financial profit for shareholders (i.e., extrinsic values) can lead boards and Chief Executive Officers (CEOs) to make decisions that harm overall environmental or societal well-being. Proposals to replace this dominant business model with cooperatives, benefit corporations, and stakeholder-based organizations all hold promise because each involves tempering the concern for profit with more intrinsic concerns, such as the democratic participation of workers and the good of the community.[21]

Conclusion

Despite the fact that these six existing efforts all share a common value base, it is relatively rare that people who practice mindfulness meditation sit down with those trying to create benefit corporations, that voluntary simplifiers converse with people promoting policies for more generous parental-leave laws, or that organizations developing alternative indicators of national progress combine forces with those trying to ban advertising to children. But there is good reason for these diverse groups (as well as others not mentioned here) to recognize that they all are, at base, trying to discourage a focus on extrinsic values and to encourage the successful pursuit of intrinsic values. For if individuals and organizations were to acknowledge these shared goals, perhaps the compartmentalization and competition that seem so prevalent in today's civil society can be avoided. Instead, perhaps the next generation will work to coordinate and jointly design interventions, communications, and campaigns that discourage values such as money, image, and status and that instead provide many opportunities to pursue values such as personal growth, close connections to other people, and contributions to the larger world.[22] As I hope to have shown here, a solid empirical base suggests that if such broad coalitions were to use the values-based approach articulated here, substantial progress could be made toward solving society's most pressing problems.

References

1. Grouzet, FME *et al.* (2005). The structure of goal contents across 15 cultures. *Journal of Personality and Social Psychology*, 89, 800–816.
2. Schwartz, SH (1992). Universals in the content and structure of values: Theory and empirical tests in 20 countries. In *Advances in Experimental Social Psychology*, Vol. 25, M Zanna (ed.), New York: Academic Press, pp. 1–65.
3. Maio, GR, A Pakizeh, W-Y Cheung and KJ Rees (2009). Changing, priming, and acting on values: Effects via motivational relations in a circular model. *Journal of Personality and Social Psychology*, 97, 699–715.
4. Feather, NT (1995). Values, valences, and choice: The influence of values on the perceived attractiveness and choice of alternatives. *Journal of Personality and Social Psychology*, 68, 1135–1151.
5. Kasser, T and RM Ryan (1996). Further examining the American dream: Differential correlates of intrinsic and extrinsic goals. *Personality and Social Psychology Bulletin*, 22, 280–287.

6. Kasser, T (2002). *The High Price of Materialism*. Cambridge, MA: MIT Press.

7. Kasser, T, M Vansteenkiste and JR Deckop (2006). The ethical problems of a materialistic value orientation for businesses (and some suggestions for alternatives). In *Human Resource Management Ethics*, JR Deckop (ed.), Greenwich, CT: Information Age Publishing, pp. 288–306.

8. Duriez, B, M Vansteenkiste, B Soenens and H De Witte (2007). The social costs of extrinsic relative to intrinsic goal pursuits: Their relation with social dominance and racial and ethnic prejudice. *Journal of Personality*, 75, 757–782.

9. Vohs, KD, NL Mead and MR Goode (2006). The psychological consequences of money. *Science*, 314, 1154–1156.

10. Kasser, T (2011). Ecological challenges, materialistic values, and social change. In *Positive Psychology as Social Change*, R Biswas-Diener (ed.), Dordrecht: Springer, pp. 89–108.

11. Sheldon, KM, CP Nichols and T Kasser (2011). Americans recommend smaller ecological footprints when reminded of intrinsic American values of self-expression, family, and generosity. *Ecopsychology*, 3, 97–104.

12. Chilton, P, T Crompton, T Kasser, G Maio and A Nolan (2011). Communicating bigger-than-self problems to extrinsically oriented audiences [online]. Available at valuesandframes.org/downloads [accessed on 8 August 2013].

13. Kasser, T (2011). Cultural values and the well-being of future generations: A cross-national study. *Journal of Cross-Cultural Psychology*, 42, 206–215.

14. Kasser, T (2011). Values and human well-being [online]. Available at www.bellagioinitiative.org/resource-section/bellagio-outputs/#papers [accessed on 8 August 2013].

15. Brown, KW and T Kasser (2005). Are psychological and ecological well-being compatible? The role of values, mindfulness, and lifestyle. *Social Indicators, Research*, 74, 349–368.

16. Brown, KW, T Kasser, RM Ryan, PA Linley and K Orzech (2009). When what one has is enough: mindfulness, financial desire discrepancy, and subjective well-being. *Journal of Research in Personality*, 43, 727–736.

17. de Graaf, J (ed.) (2003). *Take Back Your Time: Fighting Overwork and Time Poverty in America*. San Francisco: Berrett-Koehler Publications.

18. Schor, JB (2004). *Born to Buy: The Commercialized Child and the New Consumer Culture*. New York: Scribner.

19. Jackson, T (2009). *Prosperity without Growth: Economics for a Finite Planet*. London: Earthscan.

20. Korten, DC (1995). *When Corporations Rule the World*. West Hartford, CT: Berrett-Koehler.

21. Cavanagh, J and J Mander (2004). *Alternatives to Economic Globalization (A Better World Is Possible)*, 2nd Ed. San Francisco: Berrett-Koehler.

22. Crompton, T (2010). Common cause: The case for working with our cultural values [online]. Available at valuesandframes.org/downloads [accessed on 8 August 2013].

45

Teaching a University Course in Sustainable Happiness

Catherine O'Brien

Can 10th grade Inuit students in Repulse Bay (Nunavut, Canada) teach the world governments something about ways to measure progress?

In a recent classroom project taken from *Sustainable Happiness and Health Education Teacher's Guide*, these students created a video celebrating what makes them happy: fresh air; spending time with family and friends; sports; home; a peaceful place; ice hockey; listening to music; square dancing; and loving someone, something, or yourself. It is an important lesson for world leaders considering ways to measure progress other than traditional financial indicators such as gross domestic product (GDP).

While some might think that happiness is too lightweight to merit serious attention, others have recognized that it is a vital link to sustainability. Sustainable happiness — which I define as happiness that contributes to individual, community, and/or global well-being without exploiting other people, the environment, or future generations — can be used to encourage sustainable behavior, even among people who have no apparent interest in sustainability or initial desire to be environmentally friendly.

> *While some might think that happiness is too lightweight to merit serious attention, others have recognized that it is a vital link to sustainability.*

It is a powerful hook. The universal human desire for happiness becomes the entry point for individuals to discover that their well-being is inextricably linked with the well-being of other people, other species, and the natural environment. The growing interest in a universal happiness index represents a huge opportunity for sustainability education.

During the United Nations' Decade of Education for Sustainable Development (2005–2014), educators are taking a critical look at the role that education plays in forging sustainable societies. The question has been raised whether education is part of the problem or part of the solution, as the education sector has been slow to introduce sustainability across curricula, to model it in our schools, and to train our teachers for sustainability education. We are taking a bold step forward with the introduction of sustainable happiness.

Happiness and well-being have not traditionally been components of formal education curricula and so we might ask, beyond parents and guardians, who or what is teaching us about happiness? And what are we learning? With many students spending more hours per week on "the three screens" (computer, television, smartphones) than they do in the classroom, their informal education from the media often reinforces a worldview of achieving happiness through material consumption.

We are working to change this at Cape Breton University where we have introduced an innovative and engaging course on sustainable happiness for undergraduates and teachers-in-training. The aim is for students to understand sustainable happiness so that they apply it both personally and professionally. Weekly readings, classes, and activities prompt the students to examine how their daily lifestyle choices, for better and worse, can impact themselves, other people, and the natural world. Some of these activities include a happiness interview (interviewing the happiest person they know) and the completion of a baseline chart that tracks their actions for one day and captures some of the implications for their well-being as well as possible consequences for others and the environment. We explore genuine wealth; reducing consumption of nonrenewable resources; drawing an "interdependence map," which outlines the web of connections to people and the resources that sustain them; expressing gratitude; and becoming "happiness literate." We conclude the course with a sustainable happiness project.

The sustainable happiness project has to be consistent with the definition of sustainable happiness and achievable in less than a week. Typically, students select a project that is personally meaningful. One student decided to educate all of us about how to make a pizza from ingredients produced within a 100-mile radius. Another organized a community cleanup with her daughters and girlfriends. They called themselves Girls Against Garbage, or GAG. A student who referred to herself at the outset of the course as a "shopaholic" established a clothing exchange with her friends. Many of the students strive to reduce their ecological footprint through shifting to more sustainable transportation, minimizing junk food, eliminating their use of plastic water bottles, conserving water and energy, and purchasing fair trade and organic products. One young woman set out to heal the relationship with her mother-in-law, and an aboriginal student initiated an after-school language program in her native language. Students come to understand the relationship between their actions and well-being for all. As one student said, "There are aspects of my life that have changed for the better since the onset of this course, such as my physical activity levels, my eagerness to purchase local and fair trade products, and my outlook on life and the well-being of others."

The sustainable happiness course assists them to reflect upon their happiness footprint. How do their daily decisions and consumer activities impact their well-being? How might a single cup of coffee be connected to the well-being of those who produced it? The overarching themes are interdependence and interconnection. Perhaps the most compelling and gratifying aspect of teaching this course is that most of my students voice the realization that an individual's actions

> *Perhaps the most compelling and gratifying aspect of teaching this course is that most of my students voice the realization that an individual's actions can and do make a difference.*

can and do make a difference. They discover that their happiness footprint is not just relevant to how they thrive but also relevant to how our planet thrives.

Teaching sustainable happiness has convinced me that sustainable happiness should be both a vision and a goal for education — elementary, secondary, and postsecondary. We can use the concept to help our students flourish by giving them the sustainable happiness skills that enhance their well-being; developing happiness literacy to critically analyze media messages; exploring options for making lifestyle choices that contribute to their well-being, sustainably; and assisting them to discover, or even create, sustainable livelihoods by learning about sustainable happiness champions. Teachers benefit, too. While many educators have been exposed to environmental education, they are generally less aware of how to incorporate sustainability into their personal lifestyles and the teaching profession. Sustainable happiness introduces opportunities for them to understand, emotionally and intellectually, that their lives touch and are touched daily by other people, other species, and the natural environment.

Sustainable happiness has an even larger sphere of influence, beyond individuals. We can use it to examine policy and practice at the institutional, governmental, and national levels. Let us consider a corporation, for example. The business sector has learned that happy employees are more productive because they demonstrate less absenteeism, increased creativity, and more cooperative behavior. The January/February 2012 cover of the *Harvard Business Review* proclaims, "The Value of Happiness: How Employee Well-Being Drives Profits." Employee happiness is important, of course, but what if those happy workers are increasing the productivity of companies that are not practicing corporate social and environmental responsibility? Sustainable happiness reinforces the relevance of making that big picture connection. This applies to national pursuits as well. Being named in the top list of happiest countries should not be a nation's claim to fame unless the happiness of its citizens is sustainable happiness, ensuring that their prosperity has not been attained at the expense of exploiting other people and the unsustainable use of natural resources.

Municipal planning is being transformed in municipalities that have overcome the fear of using the h-word, understanding that happiness and well-being are components of successful cities. The positive emotions that children experience while walking to school are an example of sustainable happiness. Walking is also active transportation, an important source of physical activity and a contributor to cohesive neighborhoods. Imagine designing cities that enhance well-being, sustainably! I am working with colleagues at 8–80 Cities, a Canadian based nonprofit organization working to create vibrant cities with happy, healthy communities, to develop a resource for municipalities to incorporate sustainable happiness.

It is time to take happiness to the next level and merge it with sustainability. There are thousands of examples worldwide of lifestyles and livelihoods that represent sustainable happiness. There are businesses and communities that have learned how to merge well-being with economic development. We can capture these stories through initiatives such as a virtual international network for sustainable happiness. Research would be accelerated with doctoral and postdoctoral fellowships in sustainable happiness. One or more research centers for sustainable happiness could become hubs of activity that both generate and disseminate information about sustainable happiness.

I am particularly keen to involve the views of children and youth. As we learned from the 10th-grade students in Nunavut, young people have a powerful voice that needs to be shared.

Author note

My personal commitment is to collect examples of sustainable happiness champions. Please send information and stories to obrien@sustainable happiness.ca.

46

The Time Has Come to Catalyze a Sustainable Consumerism Movement

Peggy Liu

In today's global marketplace, with its ever-diminishing resource stocks, one thing is obvious: demand is outstripping supply. And here is the conundrum: increases in living standards are tightly coupled with growth in resource consumption. We have all heard the dramatic statistic that if all seven billion people on earth lived like the average American, we would need five planets to support us. But as the consumer class in developing nations explodes, with China alone forecasted to add the equivalent of another one and a half United States to its middle class over the next 13 years, we are going to need to update that statistic soon. We must eliminate the link between the rise of the developing nations' consumer classes and resource devastation (let us call it what it is). It starts with reimagining prosperity for sustainable consumerism.

Box 1 describes strategies for encouraging sustainable consumerism. In the first four categories, major progress has been made, mainly by a few corporate thought leaders. But we have a long way to go. In 2008, Caroline Savery, a consultant at Keystone Development Center, tried to lead a 100% environmentally sustainable lifestyle within urban Pittsburgh. She concluded that "it is functionally impossible to live environmentally sustainably today because corporations do not yet serve … sustainable business practices."[1] This is still true in 2012.

Box 1. Strategies for Encouraging Sustainable Consumerism

Difficulty of implementation is tied to collaboration required	Requirement for sustainable consumerism		Stakeholders driving change
EASIEST	WHOLE FOODS	Heavy-handed choice editing by retailers to guide consumerism rather than relying on consumers' values to drive them to purchase green (e.g., Whole Foods grocery stores)	Retailers
EASIER	HAWORTH Furniture For What's Next	Innovations in the way products are sold, including shifting customer value from "products" to "experiences" (e.g., Haworth Office Furniture)	Sellers
HARD	YOUR M&S	More sustainable product offerings (e.g., Marks & Spencer department store)	• Sellers • Manufacturers
HARDER	FLOR	Better resource management in the supply chain, including circular economy loops between production and consumption (e.g., Interface/FLOR carpet company)	• Supply-chain companies • Consumers • Waste handlers
HARDEST		Activating new social norms around consumption and fulfillment	• Government • Mass and social media • Advertisers • Friends

But the burden can not be on companies alone to create sustainable consumerism. Only by vastly increasing customer purchases of sustainable products can economies of scale allow retailers to offer green goods at the same prices as (resource) greedy ones.

To do this, we need an actionable way to address the fifth and most elusive category: creating well-behaved sustainable consumers. We need a social movement that changes society's attitudes toward consumption.

Getting into the heads of consumers and increasing their desire for sustainable products will require cross-sector collaboration to deploy a mix of hard and soft power tactics (i.e., government nudges and savvy marketing), activated in parallel.

A green-gilded life

In his speech, "Death of Environmentalism and the Birth of the Commons Movement," Adam Werbach[2] says that the environmental movement has thus far failed because it has forgotten to connect sustainability to the aspirations of everyday people.

Any alternative green lifestyle needs to compellingly compete with the lifestyles presented in the Paris Hilton- and Kardashian-style reality TV shows — those shrines of conspicuous consumption that are the nails in the coffin of environmentalism. Fashion icon and eco-advocate Alexa Chung sums up the problem nicely in British *Vogue*: "Ethical Fashion: surely the least sexy words in fashion. Sustainable, ecological, organic … The language of conscience-free shopping is a clunky vocabulary that instantly brings to mind images of hemp kaftans, recycled tin-can bags, and other things I'd rather not swathe my body in, thanks."[3]

People do not want green — they want green gilded. To offer a compelling alternative to the American Dream, we need a sustainable lifestyle that excites people. It should not ignore alarming statistics or the need for sacrifice, but it should not make

> *To offer a compelling alternative to the American Dream, we need a sustainable lifestyle that excites people.*

these statistics the center of its marketing campaign. A green-gilded movement is not a moral-imperative campaign for energy savings, waste reduction, or dealing with the water crisis; it is a buzz-worthy lifestyle that taps into consumers' desires and aspirations. It is a campaign that taps into people's deepest fears of not fitting in — showing not only what is cool, but also what is not. It speaks in a currency that the average person can understand — whether it is sex, health, jobs, or iPads.

Start with the developing world's emerging middle class

The real hope of sustainable consumerism is that China, India, and the other gargantuan developing nations will actively choose a different path than the industrialized countries. Here is where dreams have not been cemented, and people are eager to absorb new ideas. The change required will not be easy, but history points to other places — such as Japan, Taiwan, and Germany — that have successfully decoupled rising gross domestic product (GDP) and energy use.

For China, the moment for such change is upon us. According to Helen Wang, author of *The Chinese Dream*,[4] China's middle class will grow to 800 million by 2025. As Group M's YouTube video, *Unholdable China*, says, "China is shifting from 'made in China' to 'consumed in China' and it is changing the world. Every three days, two new Starbucks open in China. In Beijing, the sales at one shopping mall reached RMB 6B [about US$1 billion] in 2011."[5] And China's emissions are on track to equal those of the United States in just five short years, by 2017.

The good news is that China's central government understands the need to find a new, greener path. Xie Zhenhua, China's minister for climate policy, rightly notes that "if we allow China's per capita carbon emissions to rise to US levels, it will be a disaster for the world."[6] China is continually improving its energy and environmental policies and is actively searching internationally for best practices. China's 12th Five-Year Plan (see Box 2) has ambitious targets for resource and environmental

---

Box 2. China's 12th Five-Year Plan

Energy: Cut energy intensity by 16% per unit of GDP, increase non–fossil fuel energy sources from 8.3 to 11.4% of primary energy consumption.

Pollution: Cut carbon intensity 17% per unit of GDP, reduce sulfur dioxide and chemical oxygen demand by 8%, reduce ammonia nitrogen and nitrogen oxides by 10%.

Water: Cut water intensity per unit of value-added industrial output by 30% by 2015.

Forestry: Increase forests by 600 million cubic meters and forest cover to 21.66%.[17]

protection. City officials' careers are tied to their ability to meet these targets, so they are extremely motivated to try consumption shaping policies that can be implemented locally.

Are China's efforts to increase domestic consumption at odds with sustainability goals? Not necessarily, says Vijay Vaitheeswaran, the *Economist*'s Shanghai bureau chief and China business editor. He contends that "in macroeconomic terms, it is uncontroversial to observe that China grossly over invests [in infrastructure] and [its citizens] underconsume, so increasing consumption per se is not bad. What matters is the quality of the consumption."[7] As Chinese consumers start to spend more money, we need to ensure that they avoid the trap of cheap disposables, resource-greedy goods, and wasteful splurging and instead buy higher value sustainable products and services.

As a regional testbed for sustainable consumerism, China's unique dynamics present a singular opportunity to mobilize consumers in ways never before possible. China is under huge pressure to change; it has the willingness and persistence to change; and it can use government and social-media levers to activate the masses at a large scale. But the window of opportunity for a new lifestyle to take hold will not last forever. If we wait too long, the emerging middle class will have already developed their tastes and habits. It will be too late to steer the masses to greener pastures.

The China Dream

I lead the Joint US–China Collaboration on Clean Energy, or JUCCCE, a nonprofit whose mission is to accelerate the greening of China. JUCCCE is seizing this moment to catalyze a new, sustainable lifestyle in China through the China Dream campaign.[8] The goal of the China Dream is no less than to reimagine prosperity arising from a healthy and fulfilling way of life. Status symbols must be realigned around living more rather than just having more. The lifestyle promoted by the China Dream happens to be sustainable, but the campaign does not mention sustainability directly. It does this on purpose.

At the heart of the initiative is an actionable framework for changing consumer habits en masse. While we cannot change human nature, we can change social norms for what is desirable and acceptable behavior and also for what is not. The China Dream incorporates parallel efforts to use peer pressure and new government policies to create widespread desire for a sustainable life.

The China Dream framework is a collaborative effort between JUCCCE, Marks & Spencer, the World Economic Forum's New Energy Architecture Global Agenda Council, the Urban China Initiative, Shanghai Jiaotong University, Real Pegasus (Edelman China), WPP, Saatchi & Saatchi, and other experts. The bulk of the initiative will take place over three years, started in late 2012.

Crafting a different dream

The China Dream seeks to change the social context of consumer decisions. It will involve developing and seeding imagery for a new lifestyle, leveraging mass media and mobile technology. In retail-speak, this is "choice influencing." But instead of marketers acting individually to sell products, the China Dream will require companies, ad agency creatives and planners, scriptwriters, bloggers, role models, and the press to work in unison to champion sustainable consumerism.

First, JUCCCE will work with creative directors to gather a visual lexicon to define the China Dream. This carefully edited imagery will express a better China — in the way that Norman Rockwell's iconic *Saturday Evening Post* images evoked the hopes and aspirations of America. The consistency of Rockwell's images over four decades created visual stories that led filmmaker Steven Spielberg to praise the artist for painting the American dream "better than anyone."[9]

China is ripe for this imagery. The Cultural Revolution broke up much of China's social fabric, and the Chinese have been soaking in foreign advertising images of luxury for the last two decades. Today the China Dream is a vision that does not yet exist, but it is a matter of pride for China to define its own vision for its future. Qiu Baoxing, the vice minister of China's Ministry of Housing and Urban Rural Development, opened a mayoral training session on sustainable urbanization by saying, "We cannot continue to blindly follow the American Dream. This is simply unsustainable for China and the world."[10] The new China Dream can tap into traditional Chinese values that are closely aligned with sustainability — personal health, face (respect), harmony with nature, and avoiding waste.

One of China Dream's advisors, Kaiser Kuo, who is director of international communications for the Chinese search engine Baidu, has been adamant that the China Dream imagery should not just show the good-looking, healthy guy stepping off a high-speed rail train with a briefcase. It also needs to lambaste the plump, balding guy with a cigarette and gold chains stepping out of a gas-guzzling Hummer. Because "what's not" sets social norms as much as "what's hot."

Go big, go quickly

Ultimately, the success of the China Dream hinges on mobilizing multi-stakeholder collaboration to activate consumers within a short time frame, to create the culture shift that the China Dream calls for. "To make a behavioral switch, people need to start hearing the same message frequently from the community they trust," advises Danah Boyd, an academic expert on the intersections between social media and society at Microsoft Research. "This creates cultural resonance, which makes it easier for people to flip the switch. But time lag is dangerous. Activation needs to happen quickly or the idea will lose momentum."[11]

Technology enables us to quickly mobilize the masses around new concepts. What we need is a revolution — not just awareness — and recent history shows us that social media is a major enabler of change. At a dinner at Davos, Thomas Friedman[12] of *The New York Times* pointed out that it has only been a short six years in which we have seen the rise of Facebook, Twitter, Sina Weibo, and other massive online digital platforms. It is not uncommon for bloggers in China to have 1 to 3 million followers. The top user on Sina Weibo — China's version of Twitter — has 18 million followers.

The strength of this mobile platform for shaping social norms and spreading new concepts cannot be underestimated: Twitter took four years to reach 100 million users. It took Sina Weibo 1.5 years to reach that milestone. Social media in China — if used effectively to recruit these megabloggers, as the China Dream champions — could play a significant role in ensuring the success of the China Dream project.

Learning from Hollywood

The second lever to incorporate China Dream imagery into the fabric of mainstream society consists of entertainment programs made for TV and online portals. For this stage, we at JUCCCE will take a page from Hollywood, Health & Society (HHS),[13] a joint project of the Norman Lear Center at University of Southern California–Annenberg and the Centers for Disease Control and Prevention. HHS works with experts from government, academia, and nonprofits to consult with TV writers on health issues in storylines.

"Every day millions of viewers worldwide learn something new about health from TV storylines and take action on what they've learned," says director Sandra de Castro Buffington.[14] "Recognizing the profound impact of TV storylines on health knowledge, attitudes and behavior," she says, HHS works with writers and producers to weave accurate health messages into their storytelling. In a similar way, the China Dream project can work with TV writers and top Web portals in China to weave imagery about sustainable consumerism into entertainment.

Nudging behavior through policies

Desire alone will not create sustainable behavior. Studies show that consumers need institutional guidance in order to make sustainable choices. In the absence of a strong government push, public-service marketing campaigns can fall largely on deaf ears.

The China Dream effort will introduce local government policies that shape consumer behavior toward sustainable choices at the point of purchase or during product use. The concept of "nudges," introduced to me at the Harvard Kennedy School by Professor Iris Bohnet, inspired me to look at policies such as refunds for bringing your own cup to the coffee shop, green office-procurement policies, and unit-pricing programs for residential waste collection. Culturally specific policies, such as mandating mooncake gifts to be in the form of gift certificates rather than heavily regifted packages, are particularly ripe for exploration (small changes, enacted on a large scale, add up).

China's nimble government structure is an advantage in that cities are able to quickly pilot policies that get scaled up to the national level if they are effective. Witness China's banning of free plastic bags at grocery stores. This was initially tried in a couple of cities before being introduced nationwide in 2008. In the first three years after that, China reduced usage by 24 billion bags.[15]

JUCCCE is working with researchers to come up with consumption-shaping policy recommendations that make sense for China and that are easy to implement within the average three- to four-year time frame of one mayor's tenure. JUCCCE will leverage our mayoral training arm,[16] which is based on mandatory annual retraining for government officials, to distribute these recommendations across the country and to identify pilot cities. China's mayors are motivated to experiment with local policies in order to meet their local 12th Five-Year Plan targets and, possibly, to obtain one of a variety of "sustainable model city" designations by the national government.

To China and beyond (or, it is time to collaborate or croak)

The truth is, few sustainable-consumerism campaigns have succeeded to date. But the elements that can enable societal change are now aligning. For one thing, people are more open than ever to a lifestyle change. The current economic squeeze leaves consumers eager for alternatives to conspicuous consumption. As a result, governments are working with nongovernmental organizations (NGOs) to look beyond GDP growth to "sustainability indices" and "happiness indices."

And, second, consumer-facing Chief Executive Officers (CEOs) are getting more earnest about working together on driving consumer demand for sustainable products. I presented the China Dream project at a series of World Economic Forum sessions in Abu Dhabi and Davos to company titans from Marks & Spencer, Kingfisher, TESCO, DESSO, Nike, and others, and I noticed a clear expansion in corporate talk from supply-chain sustainability to how best to engage consumers in social change.

These two factors, together with the rise in social media and the unique conditions in China that prime that country for a change, mean that this is our moment. In the year of Rio+20, we have for the first time an opportunity to activate sustainable consumerism at a large scale. We have openness to change, bourgeoning corporate-consumer engagement, large-scale digital activation, and China as a test bed.

But we only have one chance to engage the emerging middle classes in China and India while they are still searching for a vision of prosperity. If we miss this window, corporations will miss the opportunity to create the customer they want to sell to.

So let us use this platform of Rio+20 to jointly commit resources to this effort. If we succeed, the China Dream is a framework that can show how sustainable consumerism can be created in countries around the world.

> *We only have one chance to engage the emerging middle classes in China and India while they are still searching for a vision of prosperity. If we miss this window, corporations will miss the opportunity to create the customer they want to sell to.*

References

1. Savery, C (2008). Widespread sustainable consumerism is more vital than taking individual actions. *Sustainablog* [online]. Available at http://sustainablog. org/2008/07/widespread-sustainable-consumerism-is-more-vital-than-taking-individual-actions [accessed on 8 August 2013].

2. Meyer, J (2005). Does environmentalism have a future? *Dissent Magazine* [online]. Available at www.dissentmagazine.org/article/?article=250 [accessed on 8 August 2013].

3. Chung, A (2012). April's green special. *Vogue*. Available at http://www. vogue.co.uk/blogs/the-green-style-blog/2012/03/april-vogue-issue [accessed on 8 August 2013].

4. Wang, H (2010). *The Chinese Dream: The Rise of the World's Largest Middle Class and What It Means to You*. New York: Bestseller Press.

5. Group M (2012). Unholdable China. *YouTube* [online]. Available at www.youtube.com/watch?v=-isnhstF-rU [accessed on 8 August 2013].

6. Black, R (2011). China 'won't follow US' on carbon emissions. *BBC News* [online]. Available at www.bbc.co.uk/news/science-environment-15444858 [accessed on 8 August 2013].

7. Vaitheeswaran, V (2012). Personal communication.

8. China Dream (2012). *JUCCCE* [online]. Available at http://juccce.org/chinadream [accessed on 8 August 2013].

9. PBS (American Masters) (2006). *Norman Rockwell* [online]. Available at www.pbs.org/wnet/americanmasters/episodes/norman-rockwell/about-norman-rockwell/689 [accessed on 8 August 2013].

10. Baoxing, Q (2009). Speech given at a JUCCCE mayoral training program at the Mayoral Training Academy for Mayors of China.

11. Boyd, D (2012). Personal communication.

12. Friedman, T (2012). Personal communication.

13. Hollywood, Health & Society (2012). *Norman Lear Center* [online]. Available at www.learcenter.org/html/projects/?cm=hhs [accessed on 8 August 2013].

14. Heasley, S (2011). 'Parenthood' honored for Asperberger's storyline. *Disability Scoop* [online]. Available at www.disabilityscoop.com/2011/08/26/parenthood-honored/13822 [accessed on 8 August 2013].

15. Liu, P (2010). China as the cleantech laboratory of the world. *TEDxTalks on YouTube* [online]. Available at www.youtube.com/watch?v=_yP9IRbxtEw [accessed on 8 August 2013].

16. Mayoral training (2012). *JUCCCE* [online]. Available at www.juccce.org/mayoraltraining [accessed on 8 August 2013].

17. Seligsohn, D and A Hsu (2011). How does China's 12th Five-Year Plan address energy and the environment? *World Resources Institute* [online]. Available at www.wri.org/stories/2011/03/how-does-chinas-12th-five-year-plan-address-energy-and-environment [accessed on 8 August 2013].

Index